9254/12

822.08

NEW
ENGLISH DRAMATISTS
5

INTRODUCED BY ALAN BRIEN
EDITED BY TOM MASCHLER

STOP IT, WHOEVER YOU ARE
Henry Livings

PROGRESS TO THE PARK
Alun Owen

MARCHING SONG
John Whiting

PENGUIN BOOKS

Penguin Books Ltd, Harmondsworth, Middlesex, England
Penguin Books Australia Ltd, Ringwood, Victoria, Australia

—

Stop It, Whoever You Are
First published in Penguin Books 1962
Reprinted 1967
Copyright © Henry Livings, 1962

—

Progress to the Park
First published in *Plays and Players* July and August 1961
Published in Penguin Books 1962
Reprinted 1967
Copyright © Alun Owen, 1961

—

Marching Song
First published by Heinemann 1957
Published in Penguin Books 1962
Reprinted 1967
Copyright © John Whiting, 1957

—

Made and printed in Great Britain
by Western Printing Services Ltd, Bristol
Set in Monotype Bembo

CONTENTS

INTRODUCTION

CRITICS are also journalists – all dressed up with only one place to go. Their motto sometimes seems to be 'Have dinner jacket, will cavil.' But it is their job to be readable as well as right, and part of their function is to identify, for readers who are often only occasional theatregoers, new trends in the drama with brisk, snappy, shorthand slogans. Thus the spread of such portmanteau terms as 'dustbin drama', 'kitchen-sink realism', and 'chamberpot comedy' for the kind of play which has bobbed up in the wake of LOOK BACK IN ANGER.

Some of the catch-phrases are older than they sound. That censorious moralist of the Victorian *derrière-garde*, Clement Scott, invented 'the drama of the dustbin' as long ago as 1900, to denounce Frank Harris's MR AND MRS DAVENTRY. What apparently aroused his indignation was the scene in which a lecherous gentleman forced his unwelcome attentions on a pure lady in a locked drawing-room. The whole thing was impeccably upper middle class, and the dustbin was metaphorical. But metaphors in controversial journalism have a dangerous habit of taking themselves literally. If Mr Scott had remained the *Daily Telegraph* critic until 1959, he would have seen his dustbins physically present on stage in Beckett's END GAME where they were the homes of the two legless, abandoned parents.

The kitchen-sink tag was probably borrowed from the art criticism of the fifties, when it was coined to describe John Bratby's paintings. Here the description was quite precise, and Arnold Wesker's ROOTS included a sink as a necessary prop. There was also the disconnected gas stove in THE CARETAKER and the attic water-tank in LOOK BACK IN ANGER.

Some partisans of the new drama have felt that the more traditional-ist critics were unfair in continually pointing out how the stage was becoming cluttered with domestic paraphernalia. But they were simply reporting the facts. The mass-observers at the Royal Court

Theatre and Stratford East have almost always framed their people in a still-life of things. What some of the critics didn't realize was that the sauce bottle, the fried liver, the ironing-board, the case of light ale, the drying-up cloth, and the old newspapers under the moquette cushion were objects as emotive of a way of life and a habit of mind as the whisky decanter, the cold grouse, the french windows, the rose garden, the fur stole, and the first edition bound in calf.

In the plays of today, notably in the Brechtian productions of the Berliner Ensemble, the objects themselves can take on a positive, almost speaking, part in the action. They are at once symbols and totems, prizes and stigmas, precariously won and sometimes capriciously sacrificed.

The final despairing epithet, popularized only in the last couple of years, was 'chamberpot', though at the time no unfriendly critic proved able to produce a concrete (or china) example. In 1961, however, Henry Livings obliged by setting two of his five scenes in STOP IT, WHOEVER YOU ARE in a factory lavatory. To those who have neither seen nor read the play, this is the nadir of pointless vulgarity. Such an opinion is unlikely to survive exposure to the play itself. '*The factory washroom and lavatories*' is no more outrageous or for that matter more fascinating a stage direction than '*Before Pomfret Castle*', or '*Sebastian's Room in Albany*'. Mr Livings knows, just as his critics know when they stop protesting, that in any small world where one sex is temporarily segregated this is often the only place in which the inmates can retire to smoke, gossip, plot, slack, quarrel, and relax, away from authority.

Both he and his characters use the lavatories naturally and unashamedly. The pub, the canteen, the factory yard, or the street would not satisfy his dramatic need for a site where his worm could turn. His working men find themselves there far more plausibly than many a stage duke finds himself in his library full of painted books.

What is unexpected about this play is that it is a work of propaganda for the beetle and against the boot, for the worm and against the spade, which does not caricature Them while sentimentalizing Us, as did the

Party-line satires of the thirties. All Mr Livings's people are just one remove from the traditional butts and butties of the seaside postcard and the music-hall sketch. In other words, they appear exactly as ludicrous, messy, bewildered, selfish, pitiable, and sinister as would any one of us if the fourth wall of his house turned transparent and revealed him in a posture guaranteed to make sensational copy for the *News of the World*.

William Perkin Warbeck is as much one of the wounded veterans of the ant-hill war as Beatie Bryant or Jimmy Porter. He is in many ways a more difficult combatant to dramatize because his rank is more obscure and his armament more feeble. Warbeck is the lowest brick in the base of the social pyramid. His only possible form of protest is to move suddenly to one side and hope that part of the roof will fall in. His heroism, like that of the Good Soldier Schweik, consists in being cowardly enough to run away.

STOP IT, WHOEVER YOU ARE invites laughter – the straightforward, unsophisticated belly-laughter of the mass audience as they recognize sudden incongruities, the primitive slapstick, the familiar reiterations and confusions and embarrassments of everyday existence. But it is also an experimental play – much more unorthodox in form than ROOTS and LOOK BACK IN ANGER – which tumbles over the edge of farce into fantasy. And it ends up as a plea for love between human beings, for the naked lonely creatures beneath the panoply of petty power or the livery of base employment.

PROGRESS TO THE PARK is superficially a Romeo and Juliet story of young lovers torn apart by the religious antagonisms of middle-aged Papes and Prods in working-class Liverpool. The author, Alun Owen, has guided his play through three different productions (and one radio performance), unveiling it in turn at each of the key theatrical shrines, the Royal Court, Stratford East, and Shaftesbury Avenue. With each version, the balance of forces has shifted slightly.

Finally, Mag has become more of a Cressida than a Juliet. A warm-blooded creature, whose promiscuities are cosily affectionate rather than sensually passionate, her tragedy is not so much the opposition of fanatical parents as the moral disapproval of an amoral gang of her schoolfellows. She discovers that love is a four-letter word in a world of casual sex.

Bobby, the Romeo of Mr Owen's Liverpool, never matches her in spirit or individuality. Instead, Teifion, the bawdy, tart, mocking Welsh Mercutio, supplies the steam power which drives street-corner and park-bench courtship to its climax. Originally, he was a kind of chorus who inspected the squabbling clans from the outside. By the last revision, he had become the hub and centre upon which the whole drama turns. His summing up is not 'a plague on both your houses', but 'I cherish the differences: they mean people are alive'.

PROGRESS TO THE PARK exists beyond, and to some extent in spite of, its plot. Its value lies in that meaty Liverpool-Irish stew which Alun Owen has mixed with honesty and compassion, of boasts and confessions, ambitions and fears, when the gang are alone together. It is a first-class scouse.

John Whiting's MARCHING SONG is a deliberately denuded, bone-bare skeleton of a play, in style and theme very far from the working-class drama of most of the new post-war playwrights. Its affinities are rather with John Arden in his SERGEANT MUSGRAVE'S DANCE vein than with Livings, Wesker, or Owen. Mr Whiting has deprived himself of all the warmth and realism obtainable by reproducing contemporary speech idioms and living habits.

The setting is described as 'a house set on the heights above a capital city in Europe', but the action takes place in the timeless, faceless world of the Either/Or choice, where each man defines himself by his deeds and becomes his own epitaph, where no example furnishes a pattern for imitation, and the summing-up is: 'It isn't what he was, it was what he did.' This is the best manifestation so far of English existentialism. But where Sartre would have particularized the political beliefs of his characters, and heightened the emotions to produce philosophical melodrama, Mr Whiting has concentrated on what he has called 'formality of pattern and austerity of movement'. It is, in fact, anti-theatrical in its cold asceticism.

In some ways, I think this is a mistake. Now that Mr Whiting has shown us in THE DEVILS that he realizes what an intoxicant language can be, MARCHING SONG has a flatness which is almost too sobering. What is impressive and interesting about the play is the shaping intelligence and chiselled craftsmanship of the playmaking, which refuses to botch and scamp under the pretence that inspiration excuses all shoddiness. John Whiting has had a rougher critical reception for some of his early plays than any other serious writer in the theatre except perhaps Harold Pinter. It is a welcome sign that the British stage is now reaching maturity when the supporters of one genre no longer feel obliged to mass forces and drive their rivals off the boards, so that Whiting, Livings, and Owen can appear within the covers of a series which has already included Osborne, Lessing, Kops, Wesker, and Arden.

ALAN BRIEN

HENRY LIVINGS

Stop It, Whoever You Are

STOP IT, WHOEVER YOU ARE

First produced at the Arts Theatre Club, London, on Wednesday 15 February 1961 with the following cast:

WILLIAM PERKIN WARBECK	Wilfred Brambell
ROSE WARBECK, *his wife*	Rosamund Greenwood
MR HARBUCKLE	John Rutland
MARILYN HARBUCKLE, *his daughter*	Sydonie Platt
LES WARD, *his friend and lodger*	Ray Mort
CAPTAIN BOOTLE	Brian Oulton
ALDERMAN MICHAEL OGLETHORPE	Arthur Lowe
POLICE CONSTABLE (Syd)	Edmond Bennet
TWO APPRENTICES	Roger Kemp and Ronald Lacey
HIS EXCELLENCY	John Saunders
(REPORTER	This part was later cut)

Directed by Vida Hope
Settings and lighting by Brian Currah

SCENE: The parlour of Mr Warbeck's house or its tiny front garden; and Mr Warbeck's place of work, the washplace and lavatory of a factory.

SCENE ONE

The tiny patch of garden in front of Warbeck's house, looking from the outside. On one side a narrow arched passage between houses. A straggly hedge, which WARBECK *is at this moment supposed to be trimming, i.e. he has the clippers in his hands and occasionally gives a dispirited click with them. He is quite bald and very insignificant.*

[MARILYN HARBUCKLE, *a buxom fourteen-year-old, is outside the garden. She has her arms wrapped round her and, unaware that* WARBECK *is there, sings to herself.*]

MARILYN [*sings*]:
> I've got a song, for the winter weather.
> We two belong, we're warm in the frost –
> The street is empty, and the wind turns the leaves,
> But in our blood there runs along
> Runs a sweet warm longing.
>
> The mills are still, and their fires are dampened –
> Out on the hills, the sheep hug the wall –
> The wind is driving and the curlew's alone,
> But in our bodies moves a thrill, moves a tender thrilling.

[*She finishes the song and cuddles herself.*]
> Ooh, darling, will you hold me as close as this always?
> Darling, darling, darling. It's wonderful to be with you alone.

[MARILYN *sees Perkin Warbeck peering at her over the hedge, and begins very seriously to hop in a complicated child's game, earnestly scoring for herself.*]

WARBECK: Marilyn, where did you pick up that song?

MARILYN: Wireless.

WARBECK: Well I never. Makes you think, doesn't it? She's nobbut fourteen, though you wouldn't think it. Ahem. My name's William

15

Perkin Warbeck. William after my father, and Perkin after the famous revolutionary. If it's all the same to you, I'd prefer to be called Perkin. It's a good name. Perkin. Or else Mr Warbeck. I'm getting on now, though you wouldn't think it to look at me. I retired five year ago. It's true. I was in packing and dispatch. Of course you can't go on doing that sort of work for ever. I had twenty-five year in the same job. But you can't go on humping them boxes. No. Fifty-six pounds in the boxes, and up to sixteen stone in the bags. Tins of fruit and jam, and beans and such – Mm.

MARILYN: Mr Warbeck, do you get into the same bed with Mrs Warbeck every night?

WARBECK: Oh yes, my dear. Eh?

MARILYN: You're not retired, anyway. I don't care what you say.

WARBECK: Oh yes I am, Marilyn, my love.

MARILYN: You're not.

WARBECK: I am.

MARILYN: Not, not, not. You go out to work every day, I've seen you. And I've seen you empty the cat's dirt-tray in the dustbin every morning as you go. I can see you when I get up, and I'm taking my nightie off. You go to work, you go to work, you go to work – [*She goes back to her hopping.*]

WARBECK: My work in the sanitary is a personal favour to Captain Bootle. And I can leave any time I want, and have my pension back. I've still got my tobacco coupons, look.

[*She ignores most of this. Leans back against the hedge, lifting her head impudently to look into Warbeck's astonished eyes. After a pause, she speaks again.*]

MARILYN: Won't you cop it, when Mrs Warbeck comes back and sees how much hedge you've clipped?

WARBECK [*jumps, and then recovers*]: Why, you little monkey.

[*He comes purposefully out of the garden, hoping she'll run off. She stands her ground. He pretends that he came out to clip the outside of the hedge.*]

As you get older, my lass, you'll find that the whole secret of life is to have a decent and dignified relation with people.

[*The* REPORTER *enters.*]

REPORTER: Good morning. Mr Warbeck?

WARBECK: My wife is a fine woman, and I respect her. And I'll thank you to study my feelings when you speak of her.

MARILYN [*put down*]: Well, that's what I think, anyway. And I think you're heavenly. So there. [*She goes off down the ginnel.*]

REPORTER: Mr Warbeck? I'm from the *Chronicle* –

WARBECK: There's two people in this world I won't hear a word against: Mrs Warbeck and Captain Bootle. My wife and my boss. Finest man that ever breathed. A soldier and a gentleman – I expect she'll want a cup of tea when she comes back from service. [*Turns to go into the house.*]

REPORTER: Mr Warbeck?

WARBECK: William Perkin Warbeck. Yes. Have been for years.

REPORTER: I'm from the *Chronicle*. We're doing a spread on Alderman Oglethorpe, to coincide with the opening of the municipal library. I understand, Mr Warbeck, that you were at school with Alderman Oglethorpe?

WARBECK: I prefer to be called Perkin.

REPORTER: Have you any reminiscences, Perkin, of Alderman Oglethorpe at school?

WARBECK: Alderman Oglethorpe?

REPORTER: Yes.

WARBECK: D'you know how he started?

REPORTER: Yes, he told me. Bricklayer's mate in the firm he now owns. Marvellous, isn't it?

WARBECK: Him and another lad had an old pram.

REPORTER: Old pram. Yes, go on. This could be interesting.

WARBECK: They used to go out nights round the fields.

REPORTER: In the long cold winter evenings, on to the desolate moors – Yes. Go on.

WARBECK: Pinching horse muck.

REPORTER: Pinching horse muck.

WARBECK: Pinching horse muck.

REPORTER: Eh? We can't print that.

WARBECK: Aye, he used to pinch horse muck and sell it back to t'farmers for manure in the morning.

REPORTER: Sell it back to the – Would you credit it? Marvellous. The old rogue. The Editor'd have a fit if I sent it up – Couldn't be printed.

WARBECK: D'you never say anything you've not already said before?

REPORTER: Well, I sometimes say things that other people have said before – Can't you give me something we can print? Anything?

WARBECK: It's all the same to me what you print.

REPORTER: Just a minute, have some respect. The press has its duties, you know. We don't just print anything. We present the facts.

WARBECK: Well it's a fact that Alderman Oglethorpe started by pinching horse muck.

REPORTER: I daresay, but we can't print it.

WARBECK: Sithee here: you could print the end of the world starting at our house, and when you come back from doing it, I'd still be standing here.

REPORTER: Not if it were true, you wouldn't.

WARBECK: Well if it were, printing it wouldn't start or stop it.

REPORTER: Don't you care about anything?

WARBECK: I've got principles. I just keep standing here. It's right what I said about Oglethorpe.

REPORTER: Well, you'll not bother Oglethorpe standing here, nor saying what you say. We can't print it. If everybody took your attitude – just a minute. You've got something there. If I took your attitude, in my job, I'd see it was printed. I'd just keep standing here – Only in my case, I'd have to dart about a bit. But I'd keep on doing what I was doing, regardless.

WARBECK: That's principles, isn't it?

REPORTER [second thoughts]: No. No, it wouldn't work. We'd be

crushed by the Editor and Oglethorpe. All our hopes'd be blasted.
[*Pause.*]

WARBECK: I haven't got any blasted hopes.

REPORTER: Is that what it is? Now I mustn't get too excited, or
something terrible'll happen – [*Third thoughts.*] No, they'd have the
laugh on us.

WARBECK: Who?

REPORTER: People like the Editor and Oglethorpe scorn little people
like us. They always get their own road.

WARBECK: Well, what if they do?

REPORTER: What if they do? You have to respect them, don't you?
That's what!

WARBECK: Respect? For pinching horse muck? For not printing facts?
How d'you mean?

REPORTER: – he's right. I've met a prophet. I'll do a full-page article
on you, and sod 'em. Perkin, if a big bloke comes and hits you,
Perkin, what d'you do?

WARBECK [*automatic*]: Lay down till he goes away.

REPORTER: It's too much. I can't bear it. If a big parade goes by, with
thousands of soldiers and missiles and that, what d'you do?

WARBECK: Go and have a look.

REPORTER: No, that was too difficult – I'll ask you that one again
later. Russia sends a missile that obliterates England; what d'you do?

WARBECK: Get obliterated.

REPORTER: It's difficult, your principle, isn't it?

WARBECK: It comes natural to me. I just keep standing here.

[*The* REPORTER *stands gazing fervently at Perkin for a second, then
grasps his hand and shakes it vigorously, and departs suddenly, leaving
Perkin a little off balance. The* REPORTER *stops just before disappearing.*]

REPORTER: I don't like my job, you know, Mr Warbeck. Perkin.

[*The* REPORTER *goes off the way he came.* PERKIN *goes into the
house. We hear* MRS WARBECK'S *voice down the ginnel:* Yak yak
yak.]

MRS W: Ooh Mrs Harbuckle, don't I know it. I bought Mr Warbeck a pair of slippers only the other day. Seventeen and six.

[MARILYN *slips back to warn Mr Warbeck.*]

Well, you can tell – I gave him a pound note and I only got half a crown change. Well, I must be going else I shall never get the dinner on. Ooh look, there's Mitle Oglethorpe coming along, Mrs Harbuckle! I wonder if he's come to have a look at our repairs. I've asked Mr Warbeck to go to him time and again. It leaks, you know. Yes, I know, so must I, else Mr Warbeck'll be wondering where his dinner is. [*Calls out shrilly.*] Morning, Mr Oglethorpe!

[WARBECK *comes out of the house.* MARILYN *gestures her warning about the imminent* MRS WARBECK.]

There now, he hasn't seen me. Such a nice man. Ever such a nice man. Yes, well, cheerio, Mrs Harbuckle, so must I – It's always the same Sundays, isn't it? Rush rush rush.

WARBECK: It's perfectly all right, Marilyn, my dear.

MRS W [*entering*]: She'd no need to rush off like that, *I* know. She's rude.

MARILYN: Who's rude, Mrs Warbeck?

MRS W: Oh, it's you, Marilyn, is it? Your mother's just gone in; don't you think you'd better go and help her now? I know she says you're a bit young for service, but you're not so soft you can't peel a few potatoes for Sunday dinner. Morning, Mr Warbeck. I see you're up. Off you go now, Marilyn, there's a treasure.

[WARBECK *has been mumbling his greetings and explaining about the hedge and putting the kettle on.* MARILYN *goes.*]

MRS W [*continues*]: There's that Mitle Oglethorpe coming along. You'd better catch him about those repairs. It doesn't matter what you're dressed like. Good heavens, when I think you two went to school together, and the way he's got on – [*Speaking down the ginnel*] Morning, Mr Oglethorpe! We were just speaking about you, fancy!

WARBECK: Howdo, Michael. Have you a moment?

OGLETHORPE [*off*]: Howdo, Warbeck. Shall I come up?

WARBECK: If you will.

OGLETHORPE [*genially, as he enters*]: Good morning, good morning. Or should I say good afternoon, Mrs Warbeck? Eh? Ha ha! Lovely day. At least, it was at six o'clock. Early to bed and early to rise –

WARBECK: Gives a man little black circles under his eyes.

OGLETHORPE [*a bit false*]: Ha ha. I don't know, Warbeck, I don't know. The old saying is good enough for me. You don't see black circles under *my* eyes, now do you, Mrs Warbeck, eh?

MRS W [*simper*]: Oh, Mr Oglethorpe, it's not for me to say.

OGLETHORPE [*roguish*]: Oho. You've as much right as anyone. Come now, say whether I've got black circles under my eyes.

MRS W: Oh, Mr Oglethorpe!

OGLETHORPE: Well, I don't know! Still I don't suppose I can fairly ask a wife to testify against her husband. All right; you, Warbeck, will you admit I haven't got black circles under my eyes?

[WARBECK *looks earnestly.* OGLETHORPE *gets edgy.*]

I never heard of anything so daft! Will you admit it? Here, Mrs Warbeck, fetch us a mirror.

[MRS WARBECK *laughs nervously.*]

Black circles my foot.

[WARBECK *nods his head.*]

What d'you mean? Yes I have, or yes I haven't?

WARBECK: Yes, you haven't got black circles under your eyes.

MRS W: Well, of course not. What a question!

OGLETHORPE [*with solemnity*]: Early to bed and early to rise makes a man –

WARBECK: Healthy.

OGLETHORPE [*with a quick glance at Warbeck*]: I think I may say, considering my work and my responsibilities – Yes. Healthy, wealthy –

WARBECK [*muttering*]: I'll give you wealthy.

OGLETHORPE: Thanks very much, I'm sure. Healthy, wealthy, and –

MRS W: Mr Warbeck, I think that kettle will be boiling, don't you? D'you fancy a cup of tea, Mr Oglethorpe?

OGLETHORPE: Healthy, wealthy, and wise.

MRS W: Mr Warbeck, are you going to make that cup of tea?

[WARBECK *goes into the house.* OGLETHORPE *is abstracted and ruffled; he looks vaguely up to the sky, gaping.* MRS WARBECK *continues brittle and sociable.*]

He always has a cup of tea ready for me when I come home from service, so you might as well join us. I'll not ask you in, seeing it's such a lovely day. I see you're looking at our roof.

OGLETHORPE [*coming out of trance*]: Clouding over. Yes, that would be very nice, I'd like one.

MRS W: I knew you would.

OGLETHORPE: That's right, Mrs Warbeck. You know me.

MRS W: Mm. It leaks, you know.

OGLETHORPE [*looking at her blankly*]: Pity it's clouded over. I plan to have a round of golf with the mayor after dinner.

MRS W: Fancy.

OGLETHORPE: Nothing like golf for business – or business for golf, for that matter, eh? Ha ha.

MRS W [*politely*]: Ha ha. Oh yes. Guinness and bolf. [*She develops a nervous giggle.*]

OGLETHORPE: No, seriously though, this'll be the proudest, and the busiest, week of my life. The mayor and I will be hard at it from morning till night. I really don't see what's entertaining you, Mrs Warbeck. This new library's going to be the finest municipal library in the whole of England.

MRS W: Oh, the libry!

OGLETHORPE: The Library.

MRS W: I thought you were speaking of golf. Oh, I'm ever so sorry. Whatever must you think of me? You must be very proud. Excuse me.

OGLETHORPE [*hurt*]: It'll be my moment, Mrs Warbeck.

MRS W: Call me Rose.

OGLETHORPE: Very well then, Rose. It's taken eight years to build, it incorporates three smaller libraries, and adds a technical, a commercial, and a musical library, a theatre, an art gallery, and a civic information centre to the city's amenities. And though it will never be given, except privately of course, I believe I deserve as much credit as anyone. In my speech, which will be a short introduction to His Excellency, who is to perform the opening ceremony, I intend to say: 'The City Praises Itself.' What d'you think of that?

MRS W: I think it's absolutely lovely, Mr Oglethorpe.

OGLETHORPE: Call me Michael. Go on! Or Mike.

MRS W: Oh no, Mitle is quite good enough for me. I can't tell you how much I admire how you've got on, Mitle.

OGLETHORPE: Bless you for that, Rose.

MRS W: And God bless you, Mitle.

[*Their conversation has become quieter and more confidential. They glow with admiration for Oglethorpe. WARBECK edges between them with a cup of tea in each hand, his face expressing an elaborate and gloomy disapproval.*]

WARBECK: Tea up.

[*He hands them a cup each and then goes back into the house. They carefully pour the tea out of the saucers back into the cups. Nervousness has reappeared.*]

OGLETHORPE: You know, your husband worries me.

MRS W: Don't give it a thought, Mitle. He's funny sometimes. He doesn't mean anything, I'm sure. He's passionate, you know.

OGLETHORPE: No, I mean, he never seems really happy in himself.

MRS W [*it slips out in a moment of bitterness*]: Well, if he isn't, he's nobody to thank but himself. He's never done a thing he didn't want to, and he's always gone his own way so what I said. He had the same start as what you had exactly, and if he hasn't got what he wanted, it's because he didn't want it enough. [*She pulls herself up.*] Anyway, he's perfectly happy, so far as I know.

[*WARBECK has reappeared. In his hand a pint mug with a large crack which sets MRS WARBECK's teeth on edge.*]

Oh, there you are, William. [*He ignores her.*] I see you've got that old shaving-mug out again. And look at that crack, dribbling.

[*The atmosphere is constrained.* WARBECK *puts his finger on the crack.*]
Oh yes, Mitle, talking of leaks –

WARBECK: First of all, I haven't washed up from breakfast. And second, I happen to like this mug.

MRS W: I can't hear a word you say when you mumble.

OGLETHORPE: How's the Glee Club, Warbeck? We used to have some fun with that when we were lads. But I don't keep that sort of thing up now. I just can't. When you come to man's estate, you have to put away many things, I'm sorry to say, and the Glee Club was one I had to forgo –

WARBECK: I expect it'd seem childish in a mason to be singing with his mates on a Sunday night.

OGLETHORPE: That's right, Warbeck. I've always known you understood.

MRS W: Of course it would, William.

WARBECK: Don't call me William!

MRS W: He's got better things to do of a Sunday evening, I know. Don't mumble.

OGLETHORPE: Now now now, Rose my dear, I don't want your husband to run away with the idea that I've anything against the Glee Club as such. I may be busy, and I may have a certain amount of influence, but such small artistic endeavours play a part in the community life as well: a clock has to have wheels, as well as somebody to wind it.

WARBECK: And somdy's got to shovel shit before a cock can crow on it – I'm sorry, my love, it just slipped out.

MRS W: Oh! [*pause*] Oh! [*pause*] Oh! In front of all these people.

OGLETHORPE: That was very uncalled-for, my friend. I'll say thank you for my cup of tea, and good morning to you both.

[MARILYN *comes down the ginnel as if she hasn't been listening, carrying a bag with beer bottles in it.* OGLETHORPE *would like to go now, but* WARBECK *doesn't take his cup, so he can't.*]

MARILYN: 'lo Mr Oglethorpe, 'lo Mrs Warbeck, 'lo Mr Warbeck.
[*She crosses and goes off.*]

WARBECK [*mumbling*]: – could stand here all day. Nothing gets done.

MRS W: What's that you say? I can't hear a word you're saying when you mumble –

WARBECK: We get no forrader.

MRS W: Well, whose fault is that, then? Ask him, go on. [*Impatient.*] Oh!

OGLETHORPE: If you don't mind taking this cup off my hands –

WARBECK: Never you mind the cup. What're you going to do about the roof?

OGLETHORPE: Eh?

MRS W: William!

WARBECK: I'll show you. [*To his wife*] It leaks, doesn't it? You said it did, yourself. Well, I know. I know very well. So does he.

OGLETHORPE: Er, the roof?

WARBECK: Yes! It leaks, and you know it.

OGLETHORPE: Now just a minute –

WARBECK: And the gas! There'll be no justing, Michael Oglethorpe. It's high time I come out of my shell. And I'm coming out. [*He walks out of the gate. Stands at a loss. Then, with firmness.*] What you going to do about it? 'The City Praises Itself.' Typical. You've always been the same, since we were at school. All blether and show. I expect if you had your head, the triumphal columns'd be that close-packed into t'library door, nob'dy'd be able to get in to read t'books! By God!

MRS W: You'll do no good by desecrating your maker, and calling Michael Oglethorpe!

WARBECK: The way you talk, it sounds like the same thing!

[MRS WARBECK *bursts into tears and rushes into the house.*]

Now I've done it. She'll hide my bottle of ale and not speak. She can be very spiteful.

OGLETHORPE: You've hurt my feelings, Warbeck. Truly.

WARBECK: Last time it rolled off the privy roof, in a storm a week later, and smashed.

OGLETHORPE: What did?

WARBECK: My ale. She reckoned she'd put it up there to be out of the way while she dusted.

OGLETHORPE: I don't think I've ever been so cut.

WARBECK: Aye. Well.

OGLETHORPE: I try to have a happy relationship with my tenants. And that you, of all people, my old school pal, should suddenly turn on me and abuse me – I won't remind you that your rent is small, because I've no wish that it should be otherwise –

[MRS WARBECK *has switched on the wireless vindictively, and an anthem* (Balm of Giliad *or* Emmanuel) *swells up.*]

OGLETHORPE [*continues*]: But I will point out that repairs are expensive, and that if I were to insist on an economic rent – economic for me that is – you might have a right to demand repairs.

[*The music is very loud by now, and they shout over it.*]

I came round here full of goodwill. In fact I have a double grandstand ticket for the parade and the opening of the library. That'll show you.

WARBECK: I'm working.

OGLETHORPE: Eh?

WARBECK: Working.

OGLETHORPE: There you go again. Nothing but abuse. I don't know what's got into you. Well, perhaps your missus'll be a bit more gracious. Good morning.

[OGLETHORPE *hands over the tickets. Both turn and go. The music comes to an end. Both return.* OGLETHORPE *hands over his cup and saucer to Warbeck and roars.*]

Say thanks very much to Rose.

[*The pips sound out very loud.* OGLETHORPE *goes, and then stops and turns.*]

You can thank her for me, and you can thank her for yourself! She's a fine woman, and she married a skunk. If it weren't for her I'd *show* you my opinion of you. So think on. I've more money in this town than most, and money talks. I can make your life a hell, and will, if need be.

[OGLETHORPE *and* WARBECK *go off.* LES WARD *and* MR HARBUCKLE *come on from different sides. They speak as if this were their first meeting today.*]

HARBUCKLE: Morning, Mr Ward.

WARD: Morning, Mr Harbuckle.

[*Both peer up the ginnel after* OGLETHORPE.]

WARD [*continues*]: It's all right, he's gone.

HARBUCKLE: Is he going to t'door?

WARD: How do I know?

HARBUCKLE: Go and have a look.

WARD: I nearly went! Oh, my poor old heart.

HARBUCKLE: We'll hear if he knocks.

WARD: Will Mrs Harbuckle answer?

HARBUCKLE: Not the trump of doom, while she's on with the Sunday dinner.

WARD: Oglethorpe is the trump of doom.

HARBUCKLE: Well, I said she wouldn't answer.

WARD: You got a good missus there. What d'you mean, the trump of doom? He can't touch you. You haven't done anything.

HARBUCKLE: Only sublet in direct contravention of the agreement, that's all. Oh yes, and incidentally built a shed without planning permission, and also in direct contrav— It's all his pigeon, you know.

WARD: I'm a visitor.

HARBUCKLE: Just dropped in for dinner.

WARD: Yes. That's right.

HARBUCKLE: – and to give me a hand with building a shed, for my motorbike.

WARD: Yes. That's right. Where's that girl of yours with the beer?

HARBUCKLE: I haven't got a motorbike.

WARD: That's right. I have, though.

HARBUCKLE: So we just run up a shed for you while you're here for dinner?

WARD: Listen: you pay your rent, don't you?

HARBUCKLE: No. I spent it on the wood for the shed.

WARD: You filthy blackguard.

HARBUCKLE: Have I said something?

[WARD *has become aware that they are being watched. He slowly swivels until he sees* WARBECK *staring steadily out of the window. He starts.*]

WARD: Ow, mother! Oh, my poor heart.

[WARBECK *disappears.*]

The face at the window.

HARBUCKLE: Eh?

WARD: Didn't you see him?

HARBUCKLE: No. Who?

WARD: Perhaps as well. Anyroad, if we're going to have to wait – [*Pulls out the* News of the World, *reads*] 'Mr Justice Cobbler said in court today: "It would be better if some young women would stop being raped sooner than they do."' He's right, you know. Wait a bit: 'Trades Union leaders are meeting this week-end to discuss the stoppage in the Road Haulage Industry.' They'll probably have all you packers and storemen go slow in sympathy.

HARBUCKLE: Roll on tomorrow. I can't stand the pace today, and that's a fact. I don't see why the packers and storemen particularly.

WARD: Use your head. They have to watch how they go, else they'll have a general strike, and everybody against the lorry drivers for starting it. Connected unions only. With go-slows, token strikes, and so on. And only where it's effective. If my union called the engineers out at our place, that'd only make three of us, and the foreman could handle our work – Mm – That's a point. I don't think I fancy them finding out exactly how much I do.

HARBUCKLE: Well, they better watch how they get us packers and storemen going slow, because old Perky's a paid-up member, and he works in the gents now. Can't have him going slow.

WARD: I should think he'd fall on his head if he went anything else.

HARBUCKLE: He hates strikes.

WARD: Well, he can't go black all by himself in the lavatories, can he? What's he going to do? Write slogans on the wall?

HARBUCKLE: I reckon it's all right now, don't you?

WARD: I reckon so. Oh look, there comes that great big gorgeous girl of yours with the beer! Come on, my loving darling.

HARBUCKLE: Now for heaven's sake don't *you* start on about her. She's bad enough with the milkman.

WARD [*laughs lustily*]: I don't know, Harbuckle. She's like the barmaid at the Church Inn: looks all the better for a bagful of beer. Don't you worry sometimes that the landlord mightn't believe she's eighteen, when you send her for beer?

HARBUCKLE: He knows damn well she's only fourteen, but he only gets round to thinking about that after a while.

[MARILYN *is coming on, when* WARBECK *comes purposefully out of the house to them.*]

Morning, Perkin.

WARD: Hallo, Perky. Something about the Glee Club?

MRS W [*screaming from the house*]: William! Dinner's ready!

[WARBECK *turns round and goes back in. The others go off.*]

CURTAIN

SCENE TWO

The factory washroom and lavatories. A corridor, alongside of which are the WCs, runs off to one side; the major part of the scene is the wider part of the room where there is a washbasin and a roller-towel. There is a mirror on the wall and a frosted-glass window that can be opened a little.

[*Two* APPRENTICES *enter, the first carrying a racing newspaper.*]

FIRST APPRENTICE: You'd think there'd be *somewhere* in a works this size where you could skive off for a read of the racing.

SECOND APPRENTICE: We're all right here.

FIRST APPRENTICE [*checking round*]: Old Warbeck doesn't seem to be here. Idle beggar.

SECOND APPRENTICE: I'd like to see him offer to stop us. Where's the paper? We'll get us bets sorted, and then we'll be able to get 'em on dinner-time.

[*The* FIRST APPRENTICE *has heard a movement and gestures conspiratorially.*]

Come on, give us it here. I think Loppylugs is running.

FIRST APPRENTICE [*mouthing the words*]: There's som'dy here.

SECOND APPRENTICE: Give us the paper –

FIRST APPRENTICE: Don't you see? With the branch meeting on, the only people likely to be in here'll be staff.

[*One of the cubicle doors opens, and* BOOTLE, *the manager, comes out. The* FIRST APPRENTICE *hauls the other into the nearest cubicle.* BOOTLE *comes along to the outer door; as he passes the open cubicle door, they see who it is and shut the door rapidly.* BOOTLE *spins round.* WARBECK *comes in from the factory with fresh water and a mop in a bucket.*]

WARBECK: Oh, good morning, sir.

BOOTLE: Good morning, Warbeck. Look, you can drop the 'sir'. I've told you umpteen times, we're not in the army now. Call me Captain Bootle, like everyone else does. Dammit, man, we were in the same depot together.

WARBECK: Yes, sir. I mean Captain. Some of the happiest days of my life.

BOOTLE [*kindly, as he goes*]: Well, no sense sentimentalizing, Warbeck.

WARBECK: My heart's not in this business, Captain.

BOOTLE [*stops*]: Eh?

WARBECK [*his glazed and heroic stare encountering something on the wall*]: Token strike. We just had a branch meeting. Excuse me.

[*He goes and has a look at the wall and speaks righteously.*]
Captain, I just want you to come and look at this, and you'll see for yourself the sort of thing I have to put up with. It's not on, you know, I mean –

BOOTLE [*looks*]: Mm? Oh yes. That's rather good, isn't it?

WARBECK: And this. And this. Just look.

BOOTLE: Can't think how I came to miss them.

WARBECK: And it's all fresh from last night. Every inch was scrubbed.

BOOTLE [*looks more closely*]: I'd never thought of that one.

WARBECK: They come in here, strewing fag-ends all over my floor. And I don't know what they've done to the flush in there, but they've done something. [*Tries the first cubicle, which resists.*] I beg your pardon! If you jerk it just that little bit too vigorous, you get a shower-bath. It comes squirting out o' t'cistern. It's the ball-cock.

BOOTLE [*vague*]: Captain.

WARBECK [*shouting to the occupant of first cubicle*]: You want to watch yourself wi' that flush! It comes squirting out if you pull too hard on t'chain! [*Looks round for more evidence.*] And then if I'm not watching them every minute – Look at that. 'City for Cup'; they're lucky to be in t'first division.

BOOTLE [*seeing some writing that isn't amusing*]: 'Bobo Bootle is a . . .' Yes. Well –

WARBECK [*looks*]: Aye. And the insulting references to your person are Singularly Unfunny.

BOOTLE: Mm. Well, Warbeck, you know what to do?

WARBECK: Yes, sir.

BOOTLE: Captain, Corporal.

WARBECK: Warbeck, Captain.

BOOTLE: Carry on, Warbeck.

WARBECK: Yes, Captain.

BOOTLE [*stopping on his way out*]: Warbeck, what was that remark you made just now?

WARBECK [*after a think*]: They don't think, you know. I don't know what their homes are like. They have no consideration.

BOOTLE [*trying to avoid Warbeck's Ancient Mariner gaze*]: Yes. Yes, yes.

WARBECK: They don't know what they *do* want, only they want something. Take this token strike –

BOOTLE: Strike.

WARBECK: I don't see as it'll get anybody owt. The drivers stop; they get the soldiers in. They get the soldiers in; us that does the loading stops. It's like a game you play to relieve your feelings. The old battles was good battles, as well you and I know. The Somme, Hill 60 –

BOOTLE: Ah yes. Magnificent, titanic. I well remember the warm glow it gave us chaps –

WARBECK: Er – er – Ypres.

BOOTLE: Thirty thousand fallen – a noble sacrifice –

WARBECK: And then there was the General Strike –

BOOTLE: That's right. A great time – we worked the trams, drove the lorries, made sure the kiddies got their milk – d'you remember?

WARBECK: No. I was on strike.

BOOTLE: Well, Warbeck, there was much to be said on both sides; but we won through in the end. And it was an *honourable* struggle, between *men*; not a few malcontented individuals – er – er – sort of – well – we might not necessarily have been much better off, or happier, when we finished, but at least we had *hope*. And we fought as if we could really win something.

WARBECK: That's just what I'm saying. Think of the Spanish War.

BOOTLE: Exactly. Some of those reds were real heroes. Fine men, I shouldn't wonder.

WARBECK: – and Dunkirk and all that.

BOOTLE: We wouldn't have done it if we hadn't been hundred per cent sure that it was worth doing. Worth while.

[*A doubt has been growing in* WARBECK's *mind about the way this conversation is going. A slight pause.*]

WARBECK: Come to think of it, I don't see the difference.

BOOTLE: No. Mmm?

WARBECK [*speaking into Bootle's ear*]: Come to think of it, it doesn't seem all that different, now I come to think of it. You still get some daft nellie getting all worked up about battles he's not fighting, any more than we were in France fourteen–eighteen. I mean, it was all right for us in the depot; but I don't suppose them as were actually shooting bullets were bothered who they shot at or why. If they had an R.S.M. like ours, they'd have more to think about.

BOOTLE [*vaguely and without conviction or comprehension*]: Daft nellie? – I've always thought of you, Warbeck, as a noble great-hearted Englishman.

WARBECK: No need for me to tell you how I look up to you, sir.

BOOTLE [*absently*]: Captain, Warbeck.

[*There is an awkward hiatus. They face each other coughing slightly. Suddenly* WARBECK *reaches out for his broom, which is directly behind Bootle.* BOOTLE *mistakes this for a clumsy embrace and is hotly embarrassed.* WARBECK *obstinately disentangles himself and the broom, and goes off, sweeping, without a backward glance.*]

BOOTLE: I shall, er – think over what you say Warbeck, and er – give you an answer. You say they've decided on a strike?

[WARBECK *doesn't turn.* BOOTLE *escapes.* WARBECK *sweeps all the cubicles but the nearest, which is still apparently occupied when he pushes the door. He apologizes loudly and elaborately.*]

WARBECK: I beg your pardon!

[LES WARD *comes in to wash and comb his hair.*]

WARD: Hallo, Perky. How's the powder-room staff? What's the matter with old Bootle? Old love-in-idleness. Oh those typists. I reckon a strike'd about break his heart. *We* can all go home, and he wouldn't notice; but if he had a union to call him out, and he had to leave all those lovely girls – Oh dear, oh dear. I wonder if he's heard about us?

WARBECK: I told him personally.

WARD: Well, you'd better tell *yourself* personally, hadn't you? Put that brush down, and come home with me.

WARBECK: I haven't finished.

WARD: You haven't finished? Well neither have I finished, I'm happy to say. Stop mucking about, it's home-time now, old maty. Look, there's a one-day token strike on today, remember? I'm not even called out, but I'm off, 'cause I can't work by myself. You're a fully paid-up packer, and you're out – or somebody might be unkind to you.

[WARBECK *is looking under the door. He straightens up.*]

WARBECK: When I was a lad, we only had the one privy to the whole terrace – and old Mary Ellen Schofield, what was used to get in there, unscrew her wooden leg (she had a wooden leg from falling up the church steps, she were that fain to leave home), anyway, she used to jam it between the seat and the door, and have about two hours' privacy, regular. Wi' all t'neighbours shouting 'Come on, Mary Ellen!' And knocking, and coughing, you know.

[WARBECK *is slowly realizing that he has seen two pairs of shoes in there. He does a vast double-take that jack-knifes him up and down.*]

WARD: Yes, you get some people who only really live in there. In Palestine a bloke blew his brains out in the next one to me. With a rifle. Put it in his mouth and then trod on the trigger. First thing I knew was this bang, and all this red on the ceiling. While I was in there!

WARBECK: Just a minute. Just a minute. Come out of there at once, d'you hear me? D'you mind coming out of there? [*Getting worked up.*] I want you out of there this minute! The two of you! [*He kicks the door, and immediately smooths the paint down. Bangs with his fist.*] Excuse me!

WARD: You're getting a bit overloaded, Perky, aren't you? Calm down, there'll be nothing you'd fancy in there, anyway.

WARBECK: There's two on 'em in there!

[*The* APPRENTICES *come out of the cubicle. One carries a racing paper. The first addresses* WARD.]

FIRST APPRENTICE: Never heard so much fuss. Old Bootle wasn't so soft, when he got Perky in here. You used to be able to have a read of the racing in peace.

34

WARD: You can go home and have a read now, anyway.

FIRST APPRENTICE [*vaguely imagines he's sacked*]: Eh?

WARD: There's a one-day token strike on.

FIRST APPRENTICE: Oh. So what you doing still here, if you're supposed to be on strike? [*Indicating Warbeck.*] Him as well?

WARD [*nods*]: If I can prise him off the job, that is.

WARBECK: I shall come in my own good time.

FIRST APPRENTICE: Anyhow, it's got nothing to do with us.

WARD: If you'd take a glance at the *other* side of that paper, you'd see it's got everything to do with you.

[*After a suspicious look, the* APPRENTICE *innocently looks at the front page of the paper he is holding.*]

FIRST APPRENTICE [*reads*]: 'Stylish Win for Red Plush.'

[WARD *snatches the paper, turns it over, and glances at it, before thrusting it back.*]

WARD [*in disgust*]: The Pony Express.

FIRST APPRENTICE: That's right. The bible.

[*The other* APPRENTICE *has been looking out of the window. The first one now goes over for a look.*]

He's right, you know. There's the picket already. [*More cheerfully.*] And feel how quiet it is.

[*The* APPRENTICES *start to go.*]

You'd better bustle about, Perky. Else the milk monitors out there'll think you're black. He comes in at half past nine and he's away before twelve – Cripes. They ought to have him on the board of directors.

WARBECK: Don't let me catch you at it again, that's all.

FIRST APPRENTICE: Why don't you belt up? [*Flaring.*] Where else are we supposed to have a look at the news? [*Going.*]

WARBECK: It's nothing to me what you were up to. I won't have two together.

FIRST APPRENTICE [*stops*]: What's that?

WARBECK: Dirty young beggars.

[*There is a freeze.* WARD *stands easily, mild and muscular. The*

35

SECOND APPRENTICE's *eyes are bulging, but he draws the other away.*]

FIRST APPRENTICE: You'll get yours, my old friend. You'll get yours.

[*The* APPRENTICES *go.* MR HARBUCKLE *comes in.*]

WARD: Nasty pair of kippers.

HARBUCKLE: Eh? Those two? They're all right. Nothing wrong with 'em that hard work wouldn't mend. Where's Mr Warbeck?

WARD: He's just finishing.

HARBUCKLE: Are you coming home, Mr Warbeck?

WARBECK: I'll not be a minute.

HARBUCKLE: Hurry up, I want to catch the girl before she comes all this way with us lunch.

WARBECK: Oh, aye.

WARD: I'll wait outside for you. I could do with some fresh air.

HARBUCKLE: We'll wait for you outside, Perkin.

[WARBECK *is just outside the cubicle, and resents the 'fresh air' line.*]

WARBECK: Oh, aye.

WARD [*mildly*]: It's nearly dinner-time, for heaven's sake. Marilyn'll be on her way.

HARBUCKLE: It doesn't matter a great lot, so long as we don't miss her altogether.

[WARD *and* HARBUCKLE *go. The* APPRENTICES *come in after a second. The second walks past Warbeck to check that there's nobody about. The first bars Warbeck's way out. The* FIRST APPRENTICE *is frightened, and the silent struggle with the uncomprehending old man is weak versus weak. The* SECOND APPRENTICE *comes up from behind Warbeck, grips him efficiently, puts him into the cubicle, and follows. There is a thud. The* SECOND APPRENTICE *comes out. The* FIRST APPRENTICE *is left behind in all this. He begins to giggle.*]

FIRST APPRENTICE: Look at him in there. He looks as if he's praying.

SECOND APPRENTICE [*stops on his way out*]: What's up with you?

FIRST APPRENTICE: Just look at him kneeling there and wagging his head up and down! Creeping Jesus!

[*The* FIRST APPRENTICE *is nearly hysterical. The other comes back, goes into the cubicle again, comes out again. This shuts the* FIRST APPRENTICE *up. They both leave soberly and swiftly.* WARBECK *emerges, very slowly, his chest heaving and his legs weak, gasping a conversation with himself about what he's doing.*]

WARBECK: Eh. Eeeh. Oh my goodness, it's difficult. Every step's agony. All very quiet – Hey! Nob'dy about, o' course.

[*We hear* MARILYN *outside.* WARBECK *can't call out or get to the window. He struggles to get his jacket on back to front.*]

MARILYN: Mr Warbeck! Here's my dad's dinner and Mr Ward's! Mr Warbeck! Yoohoo!

WARBECK: She's brought her dad's dinner round here. There now. Can't get into t'works, I shouldn't wonder. All right, Marilyn, my love.

MARILYN: Yoohoo! It's Marilyn! Mr Warbeck! Yoohoo!

WARBECK: Yes, well, it's all very well yoohooing. Just wait your sweat. Phew! I feel right funny.

MARILYN: Mr Warbeck, darling, here y'are! Yoohoo!

WARBECK: Can't you hear me when I tell you? I'm coming, I tell you.

[WARD *comes in, and falls flat over the broom.* HARBUCKLE *follows.* WARBECK *falls down.* HARBUCKLE *trips on the broom and steadies himself on Ward.*]

HARBUCKLE: What's going on here?

WARD: Skittles. [*He helps Warbeck.*] Come on, old lad. There's nothing down there, I've just been.

HARBUCKLE: Hey. Poor old Perkin's been took bad. D'you think somebody hit him, or what?

WARD: Go and get the nurse.

[HARBUCKLE *goes out.*]

Don't try and sit up until we know what's wrong.

WARBECK [*very quietly*]: I'm perfectly all right, I tell you. Marilyn.

WARD: What's that? Did you pass out?

WARBECK: The girl's outside the window.

MARILYN [*off*]: Yoohoo! Yoohoo!

[BOOTLE *comes in with* HARBUCKLE. *They both trip over the broom together.*]

HARBUCKLE: That's the second time.

BOOTLE: Well, pick it up then. How is he? This could be a very nasty business. Cause a lot of trouble, if this is a piece of strike violence, you know.

HARBUCKLE: The nurse has gone for her dinner. Is he all right?

BOOTLE: Can you move your legs, Warbeck?

WARBECK: Course I can move my legs. Marilyn's –

BOOTLE: Mmm. Black eye, symptoms of shock. No, don't try to move. Can you hear what I'm saying? Try to move your feet.

WARD: What the hell's his feet got to do with a black eye?

WARBECK [*suddenly clear and loud*]: Yes, that's right. What's my feet got to do with a black eye?

[*They all look at him and then resume their conversation.*]

BOOTLE [*to Ward*]: A black eye is a symptom, not a cause.

WARD: Sounds pretty rum to me.

BOOTLE: Don't argue. [*To Warbeck*] Twiddle your feet. [WARD *looks up.*] Hm.

HARBUCKLE: Do as he says, Perkin. He knows what he's doing.

[*With a great effort* WARBECK *says, like an oracle.*]

WARBECK: All I know is one thing. First, if my feet rot and drop off I shan't get a black eye. And second, if I did, twiddling them wouldn't cure it.

WARD: First bit of sense I've heard.

BOOTLE: Look, I don't know who you are, but whoever you are –

MARILYN [*off*]: Yoohoo! Mr Warbeck!

BOOTLE: Be quiet! Who was that?

HARBUCKLE: I think it's my little daughter, sir, with us dinners.

BOOTLE [*mastering himself, and returning to Warbeck*]: I'm asking you to twiddle your feet, Warbeck, because I want to be sure that your back is all right.

WARD: First it's black eyes, now it's his back. Why don't you twiddle your feet and we'll see if the lights go out?

BOOTLE: His spine, you fool. His spine. How dare you speak to me like that?

WARD: His spine. Twiddle your feet, Perky.

[WARBECK *twiddles his feet.*]

MARILYN [*off*]: Yoohoo!

BOOTLE: Pick him up, you two. We must get him out of here and off the premises. Might be very embarrassing. I'll tell that child to go away. [*He calls out as he goes over to the window.*] Mr Warbeck is not seeing anyone just now! Go away, pl—

[*He arrives at the window and peers down. He is struck speechless by what he sees. He turns rapidly away from the window, as if he'd seen something he shouldn't. Wipes his forehead with a handkerchief.*]

My jolly goodness gracious me!

[BOOTLE *follows the other three out.*]

CURTAIN

SCENE THREE

The front parlour of Warbeck's house. There is a small upright armchair, chairs against the walls; gasfire in the fireplace, and a mirror over it. One sash window. A door to the kitchen, and another leading to the garden. Again we see the arch of the ginnel, but this time from the other side.

[MRS WARBECK *comes in from the kitchen, confident that Warbeck is there. She is rushing to get ready to go out.*]

MRS W: You don't need to try to keep it from me that something's up. Rooting round the house. That Les Ward and Mrs Harbuckle's husband's coming round, *I* know.

[*She sees that there is no one there, and drops into a self-talking tone.*] Oh – Seems the minute I go to meeting, he makes it an excuse to get his caterwauling friends in –

[*The* REPORTER *is at the door.*]

REPORTER: Mrs Warbeck?

MRS W: Get out of my house, with your feet. Like fair and foul weather, in one of them little houses.

[*She realizes that the Reporter is a stranger.*]

Oh.

REPORTER: I just pushed the door, and it seemed to be open. I heard about your husband's heroic stand at the factory.

MRS W: Stand?

REPORTER: I understood he'd been injured in a strike incident.

MRS W: Seems you know more about it than me, then.

REPORTER: It was very fine, Mrs Warbeck, and just what I'd have hoped of him.

MRS W: Well? Go on. What was?

REPORTER: He hasn't told you?

MRS W: He doesn't tell me. I find out. In the end. Most of the time he doesn't know himself, anyway, what's happened.

REPORTER: I hoped you'd tell me.

MRS W: Oh, I haven't patience –

REPORTER: I'm a reporter, you see. At least, I was. Well, I suppose I am –

MRS W: William!

[WARBECK *appears in the doorway from the kitchen, with coaldust on his face, a quart bottle of beer in his hand, and reproach in his regard.*]

REPORTER: I did what you said, Mr Warbeck. I had Oglethorpe and you both set up. Full page each. I'm freelancing now – I'm very happy, Perkin.

WARBECK: I've just found my Sunday ale.

MRS W: Well, if you got coal in more often, you'd have found it sooner.

WARBECK: I'd have had to shovel a ton on to t'fire first. It was tucked right at t'back.

MRS W: Well, don't look at me. I don't know how it got there.

[WARBECK *goes back into the kitchen.* MRS WARBECK *shrieks.*]

And don't go putting it on the kitchen table, all over coaldust!

[*There is a crash of glass.* MRS WARBECK *feels better.*]

What's that? I can't hear a word you say!

[MARILYN *sticks her head in at the window.*]

MARILYN: 'lo Mrs Warbeck. How's Mr Warbeck?

MRS W: He's perfectly all right, so far as I know, Marilyn, my love.

MARILYN: Has he still got a black eye, Mrs Warbeck? Didn't it look heavenly, all shiny and m'room, with his eye sort of swimming in blood. I think it looked noble. Made you want to hold it in your hand. I think black eyes are nicer than rings under your eyes, don't you, Mrs Warbeck? My dad says Mr Warbeck's not in sympathy with this strike. Is that how he got a black eye? My dad says Mr Warbeck won't open his lips about how it happened.

MRS W: Oh, Marilyn, you do go on and on about Mr Warbeck's eye. I don't know whether I've got my lipstick on or my mascarara or what – I'm trying to get ready to go out.

MARILYN: Yes. My mother says to tell you she's ready.

MRS W: Not in sympathy, indeed!

REPORTER: I think Mr Warbeck'd stick up for his principles.

MRS W: Oh yes. Only stick *down* is more like. He's a cottle for sticking, is my William. That there Gandhi was a revelation to him, with his passive resistance.

MARILYN: What's passive resistance, Mrs Warbeck?

MRS W: Getting your own way with doing nothing. And he's a dab-hand at both of 'em. And that's what a strike is. And he's a dab-hand at striking too.

MARILYN [*after thought*]: You can't just do nothing.

MRS W: Exactly.

41

MARILYN: What's spiritualism?

MRS W: It's what your mother and me do every Tuesday and Sunday.

MARILYN: Yes, I know.

MRS W: William!

[*Very ostentatious busy noises off.*]

William! I'm off now!

MARILYN: Mr Warbeck doesn't like to be called William, does he, Mrs Warbeck?

MRS W: Now that'll be quite enough from you, Marilyn, my lass.

[*MRS WARBECK goes to the front door, opens it, slams it again, and stands within the room with her back against the door. WARBECK appears from the kitchen almost immediately, carrying a newspaper and a glass of beer. He is dumbfounded to see his wife still there. MARILYN giggles.*]

William, I'm off now.

[*WARBECK pretends he has left something in the kitchen.*]

Perkin! Oh, how I hate that name. You'd think after twenty years – Perkin.

[*WARBECK returns and gives her a kiss.*]

WARBECK: Goodbye, my love.

MRS W [*sniffing*]: You'd do better to have that gas leak mended, then –

MARILYN [*at the now open door*]: Mr Warbeck, was Gandhi married?

MRS W [*sharply*]: Marilyn, pull your stockings up. You look like a double-barrelled concertina.

[*MRS WARBECK goes. The REPORTER has to retreat to the window to let her by. MARILYN takes his place at the door. The REPORTER returns to his place at the door, and MARILYN turns interestedly to him. He goes back to the window. WARBECK settles himself in the chair. The REPORTER looks in at the window.*]

REPORTER: You must go on, Perkin. You've brought hope to me, and I want to be the one to bring you to the world. Some great gesture is expected of you.

WARBECK: Now then, Marilyn.

MARILYN: No, only who is it, Mr Warbeck?

WARBECK: Hush.

MARILYN: I think he's daft.

WARBECK: Marilyn!

REPORTER: The library opening and parade could be it, Perkin. I shall be there. I've still got my press card. I'll try and cover it for the nationals, if you'll just give me some idea of the line you'll take.

[MARILYN *comes and shuts the window on him. He pushes it up again.*]

Perkin, a great parade comes by for the library opening, with thousands of soldiers and that. And Oglethorpe up there in front, with his chain and all, getting all the credit. What d'you do?

[WARBECK *is impassive.*]

No. You're right. It's too difficult.

[MARILYN *leans forward and kisses him full on the lips.*]

I can't cope with everything. [*He goes.*]

MARILYN: Can I come in now, Mr Warbeck?

WARBECK: Course you can. Any time you like. Only I shall want you to run down for a quart for me shortly.

MARILYN: Oh pooh, look at these stockings. It's too hot for thick stockings anyway. I didn't want to take them off outside, in case someone was looking, but I didn't care about them, I just let them hang, all loopy. [*Taking them off.*] I don't mind them if they're pulled up tight like this, but they're better off. Don't you think so?

[*She lays the stockings on the arm of* WARBECK's *chair and seats herself. She looks down at her legs.*]

Look, they're all pink. You look as hot as what I feel, Mr Warbeck. My forehead's boiling, is yours? Let's put our foreheads together, and the one whose forehead feels hot to the other is the hottest.

WARBECK [*humbly*]: Now Marilyn, you don't know what you're doing.

MARILYN: Oh yes I do. I don't know why, though. I'm getting as close to you as I can. I'll hug you.

WARBECK: Oh, my head's throbbing.

MARILYN: From when you were bashed at at work?

WARBECK: Suppose so.

MARILYN: Kiss it better. [*She does so.*] I bet the other bloke was a mess!

WARBECK: He was a mess to start with.

MARILYN [*cuddling happily up*]: My Dad says he'll lam me if I do this to the milkman any more. But that doesn't stop me wanting to do it, does it?

WARBECK: No, but I daresay it stops you doing it, and that's something. It's very worriting for a man, when he's trying to deliver milk, you know.

MARILYN: Oh, I know. He says I haven't to do it when there's anybody watching. But I can never be bothered whether they're watching or not. Oh, it's wonderful, being with someone. I expect you know all about it?

WARBECK: I don't. That I don't. I think it's something you learn all at one go. If it had been any later for me, I'd have been dead, but I think my go's come.

MARILYN: You won't die, will you, Mr. Warbeck?

WARBECK: Not at this rate. My blood's going round me like a train in a tunnel.

[*They kiss very tenderly.* WARBECK *gets up.*]

MARILYN [*stating a fact*]: You taste sweet.

WARBECK: Nay, lass, I shall have to die after this. There's nowhere to go.

MARILYN [*getting up, after a decision, and taking hold of his hand*]: I know a place.

WARBECK [*in a trance*]: You're a scamp, Marilyn, that's what you are! Run along. Your father and Les'll be along any minute.

MARILYN: All right. But you won't forget me, will you?

WARBECK: There are just two of us in the room, aren't there? I mean, a room, and in it two different, separate people? A little girl and an old man. My head's in a daze.

MARILYN [*compassion*]: Never mind.

WARBECK: Never mind anything. Off you go. [*He gives her some*

44

money.] Get a quart. There's a bottle under the sink. I shan't want any, but we always have a drink Tuesday night.

[MARILYN *hugs him and goes*.]

Well, what d'you think of that? Disgusting. I'd never have believed it if I hadn't been there. I feel as if I were standing on my back legs for the first time. It's a disgrace. All my life I've been creeping about like a little little beetle, while everybody else seemed to be stampeding about. Like in the first war. Stampeding to kill. Or so as not to be killed. Or they were rushing after money and I don't know what-all. There was always something. Cup Final tickets was one I remember. And I thought, well, all right, if that's what they fancy. They were all shouting at me to get worked up about gas leaks and ambitions. But I was brought up in a big family, so I didn't mind the noise. Seems they couldn't just ignore me. Mind, I like things right. I mean, didn't I get my eye blacked yesterday for wanting things right? And then when they docked us money in 1926 ... Well, it stands to reason you don't work harder for getting hungrier, now do you? ... So we struck. And stood about and did nowt. I got a crack on the head from a truncheon for doing that, too. I'd do nowt again, for that matter. I've a hard nut. And then this has to happen. [*He thinks for a second*.] I don't suppose it makes any odds, but I know I'm alive now. I feel as if I'd had my ears washed out.

[MR HARBUCKLE *and* LES WARD *appear at the door*.]

HARBUCKLE: Are you in, Perkin?

WARBECK: Aye. Come in, lads.

HARBUCKLE: Had to prise him off the counter of the Church Inn. I don't know what he sees in that barmaid, I honestly don't.

WARBECK: Your Marilyn's gone for a quart for us.

WARD: Oh, that lovely creature.

HARBUCKLE [*to Warbeck*]: How are you, lad?

WARBECK: I feel as if I'd had my ears washed out.

WARD [*after a pause*]: Is that good or bad?

WARBECK [*going for glasses in the kitchen*]: I don't rightly know.

WARD: The things I do for you. Shenandoah, and then I'm off.

HARBUCKLE: Nay, Les, we'd break his heart. There's only me left of the old lot. He lives for his Tuesday nights.

WARD: I'm adamant. One song, and then off. Last time, when we finished off with 'And did those feet', and Mrs Warbeck come shrieking in, I had a very bad night's sleep. Him and his naked soul and his back teeth. I can't take much. I'm delicate.

[WARBECK *comes back in with two glasses. He pours the beer in his untouched glass into the two other glasses.*]

WARBECK: I had a slight accident with one bottle, and I only managed to save this drop. Still, barring glass splinters it should be all right. Here's to the lads of the Depot Catering Section, wherever they may be, good, dead, and indifferent.

HARBUCKLE }
WARD } : Cheers.

WARBECK [*taking off his jacket and laying it on the arm of the chair*]: Eeh, it's a long time since I felt as well. I keep on looking down to see if my feet reach the ground. Now where's my tuning-fork? You know, I often think I must look like a creature from outer space when I do this –

[*He taps the fork gently and places it on his forehead, regarding himself in the mirror.*]

WARD [*muttering*]: Looks like a creature from somewhere.

[WARBECK *emits the first note of the anthem vibrantly, rattling the pictures and ornaments, and startling Ward.*]

Oh my lord!

WARBECK [*sings*]:
      Mmmmthe lesson of history is clear
      It's safer by far to fight from the rear
      While the cooks and the crooks are baiting their hooks
      Your own side's the one you should fear.

ALL: God saves the cooks
      It's writ in the books
      La la lala, la la lala
      La la lala lah.

WARBECK: The liberating heroes storm in
          But the oppressors don't seem to be
          there to answer for their sin
          They're waiting about for a chance to come out
          And start the whole boiling again.

ALL: God saves the cooks … etc.

WARBECK: Mmmmthe machinery of freedom is refounded
          Officially the hunter is minced by the hounded
          But the new hand that turns is not much concern
          To sausages sold by the pound.

ALL: God saves the cooks
          It's writ in the books
          La la lala, la la lala
          La la lala lah.

[*They are all deeply satisfied by the song, and stand entranced for a second.* WARBECK *lays aside the tuning-fork and reaches out for a handkerchief in his jacket. His hand lights on Marilyn's stockings by mistake.*]

WARD [*mildly*]: Oh well. That's that. All over now. Thank you very much, all go home.

WARBECK: What are you talking about? We've not finished yet. [*He sees what he has in his hand, goes on speaking automatically.*] Mrs Warbeck'll not be home for a while yet.

HARBUCKLE: That's right, Les.

WARBECK: No, Les's right.

HARBUCKLE: That's what I said, didn't I?

WARBECK: No. I mean – it's a lovely night – I could just fancy a stroll down to the Church Inn – only not just now. Good night, lads.

HARBUCKLE: Eh?

WARBECK: I mustn't keep you past time.

HARBUCKLE [*to Ward*]: You've hurt his feelings.

WARD: All right, I'm sorry, Perky. What shall we sing?

WARBECK: There's nothing I'd like better. Better go. I don't want you to catch my black eye. Cold.

47

HARBUCKLE: Are you not well?

WARBECK: Aye. A cold. A cold. Very hot. Bit feverish. Good night, lads. It's not too late.

WARD: Look at him sweating! Here, where's your hanky, Perky?

WARBECK: No! It's black. Gone black. Dirty. Black eye. Cold. Good night, lads.

WARD: He's raving. Ought to be in bed.

WARBECK: So you should. Good night, lads. See you in the morning.

[WARBECK *backs off into the kitchen, one stocking stuffed in his pocket, and the other concealed behind his back. He shuts the kitchen door firmly.*]

HARBUCKLE: Just like me when I'm poorly: don't want to know anybody. Just leave me alone, that's all I ask.

WARD: Bit sudden, wasn't it?

HARBUCKLE: Hope he's all right.

[*As soon as Harbuckle and Ward have left and the front door has closed behind them,* WARBECK *looks out of the kitchen. He has the stockings in his hand. He crosses to the front door and looks out anxiously.* MARILYN *comes into the room from the kitchen. She looks round for the Glee Club.*]

MARILYN: Dad and Mr Ward not coming?

WARBECK [*swings round*]: They've gone off. Marilyn, you silly ha'porth, you left your stockings just now.

MARILYN: Oh heck them.

WARBECK: Well quick, take them now. I don't want them.

MARILYN: Oh, I see. Are you fed up with me?

WARBECK: Not a bit of it, Marilyn, my love. But what d'you think? Here, take them.

MARILYN [*clasping her hands behind his neck*]: Shan't.

WARBECK: By, it's a strain keeping this up. Give over, Marilyn. You can't leave me holding these stockings. Whatever d'you think Mrs Warbeck's going to think?

[MARILYN *is drawing him out of the house and along to the ginnel. We see them pass the window and reappear silhouetted in the passage.*]

MARILYN: Shan't. Shan't. Shan't.

[MARILYN *winds herself round Warbeck, and they lock. A* POLICE-MAN *comes cycling by. As he passes, he glances up the ginnel. He stops and gets off his bike. He speaks wonderingly to himself.*]

POLICEMAN: Young Marilyn Harbuckle –

[*He goes back and flashes his lamp up the ginnel. His suspicions confirmed, he is galvanized, and yells.*]

Marilyn!

[MARILYN *and* WARBECK *break and run, Marilyn one way and Warbeck the other, towards the house. The* POLICEMAN *gives chase.*]

Hey, you!

[WARBECK *comes into the house. He looks desperately round the room. He rushes to one place against the wall and stands rigidly, then to the armchair, where he tries to sit casually, then again to the wall in another place. The door is opened by the* POLICEMAN. WARBECK *rushes into the kitchen, the* POLICEMAN *sees him and follows. There is a tremendous clatter of pans from the kitchen.* WARBECK *rushes out again and stands rigid against a wall again. Silence. The kitchen door is opened carefully, and the* POLICEMAN *steps into the room. He stands attentively.*]

Mr Warbeck! No. Must be out. The gentleman who lives here is a personal friend of mine, and I don't suppose he'll be too pleased at you busting your way in here. Besides all your other troubles. I know you're in here somewhere. Interfering with a juvenile. Entering. Attempted evasion of arrest. Obstruction. Somebody's in trouble. Come on. I'll forget the obstruction if you come quietly. Those pans in there could have been an accident.

[*The* POLICEMAN *suddenly swings the door closed, and grabs among the coats hanging behind it. He bends down cautiously and looks under the furniture. He crawls forward, and is only a yard from Warbeck's feet when he sees them. He rises slowly, hardly able to imagine how anybody could have been just standing there in full view and not be spotted, and even more dumbfounded when he sees who it is.* WARBECK *blinks, but is no more capable of immediate comment than the policeman. The*

POLICEMAN *registers the black stockings draped over and dangling from Warbeck's fists. He puts out a hand to examine them.*]

Goodness gracious me. [*He sits down and puts his hand to his head.*] Perkin. I don't believe it. Say it wasn't you.

WARBECK: It wasn't me.

POLICEMAN: I don't believe you. Excuse me, I think I'd better go back to the station. Report. I don't know what the sergeant's going to say.

[*The* POLICEMAN *goes.* WARBECK *does not move. As he passes outside, the* POLICEMAN *hesitates, and looks in. He meets Warbeck's gaze, and hurries on. The* POLICEMAN *reaches his bike and makes a half-hearted attempt to mount, gives it up, and walks off wheeling it.* WARBECK *walks towards the kitchen. Stops.*]

WARBECK: I'll be summonsed, I shouldn't wonder.

[*He goes into the kitchen.*]

CURTAIN

SCENE FOUR

The lavatories at the factory. Outside there are crowds, marching soldiers, a distant military band.

[WARBECK *comes in with mop-bucket and mop. He sets them down, and gets a newspaper packet containing his snap out of his jacket pocket behind the door.* WARD *enters, and lights up.*]

WARD: Morning, Perky. All set for the library opening parade? Oglethorpe's great day? You should have a nice view from here. Oh, are you all right, after last night?

[WARBECK *mumbles gloomily through his sandwich that he is 'all right'.* WARD *strolls to the window to look out.*]

There's the police lining up.

[WARBECK *starts for the door.*]

Perky! Where are you going now? You can see them from here.

[WARBECK *stops and tries to speak. Chokes on his sandwich.* WARD *pounds his back.*]

You never know what's going to set him off next, do you? What did I say? I was talking about the police lining the route I think. [*Looks at Warbeck who has calmed down.*] 'Police lining the route.' No?

[WARBECK *nods conversationally.* WARD *gives up. He peers at the newspaper round Warbeck's sandwich. Reads.*]

'Chicken Sexer With Tin Legs Accused of Double Bigamy.' It's good, you know, that paper! 'She Went To His House to Watch Telly.' Mmmm. I like them 'serious offence' ones, don't you? [WARBECK *is rigid.*] The girl-friend says to me last Sunday, she says: 'Ooh, Les, I don't know what gets into you of a Sunday evening.'

WARBECK: So what did you say?

WARD: I've been thinking of answers all week. [*Reads.*] 'The Accountant and the Usherette.' I mean, that's the sort of thing you want after your Sunday dinner, isn't it? [*Reads.*] 'Duchess Claims – Playboy's Orgies –' It's all there, you know. Life. That's how people go on. The people.

WARBECK: It's not how I go on!

WARD: All right, all right. All I'm saying is, if it doesn't actually happen to you, you read about it. And it goes on. [*Indicates Warbeck's forehead.*] It goes on. You ask my girl-friend. [*Reads.*] 'He Led a Blameless Life Until He Met Her.' That's it. That's life.

WARBECK: It isn't. It's filth!

WARD: Perky, don't say that. Maybe they've been caught doing it in the wrong order, but we all want loving. That's how human beings are. That's life, isn't it?

WARBECK [*subdued*]: I don't know. But I'm living it now.

WARD: Of course you are, Perky. Don't let anybody tell you different. As I was saying to my girl-friend, we're all the same at bottom. But she would misunderstand me. You have a watch of the parade, and spit on Oglethorpe's head as he goes by. You get your head in quick, and he'll never know. [*Going.*]

WARBECK: I would, at that.

WARD [*stops*]: Here, what *did* happen to you last night?

WARBECK: Ne'er you mind. I'm a changed man now.

WARD: I hope you got good value. You look much the same.

WARBECK: I'm alive, that's what.

WARD [*thoughtful*]: Ye-es. [*Goes.*]

WARBECK: Alderman Oglethorpe's great day. [*Mops.*] When we were in standard one together, he couldn't *read*, ba'at I put them little dashes in between the bits of the words for him. Now his library's opening. I hope he tumbles down the steps. Tum-little-dash–bells down 'em. Mind, he were always good at sums.

[*Kettledrums, keeping time for the parade while the brass rests, approach along the street outside. Dum–ti–ti–dum–titi–dum–dum–dum.* WARBECK *dashes for a look. He checks himself, irritated at being caught out.*]

Dammit, I'll not watch. Couldn't see very well, anyhow.

[*The kettledrums are nearer. He sings derisively, in time with them.*]

> Our Betty Arbuckle thou dost know
> Used for t'live in Radcliffe Row
> Oo had a clock made out of steel
> Summat went wrong wi' t'owd fly-wheel
> T'owd fly-wheel come out wi' a thump
> On Betty's head it raised a lump
> Our Betty turned round she felt right queer,
> She said: 'Ee ba goom, but that's not fair.'
> Fact'ry lasses they get wed,
> Can't wash up nor make a bed.
> They make porridge thick and thin
> All full o' lumps wi' no salt in.

[*The kettledrums have been drawing nearer. As* WARBECK *puts full-stop to his song with a bit of zapateado, tum–tiddly–um–tum, the big drum comes in, and the brass blares.* WARBECK *dashes to the window.*]

Nay, blast it, all you can see is the library steps, and the stick going up and down. And Oglethorpe.

[*He turns away from the window. He contemplates the mop-head bitterly for a second. He parts the strands thoughtfully, as if brushing hair away from a face. He then lets go of the mop and spars fiercely for the split second it still stands, and at the last moment punches it. He goes back to his cleaning.*

The two APPRENTICES *come eagerly in. The second goes direct to the window and looks out.*]

FIRST APPRENTICE: Has the parade started? Hey, mate, look who's here.

SECOND APPRENTICE [*lighting up*]: I know.

FIRST APPRENTICE: That's a nasty bump you got on your eye, Perky. Fall down, did you? Want to watch you don't fall down again.

[*He shoves Warbeck and looks round for the approval of his mate. He sees, however, that his mate is gazing absorbed out of the window. He joins him.*]

Hey, look at that! We nearly missed it. The march-past! Bayonets and all. Look at that old gaffer with the sword. He'd be handy in the jungle, wouldn't he? He could dye his whiskers green for camouflage, and the sword'd come in handy for carving the Sunday elephant. What them blokes going in the new library for?

SECOND APPRENTICE: They just opened it. I expect they reckon they might as well go in and have a read.

FIRST APPRENTICE: Here come the troops. [*Halting troops are heard.*] What they stopping for? Lights agen 'em?

SECOND APPRENTICE: They'll wait here for the bigwigs to come out again, and then march off back to camp.

FIRST APPRENTICE: Seems a long way round to get nowhere, doesn't it? Is there anything more useless than the army?

SECOND APPRENTICE: Not in a war.

FIRST APPRENTICE: Oh well. In a war. But even then, they just cop a hydrogen bomb, and then, well, you might just as well have not polished your boots. Hey, look at the panic down there! What's up? All the officers looking at their watches. Oh look, they're coming out of the library again. That was a quick read. They've lost one. Him with the sword. Stayed behind for a slash, I expect. Have a look.

SECOND APPRENTICE: That's where you want to be in a war, in the army, in among 'em. A rifle in your hand. Head down, and blaze away. They darsent bomb you, because you're too close to their own lines. Rat-a-tat.

FIRST APPRENTICE: Or you could be a bomber pilot.

SECOND APPRENTICE: Yer.

FIRST APPRENTICE: Better than festering in this hole. But look out here –

SECOND APPRENTICE: You'll hear them shouting and banging their feet, before they set off again.

FIRST APPRENTICE: No, but look, the bigwigs are coming over here.

WARBECK: Who?

FIRST APPRENTICE: I don't know, but Bootle's one of them. And Alderman Oglethorpe. I expect the others'll be fight managers and agents and that. You want to see the medals Oglethorpe's carrying.

WARBECK: Aye. That's about his mark. What he couldn't get in his pocket he got on his chest.

FIRST APPRENTICE [astonished]: Hark at him.

SECOND APPRENTICE [advances coldly on Warbeck before speaking]: What's wrong wi' that? Nobody really cares what you think, you know, Perky. Not even Oglethorpe. They're not bothered. Oglethorpe is up. [Trips Warbeck.] And you're down.

FIRST APPRENTICE [nervous]: Hey, don't.

SECOND APPRENTICE: That's your mark, Perky. Down there, where you can get walked on.

FIRST APPRENTICE: Hey, mate.

SECOND APPRENTICE: Get up.

FIRST APPRENTICE: He's hurt.

SECOND APPRENTICE: Get up. Hurt? I could squash him. He's not hurt, he's just lying there. Get up. Get up before I kick you in.

FIRST APPRENTICE: I'm going.

SECOND APPRENTICE [*still to Warbeck*]: You make me sick! D'you hear me? You're just a piece of dirt, and you don't matter! [*He's beside himself, and would give Warbeck a kicking, but his mate restrains him.*] Get up!

FIRST APPRENTICE: Hey, there's someone coming!

[HARBUCKLE *comes in. He takes in the scene. Goes to help Warbeck to his feet.*]

HARBUCKLE: What's going on?

WARBECK: Hello, Mr Harbuckle. Tea break already?

HARBUCKLE: What's wrong?

WARBECK: Nothing whatever wrong with me, if that's what you mean.

HARBUCKLE: Well, what's he standing there for, like a fighting-cock with face-ache, for a start? And what were you doing, stretched out on the floor? It's no odds to me, I was only asking. [*He lights a cigarette.*] I just come here for a look at the library opening.

[WARD *comes bustling merrily in, jostling the second apprentice as he passes him.*]

WARD: Hey ho, my merry lads, here's a giggle for us all. Sorry, mate.

SECOND APPRENTICE: Don't you push me around.

WARD: Oh my goodness me, guess what's happened in the book house. What's the matter with you, my flower? I said I was sorry, didn't I?

SECOND APPRENTICE: Just don't do it.

WARD: Somebody left the gas on under you? [*To Harbuckle*] What's up?

HARBUCKLE: I just found Perkin flat on the floor.

WARD [*concerned*]: What, again? [*Referring to second apprentice.*] And he didn't like it?

SECOND APPRENTICE: It was me knocked him down.

WARD: Aren't you the raving hero. Anyway, if you didn't like it you didn't have to do it. Come to think of it, don't do it.

SECOND APPRENTICE: I'll do it any time I've a mind to.

WARD: Have a try now.

WARBECK: Leave him be. He doesn't know what he's at.

[*This is too much for the* SECOND APPRENTICE, *and he flies at Warbeck.*]

SECOND APPRENTICE: I'll kill him!

[WARD *grabs him by his shirt-front as he passes, and swings him round, intending to clout the boy. But the boy ducks away, choking with emotion.*]

My shirt! Look at that, you've ripped my shirt, you swine!

WARD: Listen to me, my little snake-charmer. You may find it hard to believe, but I don't mind your shirt being torn. Not one bit. He's a very provoking old man, I dare say, but you mustn't knock him about. Else I might tear off something else a bit more intimate. All right?

SECOND APPRENTICE: Swine.

[*The two* APPRENTICES *go.* WARD *lights a fag.*]

WARD: Love-starved. They only want loving, you know. What was I saying? Oh yes. ... Did you see the club outing going into the library just now?

HARBUCKLE: No. I missed it, I think. I only just come.

WARD: Well, I was watching with the others, in the cycle park. So anyway, after they'd been in the library a bit, a kid comes along with the story. There's His Excellency the Mayor, Oglethorpe, Bootle, and General Sir Clangsby-Ironmonger, all tramping along, see. All getting out of each other's way, and trying to look as if they're trying not to look as if they built the library themselves. And a gaggle of architects and surveyors, hovering and feeling bitter because nobody's taking enough notice of them. When all of a sudden a look of strain begins to show on H.E.'s face. Ho! What can it be? Is he not happy about our library? Would he like to read a book? H.E. murmurs to his secretary. The secretary gets so discreet he nearly disappears. He murmurs to the Town Clerk. The Town Clerk smiles that lovely smile that we all know so well. The one he uses when he's talking about the housing-list – on and off as if his teeth were uncomfy – and he murmurs to the Borough Surveyor. A nod. All is going well!

WARBECK: I know, I know. His Excellency wants –

WARD: I know you know, Perky. But do you know the full drama and agony of it all?

HARBUCKLE: Just a minute. Were you there while all this murmuring was going on?

WARD: I'm filling in the gaps here and there, I'll admit; but don't interrupt the artist. Now. The Borough Surveyor is murmuring, *murmuring* to the Chief Architect. H.E. is polite, anxious, and distinguished, in radiating waves. A development! The Chief Architect is murmuring to a junior partner, who is soon engrossed in murmured recriminations with one of the contractors. Back comes black news. Along the distinguished file it goes, slower and more reluctant in each mouth. Who will deliver the bad news to the gent? Ho deary me! Man who build big library should not forget small words. What a lesson for us all, Perky!

WARBECK: Was there one?

WARD: There was not one, Perky, my lamb. H.E.'s bladder tells him that it's time to wash his hands, and somebody's got to tell him that he can't until he gets home. Stark staring tragedy.

HARBUCKLE: Well, would you credit it? Four years building, and nobody thought of that. What did the brickies do?

WARD: They filled in chitties. But to return to the scene of the catastrophe. Whom do we see coming to the rescue, but our own galloping Captain Bootle? Has he not his own establishment but a few paces away? Shall he be found wanting, when the welcoming doors of his jam factory gape? Straight opposite and turn left down the first alleyway? Ho no! Some casual-seeming remark about sherry with the directors is dropped to the press, to whom the real story would be as good as money in the bank. And off they go. Oglethorpe, on whose brow stands a dew of honest sweat, old High Explosive, and the gallant Captain. What d'you think of that?

WARBECK: Very good. Very good. Captain Bootle's a fine man.

HARBUCKLE: He got Oglethorpe out of an embarrassment, didn't he?

WARBECK: Aye. He's chairman of t'library committee.

WARD: All right, cheer up, Perky. All is well now. To look at your face, anybody'd think you didn't feel all radiant after Oglethorpe's Happy Escape.

WARBECK: I an't.

WARD: Well, I'm not too bothered myself, but I'm bearing up.

HARBUCKLE: Hey. Doesn't that mean they'll be coming in here?

WARBECK: I don't give tuppence for Oglethorpe or any of them. Or their parades and libraries.

WARD: He's right, you know. Fags out, lads.

[*They all flap their arms to get rid of the smoke. The door opens and* BOOTLE *looks in. He stares without expression at Ward and Harbuckle, and they sidle out through what space he leaves them in the doorway.* BOOTLE's *expression grows a little kindlier, as he addresses Warbeck confidentially.*]

BOOTLE: All in good order, Warbeck? Highly distinguished visitor for us. [*He turns.*] This way, Your Excellency.

[WARBECK *stands to a kind of attention with his mop.* H.E. *enters, followed by* OGLETHORPE. H.E. *beams on Warbeck.*]

BOOTLE: May I introduce Mr Warbeck? A veteran worker with us.

H.E.: Good man. How long have you worked in this factory, mm?

BOOTLE: Thirty years, is it, Warbeck?

WARBECK: Thirty years altogether, sir. Captain.

[*He nods at Oglethorpe, who nods back.*]

BOOTLE: Warbeck *used* to be in our *dispatch* department, Your Excellency.

H.E.: Oh yes. Sending things off. Thirty years, eh? Well, it doesn't seem to have done you any harm.

WARBECK: Why? Was it supposed to?

[H.E. *turns stiffly to Bootle and Oglethorpe.* BOOTLE *smiles winningly and gestures to indicate the cubicles.* H.E. *goes along, and takes the third one.*]

BOOTLE: Mr Warbeck is quite a character with us.

[BOOTLE *and* OGLETHORPE *regard each other with mutual relief. They draw a little away from* WARBECK, *who listens unashamedly.*]

OGLETHORPE: A ticklish moment, Captain Bootle. And I've you to thank for our rescue. Do you have some sherry in your office, so that we can give off a smell that will lend colour to my evasion *vis-à-vis* the press?

BOOTLE [*nods*]: Whisky might be better.

OGLETHORPE: Aye. More smelly. You're right, Bootle.

WARBECK: If you chew peppermint and say nowt, you'll fool 'em both ways. That's what I do, when I've been rabbiting or dog-racing. One sniff, and she's more pleased that she's caught me out than what she is vexed at me enjoying myself. Mind, it's two-edged. One time I won fifteen bob by half past eight, and I had a few drinks on it. By closing time, I didn't know whether it was pepper-mints or knock-over-the-hallstand. In the event I got both barrels. She swore I couldn't have been in the Church Inn all night, else I wouldn't have had the cheek to come home reeking, and where *had* I been?

BOOTLE: Yes, yes, Warbeck.

WARBECK: Just a suggestion, Captain.

BOOTLE: Yes, all right, Warbeck.

OGLETHORPE [*heavy*]: Aye. Whisky. We're not out of the wood yet. [*Turning to Warbeck.*] Need I tell you, Perkin, that we rely on your absolute discretion in this delicate matter?

[WARBECK *glowers.*]

Do I make myself clear?

[*They both look at Warbeck's glum face.*]

BOOTLE: Everything all right, Warbeck?

WARBECK: What I think, is what I think.

BOOTLE: Of course, of course.

WARBECK: Nob'dy's forced to take note of it.

BOOTLE: If you say so.

WARBECK: But if he'd show some respect, he'd get further wi' me.

BOOTLE: Alderman Oglethorpe? He's said nothing offensive, I'm sure.
[BOOTLE *is bewildered, and looks inquiringly at* OGLETHORPE,
who draws him aside.]

OGLETHORPE: What about him?

BOOTLE: It's beyond me.

OGLETHORPE: Personal animosity towards me, I think. And envy of
my present success.

BOOTLE: You don't say so? It's an entirely new facet of him to me.
He's always been the soul of loyalty towards me.

OGLETHORPE: Has he? Has he ever had any benefit from it?

WARBECK: Roof leaks. Gas leaks. He goes in triumph through the
streets, everybody's gawping. And he's all but put his great boot
down, when he sees the worm Warbeck creeping across the route.
He daresn't strud on me when everybody's watching. So, in a tone
which makes it clear that he'll be back later, he says: 'Move over,
little worm. It's me.' Him. Well, who knows but what my
moment's come – Roof leaks. Gas leaks.

BOOTLE: You think perhaps a rise, or something?

OGLETHORPE: It's not for me to say. Anything I could do would only
lay me open even more to reproach and insult. But you know
what's at stake. The tale'll be all round t'town by now, I shouldn't
wonder. But so long as it's not confirmed, or printed, we shan't
come to much harm. The builder's having a small 'Convenience
Out of Order' notice made, and it'll be posted in a suitable and
plausible place. That, and your whisky, should be enough smoke-
screen for the present – if he can be relied on. His Excellency's a long
time. I think I'll leave you to it for an instant.
[OGLETHORPE *moves towards the cubicles.* WARBECK *has screwed
himself up to speak to him. He stands in Oglethorpe's way and squares
up aggressively.*]

WARBECK: I should be extremely glad, if you don't mind, Oglethorpe, if you'd see your way to doing something about my gas.

OGLETHORPE: Your gas.

WARBECK: Yes. And the roof.

OGLETHORPE: You choose your moment. [*Raising an admonishing finger.*] I think I've told you this before, but it doesn't seem to have sunk in. I am a man of goodwill, Perkin. And I'm amenable to any well-meant suggestion. But I will not be badgered, bullied, or blackmailed. [*He tries to get by Warbeck, who does not move.*] Is this a free passage, or do I have to tip you for this as well?

[WARBECK *stands aside.* OGLETHORPE *goes into the first cubicle.* WARBECK *looks round after him, meets Oglethorpe's eye, and steps back looking elsewhere. Something makes* OGLETHORPE *change his mind, and he goes further along the corridor. Meanwhile* BOOTLE *has been thinking of some suitable approach, and finally brings himself to tackle Warbeck.*]

BOOTLE: You know Alderman Oglethorpe, do you?

WARBECK: Aye. Captain.

BOOTLE: Very strong character. Ar-um ... you seem to have heard that there was a hitch in the opening? Of course, we don't want to talk about it, do we? I mean, I know you understand.

WARBECK: Thank you, Captain.

BOOTLE: Now what I'm wondering is, is there anything you need?

WARBECK: Well, I've only just had a new mop-head –

BOOTLE: I'll see to it.

WARBECK: There's the flush in the first cubicle. They've done something to the ball-cock.

BOOTLE: Captain.

WARBECK: If you jerk it just that little bit too hard, you get a shower bath. It comes squirting out o' t'cistern.

BOOTLE: No, you misunderstand me.

WARBECK: Do I, Captain?

BOOTLE: Yes, you do. [*With an effort.*] Would a little bonus be acceptable?

WARBECK: A bonus? What for, sir?

BOOTLE: Well, a rise, then. Time you had one. Ten shillings keep you quiet? Happy?

WARBECK: Oh yes. It's most generous of you, Captain. I hardly know what to say.

BOOTLE: Not a word, Warbeck. Yes, that's right, not a word, mm?

[*There is no light of comprehension on Warbeck's face.*]

Yes, I think I have time. Excuse me, Warbeck.

WARBECK: Certainly. Don't worry, I shan't tell anybody. Else you'd have them all putting in for rises, wouldn't you?

[BOOTLE *goes along the corridor to the cubicles, stops, turns to Warbeck with a gentle smile, and speaks very simply.*]

BOOTLE: We shall be grateful to you, Warbeck. Alderman Oglethorpe and myself.

WARBECK [*who is not following at all well*]: Aye. Well, I'm very glad for all three of you, Captain.

[WARBECK *turns away, gazing into space while his mind works over the problem.* BOOTLE'S *smile sags slightly. He goes into the first cubicle.*]

Two. What's just happened? If I'm not mistaken, I just got a rise. Why should Oglethorpe be grateful for that? He's not getting a rise. I could see it, if I'd just promised not to tell on 'em to the papers. But I wasn't going to do that in the first place, was I? It's a mystery. And somehow I don't fancy it. Oglethorpe *grateful* to me? Him. I'd like to have him in front of me now, with nob'dy about, and up to his neck in water and sinking. I'd – I'd – flick water up his nostrils. I hope to die if I wouldn't. [*Getting over-heated.*] Oh yes, he fancies himself now, I know. But he'd not feel so clever with me flicking water up his nostrils, and the water rising! He used to have a bag of marbles as big as your head, when nob'dy else had none. No good, marbles, in the water. Course, I wouldn't let him drownd ... but wouldn't I flick! And all his clothes all wet. ...

[*He is suddenly taken with a heart-clutching idea. He looks at the door of the first cubicle. Quietly he goes to the side of it and contemplates the*

[*partition. Then he sets the mop-bucket to stand on, and mounts it gingerly. He stands there for a split second and then he reaches over and pulls the flush and is down off the bucket before he dare think. He is flooded with a kind of sweet hysteria, listens to the water rushing as if it were music. His eyes glow.*]

Knowledge is power. He'll be soaked.

[*He sneaks over to the other side of the door and watches elaborately casual.* OGLETHORPE *comes out further down, i.e. not out of door number one, and passes Warbeck heedlessly. He looks for Bootle where he left him.* WARBECK *is shattered by Oglethorpe's escape; he totters forward with an arm stretched out, unable to articulate a word.*]

OGLETHORPE: Bootle. Captain Bootle! Perkin, do you know where Captain Bootle is? Oh, gracious heavens, don't say we've got more trouble. Supposing His Excellency were to come out now? Well? Oh gracious heavens. He's not gone out and left nobody here?

[OGLETHORPE *goes out into the factory.* WARBECK *has an awful feeling he knows who is in number one.* H.E. *comes down the corridor, sees that his escort has disappeared, tries the outer door and then goes out.* WARBECK *counts desperately on his fingers.*]

WARBECK: One, two, three of them come in. That feller, Oglethorpe, and – One, two, three – It's perfectly right, there was on'y them three. One, two have gone out. Oglethorpe, that feller –

[*He looks at the door of cubicle number one, and then at the remaining standing finger.*]

Go away, finger. Vanish.

[WARD *opens the outer door, looks in, and then enters.*]

WARD: All gone, have they? The old band'll be off again in a sec then.

WARBECK: Did you pass anybody coming out of here?

WARD: No –?

WARBECK: You didn't pass Captain Bootle coming out of here?

[BOOTLE *comes out like a walking slow burn.* WARD *and* WARBECK *watch him as he stalks to the outer door, there he stops and gives Warbeck a look of infinite reproach, shakes his head, shakes his legs, and goes out.*]

WARD: Like that you mean?

WARBECK: It wasn't me, sir! It was som'dy else. I don't know who! Captain!

[WARBECK *sways on his feet.* WARD *hurries out.*]

Oh heck. The room's going round. My head's pounding fit to bust. Little yellow discs, and red and m'room ones. If I'm going to faint, I'd best lie down ready – I'll only fall on my head again.

[*He lies down close to and parallel with the bottom of the wall, and pulls the mop to cover his face. Groans.* OGLETHORPE *opens the door, looks round inside, and then goes away again.* WARD *comes back in, bringing* HARBUCKLE.]

WARD: No. I'm sure of it. He's definitely ill, or something. You'd be surprised, but you can tell. Now where's he gone?

[H.E. *looks in anxiously and goes away again.* HARBUCKLE *sees Warbeck and bends to look closer.*]

HARBUCKLE: I believe this is him. Perkin. What are you doing down there?

WARBECK: I'm not doing anything down here. I come over dizzy.

HARBUCKLE: I see. What have you got the mop over you for? [*No answer.*] I say, what's the mop for?

WARBECK: I heard you. I just can't think of an answer.

WARD: Come on, Perky. Up you get. Well, let go the mop.

WARBECK: Why?

WARD: Why? Why? How do I know why? Just let go.

WARBECK: It's the on'y think I got left.

WARD: It's the only thing he's got left. [*He stumps for the door.*] I'd get more sense out of a tin of jam.

HARBUCKLE: Don't go. We can't leave him like this.

WARD: What difference is anything we do going to make to the way he is?

HARBUCKLE: Give us a hand.

[WARD *and* HARBUCKLE *hoist* WARBECK *to his feet.*]

WARBECK: Don't let anybody see me.

[OGLETHORPE *and* BOOTLE *come in from the factory.* WARBECK *draws* WARD *and* HARBUCKLE *together with the mop between them and himself behind, so that he is more or less hidden from the front. During the dialogue he hutches* WARD *and* HARBUCKLE *nearer the door, so that he can move behind them and out through the door, using the mop as a futile camouflage. The manoeuvre looks pretty odd to* OGLETHORPE *and* BOOTLE.]

OGLETHORPE: Let me deal with it, Bootle. You're not yourself. Have you two seen a distinguished-looking gentleman in morning suit and medals?

WARD [*nervous*]: Does it have to be both of us?

OGLETHORPE: Either of you!

HARBUCKLE: The man who opened the library, sir?

OGLETHORPE [*to Bootle*]: There you are. It's all round t'town. [*To Harbuckle*] Have you seen him?

HARBUCKLE: Only going in and coming out, sir. I mean, coming in and going out —

OGLETHORPE: Come on man, which? And which was first? And in and out of where?

HARBUCKLE: Yes.

BOOTLE: Warbeck!

[WARBECK *has reached what he judges to be a favourable position for his escape. He flits to the door, and is about to open it, when it is opened from the other side by* H.E.]

H.E.: Oh, terribly sorry!

[*He shuts the door again, revealing Warbeck.*]

OGLETHORPE }: Your Excellency!
BOOTLE

[H.E. *comes back in again and shuts the door.* WARBECK *has lain down at the foot of the wall with the mop over him, as before.*]

H.E.: I thought I was right. Look here, Alderman Oglethorpe, I've been completely lost.

OGLETHORPE: Yes, Your Excellency. There was a hitch. Captain Bootle.

[BOOTLE *leads* H.E. *out.* OGLETHORPE *turns.*]

Warbeck. Now where's he gone? [*Sees him.*] Warbeck, from what Captain Bootle tells me, your services will no longer be required here. And you can expect a call from me, the minute I'm free. Viper.

[OGLETHORPE *goes out.* WARBECK *gets up, picks up the bucket, and puts the mop over his shoulder. He trudges unsteadily out. As the door closes, it catches hold of the mop-head. The head slithers down as the stale end is released.* WARD *and* HARBUCKLE *hurry out.*]

CURTAIN

SCENE FIVE

The Warbecks' front parlour again. A day-bed and a short screen appear in this scene.

[HARBUCKLE *and* WARD *struggle in with the limp but conscious* WARBECK. *The* REPORTER *follows.*]

REPORTER: Steady with him.

WARD: Are you there, Mrs Warbeck?

[MRS WARBECK *comes in from the kitchen.*]

HARBUCKLE: Now then, it's all right, Mrs Warbeck. He fainted at work, that's all.

WARD: Excitement of the library opening, I expect.

MRS W: Yes, I was there. Lovely. I don't see what he had to get excited for, though. Mitle Oglethorpe had every right to get excited, and he didn't faint.

WARD: No. But he had a nasty moment.

HARBUCKLE: Hush up.

MRS W: Put him on the sofa, and I'll pull the rug over him. You do look a colour, poor lamb. Rest quiet, and you'll be all right. Look at me in my best. I've only just got in.

HARBUCKLE: We – er, we took him to the doctor's on the way home.

MRS W: Did he say anything?

HARBUCKLE: Nothing organically wrong.

WARBECK [in a hollow voice]: Nothing organically wrong.
  [MRS WARBECK gives him a sharp look.]

WARD: Nervous shock, just symptoms of shock.

WARBECK [hollow]: Shock.

MRS W [looking at Warbeck thoughtfully]: Shock. What shocked him?

HARBUCKLE [feeling a bit hot]: Oglethorpe's coming along shortly.

MRS W: What ever for?

HARBUCKLE: See Perkin's all right, I suppose.

MRS W: Well I never. Is there something I don't know about yet?

HARBUCKLE ⎫
WARD   ⎬ : No, no, no. No.

MRS W: I see. Well, I daresay I shall find out in due time. From him.

WARBECK: I'm going to die.

MRS W: Now you're not going to die, so don't talk such nonsense. [To Harbuckle and Ward] Take no notice.

REPORTER: Shouldn't he be upstairs?

MRS W: He's not going to die.

WARBECK: I'm going to die. And I'm going to go mouldy. Dig me up after a bit, and you'll see I'm alive. I could just fancy a cup of tea.

MRS W: Yes, love. [To the others] Listen to him, he's wandering. Talk to him, Mr Harbuckle. Make him see sense. [She goes into the kitchen.]

HARBUCKLE: Well, Perkin?

WARD: I think I'll nip off now.

HARBUCKLE: Sit where you are. It'll be all right. Him going funny is going to help. Make a better explanation. Just keep calm.

REPORTER: This is what happens when you stick up for your principles. He's a martyr. What happened?

WARD: I only saw the back end of it. And I could have missed that and lived longer.

REPORTER: Oglethorpe was talking to the press boys, when the official party came back from sherry at Bootle's jam. It must have been a good laugh, because they all looked pleased with themselves. They all went into a room, and I wanted to follow, but this bloke come along and put up this notice on the door. 'WC Out of Order.' And he wouldn't let me in. I couldn't understand it. Every time I started to ask anybody, somebody jogged my elbow, or jostled me, or stood on my foot. Look. [Shows his shoes, all dusty.]

[HARBUCKLE and WARD avoid comment.]

WARBECK: When I were little, I had a clock.

HARBUCKLE: How are you, lad?

WARBECK: My father hated this clock, and I loved it. I made a oak box for it, when its case come off. And I cleaned it with some sand, to get t'rust off. And when I couldn't blow all t'sand out again, I tried to wash it out wi' oil and paraffin.

HARBUCKLE: Perkin, can you hear me?

WARBECK: One way and another, this clock had had a hard time. But suddenly, as by a miracle, it took to working again. My dad hated it, all my brothers and sisters hated it, my mother hated it. But I loved it.

HARBUCKLE: Why did they hate it?

WARBECK: I used to keep it wound, and hide it in a different place all the time, so't they couldn't throw it away. And if ever there was a quiet moment, you could hear it, from the attic or the back of the hen-house, or wherever it was. And I used to listen. And they all used to listen.

[WARBECK settles back with his eyes closed, smiling secretly.]

HARBUCKLE [moved]: Poor old Perkin.

WARBECK: Chung chung chung ching choing choing chickety chakety chick chung chung chung chikety chikety chick chack ....

HARBUCKLE [*to Ward, who is not at all happy*]: Is it the end coming, d'you think? Yes. I think it's the end. Tell Mrs Warbeck. Mrs Warbeck! Will you come quickly, please!

WARBECK: I'd wrap it in rags, so't nobody could hear it but me. Or I'd hang it by a nail behind the tallboy. But they heard it, and they knew it was somewhere. They used to go mad looking for it when they thought I was asleep.

WARD: Mrs Warbeck.

[*There is a knock on the front door.* HARBUCKLE *goes. It is the* POLICEMAN, *with Warbeck's summons.*]

POLICEMAN: Oh, you, Mr Harbuckle. Is Perkin in?

HARBUCKLE: Aye but – er –

[MRS WARBECK *comes in, tearful, with a tea-cloth in her hand.*]

MRS W: Who is it? Oh, Syd. Come in, you knew him as well as anybody.

POLICEMAN: Knew?

HARBUCKLE: He's badly.

WARBECK: Come in, Syd. Rose's just brewing, and I'm like to die.

POLICEMAN: Oh well – er – I'll call back later, shall I? When you're dead. I mean better.

WARBECK: What've you got there, Syd? Something for me?

POLICEMAN [*to Harbuckle*]: He's dying?

HARBUCKLE: So he says, and he should know.

POLICEMAN: Oh heck.

WARBECK: Is it my summons?

MRS W: Summons!

WARBECK: Give it here, Syd. It's mine, isn't it?

MRS W: What ever has he been doing? No wonder they bring you home from work!

POLICEMAN: No, no. This wasn't at work.

MRS W: What wasn't? Give that to me. The shock might be fatal.

WARBECK [*grasping it*]: Give over, will you. You're nosy.

MRS W [*screaming in exasperation*]: You wicked old man!

POLICEMAN: If I knew what to do, I'd go and do it.

MRS W: Ooh, I could shake him.

WARBECK: Now, now, my love, don't take on. I shan't be long. I'm going fast.

MRS W: Pooh, smell that gas. There's a leak somewhere, I know.

WARBECK: It's me, going mouldy already.

MRS W [*with a pinched and fastidious glance at her husband*]: If we're going to have any more of this crazy carry-on, we might as well sit down to it. Come on, all of you.

[*They all sit.*]

WARBECK: Chung chung chung chick chick chikety choing choing choing –

MRS W [*standing again*]: What's that?

HARBUCKLE: He's on about his clock.

MRS W: *I* could clock *him*.

WARBECK: On and on. You couldn't stop it. I hit it once, to see if it would stop.

HARBUCKLE: Did it not stop?

WARBECK: Oh yes, it stopped.

MRS W: Oh, my heavens.

WARBECK: But it started again. Choing choing choing chikety chikety chikety –

[*There is a knock at the front door.* WARBECK *continues to tick quietly for a second.* HARBUCKLE *goes to answer the door. It is* OGLETHORPE.]

MRS W: Whoever can that be? Mitle Oglethorpe!

OGLETHORPE: Is your Perkin in?

POLICEMAN: He's – indisposed.

OGLETHORPE: Indisposed? I should just say he is. Oh, you, Constable.

[*To Mrs Warbeck*] Well, I should like a few private words of explanation with your husband, my dear, and then have done.

MRS W: So I'm going to find out what happened today, at last, am I?

OGLETHORPE: Now, Rose, my dear, I said private, I think.

MRS W: Oh, I heard. But you can't prevent me from listening.

OGLETHORPE [*with dignity*]: Now if you'll just stand apart –

WARBECK: Everybody draw close.

[*Recognizing instinctively the tone of a man about to pronounce his last words, everybody stands.*]

OGLETHORPE: Perkin, for heaven's sake, can't we have just a little dignity?

WARD [*to Oglethorpe*]: Show some respect.

OGLETHORPE [*outraged*]: Respect!

HARBUCKLE: I think you should know he's dying, Mr Oglethorpe.

OGLETHORPE: I'll believe that when I see it, sir. Now [*lowering his voice for Warbeck*] – I can't conceive what you were up to this morning, or who exactly was the target of your malice – [*raising his hand to forestall an expected protest*] – I say malice. But the net result for me, and for His Excellency, *and* for Captain Bootle, was confusion and loss of dignity. There was a pool of water, which the press was quick to seize upon, and which cost me considerable humiliation and pains to keep from publication. I hope you're satisfied – It's my opinion you ought to be certified. T'ceremony had to be curtailed.

WARBECK: Tell him the roof leaks.

OGLETHORPE: If that's the best you can think of – A brand-new library with a leaky roof –

MRS W: No, he means our roof here.

OGLETHORPE: Oh. [*Indignant*] He doesn't seem to care!

WARBECK: Oh yes I do. I put a bucket under it. You know, you're like that clock, Michael –

OGLETHORPE: What clock?

HARBUCKLE: He had a clock once.

WARBECK: Chung chung chung clatter clatter chikety clack, on and on, no matter what happens. But *I* stopped *you*, didn't I? Now if you'd been really hopeless, like my clock – [*In a matter-of-fact voice*] I'm going.

OGLETHORPE: His mind's going.

WARBECK [*distinctly*]: You hope.

[WARBECK *dies, the summons clutched firmly in his hand. Nobody notices any difference.*]

MRS W: I think you'd all better go now. They're going now, dear.

[OGLETHORPE, HARBUCKLE, WARD, *and the* POLICEMAN *all say* Goodbye, Ta-ta, lad, See you, etc. *Silence.*]

MRS W: There now. He's dropped off, poor lamb.

POLICEMAN [*coming forward to examine Warbeck*]: Excuse me, Mrs Warbeck, but I'd say – he's dead.

MRS W [*stunned*]: Oh, lord forgive us, he can't be. No.

POLICEMAN [*going*]: I'll get the doctor to call.

[MRS WARBECK *throws her arms dramatically round Warbeck's body.*]

MRS W: Oh, to die like that! After I'd said such things.

[*Warbeck's downstage leg rises vertically.* HARBUCKLE *tries discreetly to press it down again, causing Warbeck's torso to rise slightly.* MRS WARBECK *shrieks, and feels his heart.*]

He's alive! I felt him move.

[*She jumps as she sees the vertical leg. Looks round at the others, flustered. She sidles along, and tries to push it down, with a confused attempt at dissimulation.*]

MRS W: Something's the matter – Goodbye everybody. Thank you for calling – at a moment like this – so kind – I think the screen –

HARBUCKLE [*getting the screen and putting it in front of the day-bed and Warbeck, and Mrs Warbeck as well, since she does not move out of the way*]: Yes, Mrs Warbeck. I'll get Mrs Harbuckle to come round.

MRS W: You're very kind.

[*She sidles out from behind the screen to the door, pushing down the leg again as she passes. The leg rises again behind her. The others file out solemnly, shaking hands with her.*

The REPORTER *speaks in an urgent whisper to Oglethorpe, at the door.*]

REPORTER: In this tragic moment, Alderman Oglethorpe, would you care to make a statement about the late W. P. Warbeck's Principle?

OGLETHORPE [*sombre*]: Press?

REPORTER: Freelance, sir.

OGLETHORPE: Have you been here all the time?

REPORTER: I didn't hear anything, really.

OGLETHORPE: I thought I'd reached a satisfactory, and on my part generous, arrangement with the press, at the library. What d'you want, blood?

REPORTER: Oh, I wasn't in the room that had the notice 'WC Out of Order', sir –

OGLETHORPE [*whose blood pressure is rising, but not his voice*]: You yammering jackal, you. Is nothing sacred?

REPORTER: Please don't be angry, sir. Just a brief statement. I've been dismissed from the *Chronicle* already.

OGLETHORPE: Oh, it was you, was it? In league with *him*, eh? Egging him on? You see the results, I hope? Well, you won't be causing any more damage. Get out.

REPORTER: Maybe not, but I can still – I can – [*To himself*] What can I do? [*He goes to the screen.*] No. [*Turns back, composes himself, goes to Mrs Warbeck and shakes her hand.*] My sincerest condolences. [*Shakes Oglethorpe's hand, and goes.*]

MRS W [*watching the Reporter go*]: Thank you for being such a comfort, Mitle. [*The Reporter has gone now.*] It's all a mystery. Mitle, what happened today that I don't know about? They were all hinting. And you.

OGLETHORPE: Now then, Rose. I can't, for shame. There was a hitch in the opening.

MRS W: Well? And it was my William?

OGLETHORPE: Partly.

MRS W: – and he was summonsed?

OGLETHORPE: Summonsed? Good heavens, what d'you take me for, Mrs Warbeck? Perkin Warbeck is dead, my dear. We – that is the official party – had occasion to visit the factory – and Perkin – took the opportunity to – embarrass Captain Bootle – and incidentally everybody else in the official party. Ahem.

MRS W: Oh, I can't make head nor tail of all this! [*She goes behind the screen. She screams, and comes out again, holding the summons in her hand.*] Interfering!! [*She shows the summons to Oglethorpe.*] The wicked old man! I don't believe it! A hitch, you call it! It's a downright lie! That Marilyn Harbuckle, she wants putting in a home!

OGLETHORPE [*reading summons*]: '– did remove garments –' Well I never. They wrap it up well, but it's still there in black and white. It's a shock, I won't deny it. It's a shock to *me*. But we must be calm about it.

MRS W: You're right, Mitle. No sense flying off. That'll get us nowhere. That's just what *he* wanted!

OGLETHORPE: Nay, don't go so fast. Fair's fair. The last thing Perkin ever wanted was to be a bother.

MRS W: Never mind what he wanted. It's what I want, now. He's shamed me and defied me. Mrs Harbuckle'll be along in a minute. We'll fix him between us.

OGLETHORPE [*a bit alarmed at her vindictive tone*]: I never knew that you felt that way about him, Rose. It's your grief speaking.

MRS W: That was his wickedness. He left me without a leg to stand on. All the time, you knew he was living inside of himself, and not so much as peeping out. Like one of them beetles that are that small you can't squash them so how you try. But I knew something was going on inside his nasty little head, oh mark my words! And to crown it all, he gets himself summonsed for bothering with that Marilyn. He's gone his own sweet way all these years, without a tickle of conscience; and if he isn't suffering the tortures of the damned at this moment I shall want to know the reason why.

OGLETHORPE: Mrs Warbeck –

MRS W: *And* I'll have a word or two to say referring to the incidents at his work today, whatever they were.

OGLETHORPE: Calm yourself, Mrs Warbeck. In heaven's name, how can you do a thing like that?

MRS W: You'll see. And while we're waiting, you can calm *yourself*.

To us who believe, our loved ones are never dead; only passed over. Not lost; only waiting to be found. Mrs Harbuckle'll have no bother at all to fetch him through.

OGLETHORPE: Fetch him through?

MRS W [*impatiently*]: She's a *medium*.

[MARILYN's *voice, as she plays a game out at the back, is heard, lonely and absorbed.*]

MARILYN [*off*]: Take your lady by the hand,
Take her by the water,
Give her all the best you can
For she's the boss's daughter.

MRS W [*from the door*]: Now then, Marilyn, that'll do. I daresay you know what's happened, so just you be quiet. Where's your mother?

MARILYN [*off*]: Oh, Mrs Warbeck, Mr Warbeck wouldn't mind me playing.

MRS W: I expect not, my love; but he's dead now, so you'll just show some decency. Ah, here's your mother now.

OGLETHORPE: If you'll excuse me, Rose – There's the banquet –

MRS W: That's right, Mitle. You go and amuse yourself. Come in, Mrs Harbuckle.

[OGLETHORPE *sidles rapidly out and escapes.* MRS HARBUCKLE *comes in.* MRS WARBECK *is busily setting chairs: the armchair, and an upright chair opposite it.*]

Here's a chair.

MRS H: Where is he, dear?

[MRS WARBECK *nods, tight-lipped, to the screen.* MRS HARBUCKLE *goes reverently over. She sees the foot sticking up, glances at Mrs Warbeck, and, with the efficient air of one used to corpses, pushes it gently down. It rises up again. She doesn't feel inclined to try again, but composes herself and comes earnestly to take Mrs Warbeck's arm.*]

You won't think so in the instant of your bereavement, Rose, but you and I know – who better? – in our hearts, don't we? – not lost, but gone before.

MRS W: I sincerely trust not, Mrs Harbuckle. Anyway, wherever he's gone, I'm relying on you to get him back this instant. I hadn't finished.

MRS H: Rose, Rose dear; he's still warm.

MRS W [*very much her own mistress*]: Mrs Harbuckle, are you going to get through to my William, or aren't you?

MRS H [*composedly*]: I shall do my best, Rose.

MRS W: I'm no pharisee, Mrs Harbuckle. But I can't sit easy when God's laws have been flaunted under my nose; and I'm not going to.

MRS H: Surely you can leave that to God, Rose?

MRS W: Let God look after his own. This one's mine!

MRS H: Rose, Rose, you're beside yourself. You don't know what you're saying. Sit you down here. Take hold of my hands. Between us, we will reach out for your loved one.

MRS W: Yes. Well. Not too much messing about!

MRS H: It is not in my hands, Rose dear. I've no idea what you mean.

MRS W: Can't you skip the fiddle-faddle, just for once? Little Sambo from Matabalaland is all very well Tuesday nights, when I want something to take my mind off things, but this is urgent. I want *him*. Oh my heavens, she's off.

[MRS HARBUCKLE *is undergoing a transformation. Her eyelids droop, and her shoulders stiffen. She shudders brusquely. She is erect and attentive in her seat, concentrating on her imagination.*

The outward results of her concentration are striking. She rapidly begins to seem negro; taller, heavier in feature, more physically proud. She struggles to say a few incomprehensible words, which could be Matabele, and then becomes clearer.

The whole performance gives a vivid impression that a whole real physical action is taking place which is invisible, and that the words are only half the story.]

MRS H: Mbaba – mbmba ngai chui – Greetings, you, Missy Harbuckle. Who is askin'?

MRS W: Rose Warbeck wants news of her husband. Nobody else.

MRS H: Mbaba ngai chui, greetings, you, Missy Warbeck. I see – I see – Man. Old Man – no hair – Name – William.

MRS W [*calmly*]: Yes. Yes.

MRS H: Very, very old. White hair on face, golly.

MRS W: Oh, that'll be his grandfather, I daresay. Tell him to call again. I want my husband.

MRS H [*as if violently attacked, though her body is rigidly still*]: You cheeky monkey! Golly mbaba ngai chui, greetings, old fellow – Don't harm me! Old man on Sambo's back, Missy!

MRS W: Grandad Warbeck? Never in this world!

MRS H: Aie aie! Someone new on this side. On my shoulders, lady.

MRS W: That'll be him. William!

[*MRS HARBUCKLE becomes very still and relaxed. She reclines back limply, and her dropping yet not closed eyelids and somnolent expression give her an air of insolence. She murmurs indistinctly.*]

MRS W: It is you, isn't it? Speak up! I can't hear you when you mumble. Perkin!

MRS H [*conversationally, and in Warbeck's exact tones*]: There you are. I told you so. You wouldn't have it. I told you I were going to die, and I did.

MRS W: Never mind that. What's all this about you being summonsed over Marilyn Harbuckle?

MRS H: Disgusting.

MRS W: But you did it?

MRS H: But I did it.

MRS W: Is that all you can say? You did it?

MRS H: It wern't nothing wrong.

MRS W: Nothing wrong? When you got summonsed?

MRS H: Oh, aye.

MRS W: Well? Aren't you ashamed?

MRS H [*after a pause*]: Yes. But I did it.

MRS W: I know full well you did it. What have you got to say for yourself?

MRS H: It's done.

MRS W: Why? Why? Had you no thoughts for your wife?

MRS H: Yes. But you never let me. Marilyn did.

MRS W: You're filthy.

MRS H: I daresay I am. I'd ha' been just as filthy if I hadn't done it, so I did it. Old Adam.

MRS W: Old Adam indeed. You had an Adam's apple, and that's about all you had of him.

MRS H: Ne'er mind. I did it.

MRS W: You did it, you did it! What was *I* supposed to do?

MRS H: You can do whatever you've a fancy to do. I've been a nuisance all my life. To you, me, and everybody – and I haven't had much joy of it, I can tell you – But I might have gone down to the grave not knowing what a hairy old baboon I was. I didn't. I did it. I'm entirely dead now, and you can heap words on me. You can heap six foot of dirt on me, for that matter. But I shall have been entirely alive.

MRS W: You – You Sunday-paper Casanova!

MRS H [*calmly*]: It wasn't on'y that, my love.

MRS W: There may be more, but I don't want to hear it. That's enough.

[MRS HARBUCKLE *beckons* MRS WARBECK *imperiously over to her to listen to a whisper.* MRS WARBECK *resists at first.* MRS HAR-BUCKLE *beckons again, and carries on as if her gesture had been obeyed; that is, she leans towards one side and begins to whisper. This is too much for* MRS WARBECK, *and she goes to listen. She is horrified.*]

Ah! You never!

MRS H: That I did.

MRS W: What did Mitle Oglethorpe ever do to you, to be tret like that?

MRS H: He never did owt. But he would ha' done, if I'd got in his road.

MRS W: Why should he give a thought to a worm like you?

MRS H: I showed him why, today. Alderman Oglethorpe: a giant among men. Hardheaded. The mayor's trusted friend. Influential businessman. Powerful on the council. Right up there. I expect you thought he stayed up there by magic, like the Indian rope trick? I know *he* did. Well, he doesn't. He stands on the heads of the likes of me. And I shifted over a bit – And the bottom'll be out of that kettle, if you don't take it off.

MRS W: What! [*She starts up, without fully realizing, and rushes towards the kitchen. She stops by the door, with an enraged and frustrated gesture.*] Oh!

MRS H: If you fill it up again, it'll do for a brew for Mrs Harbuckle when she comes round.

[MRS WARBECK *rushes into the kitchen, shutting the door.* MRS HARBUCKLE *sighs and relaxes. She takes out a nub-end and straightens it. She finds a loose match in a pocket and leans over to strike it on the gas-stove in the fireplace. There is a deafening bang. Everything goes dark. Then brilliant magnesium white light. Then total blackout again. There is a scream and a crash from* MRS WARBECK. *Then the light returns to normal daylight.* MRS HARBUCKLE *is still sitting where she was, contemplating the hand which held the cigarette. Her hair has all gone, so that she now looks like Warbeck in drag. She settles back as before and begins to mumble. The whole uproar is very brief, so that* MRS WARBECK *opens the kitchen door on the end of her scream.*]

Chung ke-chung chung –

MRS W: It's that gas, I know. Who did it? I told him time and again it leaked. Who was it? You? Which one of you? Sambo, Mrs Harbuckle, or him? There's some monkey business here. It's too much.

[MRS WARBECK *rushes to the screen, where the foot still sticks up, and looks over.* MRS HARBUCKLE *chants steadily on.*]

MRS H: Chung chung chung chercklikety clikety clikety chick chick chung choing choing ...

MRS W [*shaking her fists wildly*]: I can't stand it! You're driving me out of my mind; it's enough! Shut up shut up shut up! Whoever you are, stop it!

CURTAIN

P.S. In later productions of 'STOP IT WHOEVER YOU ARE' the following ending has been used:

Immediately on MRS WARBECK's last line, as the curtain is falling, the cast enters to her, and they all come downstage of the curtain, leaving PERKIN/MRS HARBUCKLE ticking away. They sing, with interjections from PERKIN when he has struggled through the curtain, to the tune 'Johnny came marching home':

OMNES: Old Perkin led us all a dance.

PERKIN: Kerchung, kerchung.

OMNES: We thought he didn't stand a chance.

PERKIN: Kerchung, kerchung.

OMNES: We got him a bucket to follow the band
And all of a sudden he chanced a stand.

PERKIN: Kerchung kerchung kerklickety choing
Kerchickety chung kerchung.

OMNES: We'd got him labelled as a clown

PERKIN: Kerchung, kerchung.

OMNES: We parcelled him up and stamped him down.

PERKIN: Kerchung, kerchung.

OMNES: And then when we undid the string
There he was the dirty thing.

PERKIN: Kerchung kerchung kerclickety choing
Kerchickety chung kerchung.

ALUN OWEN

Progress to the Park

PROGRESS TO THE PARK

First performed in London in this version at the Saville Theatre, on 3 May 1961, with the following cast:

MAG KEEGAN	Billie Whitelaw
TEIFION	Tom Bell
BOBBY LAUGHLIN	Brian McDermott
JAMIESON	Michael Coles
CHARLIE MODRYB	Norman Rossington
MR LAUGHLIN	Patrick Magee
MRS LAUGHLIN	Julie Jones
MR KEEGAN	James Mcloughlin
MRS KEEGAN	Bee Duffell
KELLY	Ken Jones
HANNAH	Malcolm Taylor
NEVILLE	Keith Smith
LESLEY	Robin Chapman
TIM KEEGAN	Anthony Moore
TERRY	Royston Hodges
GEORGE DOUGLAS	Jon Croft
TERRY QUINN	Maurice Podbrey
SHAY	John Quayle
BILLY MACQUADE	Edmond Bennett
CARSON MCDERBY	Patrick Dugan
MEME	Valerie Varnam
NEWSPAPERMAN	John Quayle

Directed by WILLIAM T. KOTCHEFF

ACT ONE

A street in Liverpool. The street consists of a pub and several two-up and two-down houses, built in the Ruthin red brick that is found only in Liverpool. The interiors of the Laughlins' and of the Keegans' living-rooms can be lighted when required in Scene 2.

SCENE ONE

Saturday Evening

[KELLY, *a youngish barman, comes out of the public house. He is hot and delighted to be out of the oven of the pub, and gulps in the fresh air. He turns and beckons on* HANNAH, *his assistant barman.*]

KELLY: Let's have you. God, it's hot.

HANNAH [*joining him*]: I'm glad to be out of there, it's like a bloomin' oven.

KELLY: Aye, it's hot.

HANNAH: It's the gnats I don't like, y'know.

KELLY: Get hold of your ladder and we'll string the flags across the street.

HANNAH: Of course, if you smoke they don't bite you.

KELLY: What?

HANNAH: The gnats.

KELLY [*up his ladder arranging the flags*]: It's not going to be much of a show.

HANNAH: I don't smoke so they bite me.

KELLY: Ah, shurrup and get on with it!

83

HANNAH: This won't be a patch on the Chinese decorations in St George's Square.

KELLY: No, I don't suppose it will.

HANNAH: Eh ... d'y'remember them decorations before the war down Pitt Street?

KELLY: Aye, dragons and rip-rap fireworks and lanterns everywhere ... and all them little yellow kids sitting at the tables in the street bolting jelly and sandwiches.

HANNAH: They're very clean.

KELLY: Who?

HANNAH: The Chinese.

KELLY: Oh aye [*Pause*] ... and I'll tell you another thing and all, they're very good to their kids.

HANNAH: Do they have any Protestants and Catholics amongst them?

KELLY: Oh, don't be so daft, they're all Buddhists.

HANNAH: They used to smoke a lot of opium down there in the old days.

KELLY: I bet that kept the gnats off 'em!

HANNAH: Well [*indicating the flags*] ... I don't suppose this lot'll look as good as the Pitt Street decorations.

KELLY: Oh, definitely no comparison.

HANNAH: Funny, the Darkies down in Stanhope Street don't go in for decorations, do they?

KELLY: No. I don't think they've got anything to celebrate.

[*They are stopped by the sound of voices shouting aloud from the bowling green.*]

Right of way!

Mind me wood!

A point to starboard!

Gerrout of it, yous!

[KEEGAN *comes out of the pub, followed by* SHAY.]

KEEGAN: I'll not play with him!

SHAY: Ah, come on, it's only a game of bowls!

KEEGAN: No! That Protestant bastard moved me wood!

[LAUGHLIN *comes out of the pub, followed by* CARSON. *He crosses over to Keegan.*]

LAUGHLIN: Look here, Keegan ... am I right in thinking you accused me of moving your wood?

KEEGAN: You stood there, in me line of sight, 'twixt me and me aim, didn't y'?

LAUGHLIN: Ah, for God's sake, man, it was too dark to see what I was at ... so I just made a side-step.

TIM [*coming out from the pub*]: Eh, Dad, did he kick your wood?

LAUGHLIN: I did not!

KEEGAN: Didn't y' see him! [*Mincing*] Oh, I'm sorry, says your man, faking surprise, take it again.

SHAY: Cheeky!

LAUGHLIN: Well ... there you are! I offered to go again, didn't I? I wanted to be fair to you, you old fool!

FIRST MAN: Good man, Robert.

SECOND MAN: You were always fair.

KEEGAN [*to Laughlin*]: It was me best bowl of the match, no less! I let meself be led like a lamb to the slaughterhouse.

LAUGHLIN: Ah, go on ... we'd have won anyway!

FIRST MAN: Aye.

SECOND MAN: That's right.

THIRD MAN: Yes, Robert.

LAUGHLIN: A bad workman always blames his tools.

KEEGAN: You robbed me like you stole the six counties ... by lies and manipulations.

CARSON: Are you going to let him get away with that, Robert?

LAUGHLIN [*the martyr*]: No, it was me own fault.

TIM: Aye, that's more like it.

LAUGHLIN [*going on*]: I let me instincts for the game ruin me better judgement. I should never have agreed to play with a man who digs with the wrong foot.

KEEGAN: D'y'see that! D'y'see that! He was the first one to bring religion into it!

CARSON: Religion is it! You're just trying to make a divergence to get out of your side-bet!

KEEGAN: That's cancelled!

CARSON: It is not!

KEEGAN: Null and void!

TIM: Did you have a side-bet on? No ... just a minute, let's get this right, did you have a side-bet on?

KEEGAN: Just a little one.

TIM: I knew it ... there had to be money involved!

CARSON: Just five shillings.

TIM: It doesn't matter how much. No, Da. It doesn't matter how much ... but it's a funny thing with Protestants ... they're all great sportsmen until a bit of money comes into it!

TERRY: Tim's right.

KEEGAN: He's not wrong!

TIM: No, they're the meanest lot of sodgers ... I mean, look at that church of theirs for a start ... it's falling to bits!

KEEGAN: They've got no ...

TIM: Faith, that's what they haven't got, faith. They've all got itchy fingers and no faith ... money's all they're interested in.

SHAY: Oh God, he's right!

KEEGAN: He's not wrong.

TIM: That's why they're all for birth control ... that's why they won't have no kids.

[*They all start to move off, muttering and grumbling.*]

TERRY: It's a sin against nature!

SHAY: They're worse than the Jews!

KEEGAN: Who killed Christ with a putty knife!

[*The Protestant group move slowly into position by the ladder.*]

LAUGHLIN: Of course, those new flats her Royal Highness the Duchess is going to open is a dirty Papist plot!

CARSON [*eagerly*]: You've heard something, Robert, you've heard something?

LAUGHLIN [*elaborately*]: Has it ever struck you, as a working man,

86

has it ever struck you that although our lot and their lot take home the same amount of wages ... and even though they booze it all away ... they always wind up better off than us?

CARSON: They do so. It's a thought and they do so.

LAUGHLIN: Well ... it's the Family Allowances!

[*Chorus of 'Ohs' and 'Ahs' from the group.*]

Family Allowances! For every child each of us has, they have about seventeen! Let me tell you, when they send the old woman down to the post office to collect it, they have to send an armoured guard with her. Sure, the women are all lobsided with the carrying of so much bloody silver!

CARSON: It's a fact.

LAUGHLIN Well, you think of it, around ten bob a head! I mean, I know for a fact that old Billy O'Dwyer only got married again to have a fresh brood of allowances ... and him seventy-nine!

CARSON: Yeah, he's bleeding the State white of our money, the old goat!

LAUGHLIN: Now, if you want a Council flat, you're a unit, aren't you?

[*Chorus of agreement.*]

Well ... there you are. You're a unit, the wife's a unit, and each of the kids are units too. Well, it stands to reason that the Catholics have got a corner on all the units in this town. They're splashing knee-deep in them, they could paper the wall with them! No, they'll have the new flats, you mark my words ... and then you know what'll happen ... you know what it'll be ... Coal in the bath! You've seen it before! Coal in the bath!

[*He moves off, the group following, grumbling.*]

CARSON: Why don't they call them 'The Vatican Court'!

BILLY: Or 'Pope's Mansions'!

GEORGE: It's a disgrace to the town!

KEEGAN: I'm as loyal as the next man, but I think if they'd got a Cardinal to open them, they wouldn't have gone far wrong.

TIM: Y'what! They wouldn't have let that happen! They've no respect for the cloth!

87

TERRY: I'm giving them a wide berth.

SHAY: I'm glad I haven't paid my subscription.

[*They all laugh.*

MR LAUGHLIN *and his group appear on. They approach the ladders.*]

CARSON: Ah well, you wouldn't have us not have the flags for the Duchess?

LAUGHLIN: No. I stand behind my Queen, I'm right with the Monarchy ... but they'd have been happier if they'd have had a Cardinal doing the job ... Pomp and Splendour ... and work their Church a few bob!

[*The two groups are now standing near each other, facing one another dangerously.*]

KELLY [*calling from the top of his ladder*]: Listen, you lot, will you give us a hand, Mr Laughlin?

HANNAH: We want to move the ladders and finish off the job, Mr Keegan.

LAUGHLIN [*glaring*]: Of course we will!

KEEGAN: Aye ... you've only to say the word!

[KELLY *and* HANNAH *climb down from their ladders and direct the moving,* KELLY *with one group, the Protestants, and* HANNAH *directing the other, the Catholics.*]

KELLY: Steady the Buffs!

HANNAH: Easy the Dubs!

KEEGAN [*to the Protestants*]: Watch it, you lot!

KELLY: Tend your own furrow!

[*They rearrange the ladders as required and to an encouraging cheer* HANNAH *and* KELLY *mount the ladders again. However, the two men holding the ladders start to jostle each other.*]

KEEGAN: Who are you pushing?

CARSON: Get on with your job!

LAUGHLIN: Don't let 'em worry you boys, we always won. Ulster will fight 'cos Ulster is right.

[*The ladders start to sway about with the skirmish that is going on.*]

KELLY: In the name of God!

HANNAH: You'll have us over!

LAUGHLIN: Oughtn't to be allowed in a decent neighbourhood!

KEEGAN: Who kicked me wood!

LAUGHLIN: You miserable Catholic get!!

KEEGAN: You rotten Orange sucker!!

[*The words are about to lead to worse, when with a deafening drum beat, the Salvation Army marches on to the stage, singing and playing loudly* 'THERE IS POWER'.

The band come downstage, followed by TEIFION. *The Catholics and Protestants watch in silence. The Salvation Army Captain declaims in a loud voice* ... 'Brothers' ... *The Catholics and Protestants charge at him yelling and cat-calling, and chase the Salvation Army off the stage leaving* TEIFION *watching them amused. He looks around the stage and sees the two flag hangers.*

TEIFION *moves downstage towards the ladders.*]

TEIFION: What a place to come home to! They're still fighting the Thirty Years War up here!

[*He surveys the flags.* HANNAH *and* KELLY *come down.*]

Eh!

KELLY: Now don't you start!

HANNAH: Hello, Teifion.

TEIFION: I was only going ...

KELLY: Shut up!

TEIFION: You are a tolerant lot up here!

KELLY: All right, what's up?

TEIFION: Well, I'm reasonably divorced from racial loyalties ... but if I may point out ...

HANNAH: Go on.

TEIFION: Well ... somebody's cut the head off the Welsh Dragon on that flag and it'll play havoc in the ranks of the more ardent Welsh Nationalists! Well, what was all that about?

KELLY: Oh, the Irish element feeling their oats.

TEIFION: Aye, I thought I saw old man Laughlin and old Keegan.

89

HANNAH: It's them flats that's causing the trouble, y'see. Everyone suddenly wants a bathroom.

KELLY: What he means is, it's been put around that the Catholics are getting more than their fair share of the flats, and in this town that means trouble!

TEIFION [*leaping about the stage, yelling and shouting*]: I'm Welsh! Dragons are neutral!

KELLY [*as if seeing Teifion for the first time*]: Hullo, Teifion! How are you?

TEIFION: Eh? Oh, surprised to be home. [*Pauses. He looks at Kelly.*] Well, go on ... ask me!

KELLY: Ask you what?

TEIFION: When I'm going back.

KELLY: Oh ... aye ... when are you going back? [TEIFION *gives him a friendly push.*] Some of your mates are home, Jamieson, Charlie Modryb, and ...

[MEME MODRYB *comes on to the stage in the full gear of a teenager. A sticky-out frock with a full petticoat. She is heavily and grotesquely made up. She crosses to the group.*]

MEME: Haven't you finished yet?

HANNAH: Y'what?

MEME: The flags?

KELLY: Just about.

MEME: Hadn't you better get them ladders back before the Copry miss them?

KELLY: How do you know about them ladders?

TEIFION: Are you Meme Modryb?

MEME: Sure.

TEIFION [*admiringly*]: Well ... you've put on weight.

MEME: Ash ... leave off.

TEIFION: Is Charlie back from his last trip?

MEME: Tonight ... I'm just going to meet him.

TEIFION: Well, Charlie's in for a surprise for a start. The nymphet of Back Nile Street ... poor old Charlie.

MEME: Ah, shrup, fellow … you're only talking.

TEIFION: Yes, I'm only talking.

[*She flounces off, followed by* TEIFION. KELLY *stops him.*]

KELLY: Eh, Teif, some of your mates are home, Jamieson and young Bobby Laughlin's expected tonight.

TEIFION: He's mistimed his arrival then. It only needs him and Tim Keegan to get together and we'd have a right barney! Oh, the Irish, the Liverpool Paddies! The best Catholics, the best Protestants, and the worst Christians in the world! Well, there's one good thing about being Welsh, you don't have to join that lot.

KELLY: I'm all right too.

HANNAH: What are you then?

KELLY: Manx.

TEIFION: What?

KELLY: I'm Manx.

HANNAH: From the Isle of Man?

KELLY: Yes.

TEIFION: Where the cats don't have any tails?

KELLY: Aye, that's it.

TEIFION: Three legs of man, sort of thing?

KELLY: You've got it.

HANNAH: But they're sort of Irish, aren't they?

KELLY: Of course they're not!

HANNAH: They are.

KELLY: Look … my old fella was Manx and me old lady was too. Well, they weren't Irish … they were Manx!

HANNAH: Oh … I always thought they were …

KELLY: Well, they weren't!

TEIFION: They're more like the Welsh then?

KELLY: No … I'm sorry, Teifion … but they're more like Manx.

HANNAH: Well, you won't be getting mixed up with the Prods and the Red Necks then, will you?

KELLY: Oh no, I won't. I'm Manx.

HANNAH: Well, you're all right.

KELLY: Aye, I am, I'm all right.

HANNAH: I mean, if anybody's going to clout you, you can always tell them you're Manx.

KELLY: Oh, I've found it very useful in the past.

HANNAH: Yeah, I suppose so ... but it's funny really, cos I always thought that Kelly was an Irish name.

KELLY: What are you on about! Don't you know the song ... [*Singing rapidly*] Has anybody here seen Kelly, Kelly from the Isle of Man!

HANNAH [*after a pause*]: Then it must be Manx.

KELLY: It is.

HANNAH: Well, you're all right then.

KELLY: Aye ... but how about you like?

HANNAH: Oh, I'm all right! Y'know, you can spell my name backwards and it spells the same as frontwards. Hannah, H.A.N.N.A.H ... Either way it's the same.

TEIFION: Scotch, isn't it?

HANNAH: Dunno. The old fella came from Wigan.

KELLY: But what about your mother?

HANNAH: Her name wasn't Hannah until she got married.

KELLY: Well, I know it wasn't, y'daft sodger! Was she Scotch?

HANNAH: No. She came from Fazerckerley!

TEIFION: Well, you're all right then.

HANNAH: Oh aye, I'm all right.

KELLY: And Teifion here, he's all right, he's Welsh.

HANNAH: Well, that's what I always say, there's one good thing about being Liverpool Welsh, you don't have to join up with them lot.

TEIFION: Well ... as long as everybody knows about us ... we're all right.

KELLY [*doubtfully*]: Yeah ... we're all right.

HANNAH [*uneasily*]: Well ... it goes without saying, doesn't it?
    [*There is the sound of distant angry voices. They pause and look at each other apprehensively.*]

TEIFION: Well, here we go. Mah, Mammy, it's Teifion, rwy'wedi arrivo.

[*They pick up their ladders and rapidly disappear.* TEIFION *crosses to the door of his house. The stage is dark and the lamplight throws long shadows. A boy and girl cuddle close together in the dark.*]

TEIFION [*calling out*]: You ought to be ashamed of yourselves! Tomorrow is Sunday! God's watching!

[*He puts his hand through the letter-box and pulls out the key on the end of a piece of string. He opens the door and on a deep breath he goes into the house.*

CHARLIE MODRYB *enters in full uniform carrying his cases and a stuffed crocodile. He is refusing to look at his sister,* MEME, *who is running behind him.*]

MEME: Well, talk to us, Charlie.

CHARLIE [*furious*]: Not another word ... so don't tempt me!

MEME: Charlie!!

CHARLIE: Me mother wants her head examined! You look like a bloody maypole!

MEME [*whining*]: But I'm not wearing me ribbons!

CHARLIE [*turning on her*]: Don't you get cheeky wi' me!

MEME: I'm not being ...

CHARLIE: Yes you are!

MEME: ... cheeky!

CHARLIE: You what?

MEME [*bursting into tears*]: Charlie!

CHARLIE: You look a proper sight, you do. Honest to God, if any of the lads saw you ... I'd never live it down! I've brought you a present too. But you're not having it. I suppose you know that every time you bend down you can see the top of your stockings.

MEME [*peering over her shoulder*]: Can you?

CHARLIE: Yes, you can ... so stop it.

MEME: Well, it'll be all right when I get me high heels tomorrow ...

CHARLIE: Y'what?

MEME: Our mother's got me a pair of high heels.

CHARLIE: We'll see about that!

MEME: Oh no, Charlie!

CHARLIE: Oh yes, Charlie! Stood there in the middle of Lime Street Station like a bad woman.

MEME [*pleased*]: Is that what I looked like?

CHARLIE: Yes ... I din't know you.

MEME: Is that why you said, 'Sorry, love, I'm in a hurry'?

CHARLIE [*furious*]: Get in the house before I clout you.

MEME [*crying*]: Charlie.

CHARLIE [*as they go*]: I'll take the scrubbing brush to you!

   [*They exit.* JAMIESON *and* MAG *come into the street.*]

JAMIESON: Well, as we arrived, Bobby's ship was on the way out.

MAG: Then you didn't see him?

JAMIESON [*pretending*]: I fancy I got a glimpse of him. Look, Mag, forget Bobby Laughlin. Will we not go up to the park?

MAG: Now? At this time of night? Are you barmy?

JAMIESON: Ah, come on, we could have a sit down and a bit of a gas about old times.

MAG: Well, some other time, not tonight. I promised me mother I wouldn't be late.

JAMIESON: Mag, come on, just half an hour up by the back of the tennis courts.

MAG [*smiling*]: They've trimmed the bushes.

JAMIESON: They haven't!

MAG: They have, y'know!

JAMIESON [*furious*]: Trust them! They'd spoil everything if they had their way.

MAG: Eh, have you heard when Bobby's coming back?

JAMIESON: Oh forget Bobby Laughlin for a minute, will you?

MAG: I thought he was a mate of yours.

JAMIESON: To hell with him, Bobby's away and Jamo's here ... Ah ... come on, Mag.

MAG: No, there's no future in it.

JAMIESON: But we could have a bit of fun.

MAG: You could, you mean, not me.

JAMIESON: Ah, go on, you came with me before.

MAG: Well, not any more. No! There's no future in it.

JAMIESON: I suppose if I was Bobby Bloody Laughlin it'd be different!

MAG: What did you say?

JAMIESON [*justifying*]: I took you to the dance, didn't I?

MAG: Do you want the money?

JAMIESON: You know I don't ... but a fella's got a right to ...

MAG: To what! Look, Jamo, I'm going in.

JAMIESON: But, Mag, you've always ... [*pleading*] you've always ...

MAG: Well, not any more, tara. [*She moves off.*]

JAMIESON [*pauses then goes off after her*]: Ah ... in the name of God!
   [*He walks away.* MAG *sighs and moves further downstage. From another direction a young man enters and crosses into the lamplight. He is carrying luggage and he puts it down irritably ... he sees Mag. The young man is* BOBBY LAUGHLIN.]

BOBBY: Eh ... is that you, Mag? Hello, is that Mag Keegan?

MAG: Y'what?

BOBBY: I thought it was! It's me ... Bob Laughlin!
   [*She crosses into the light.*]

MAG: Bobby! Hello!

BOBBY: How are you then?

MAG: Oh, I'm fine. You're home then?

BOBBY: Aye, I'm home. [*They pause.*] Aye, listen, before we go any further, was that the unlikely fella you were with?

MAG: Who?

BOBBY: Come on, you know, Jimmy Smith.

MAG: Oh no, I haven't been out with Jimmy for over a year. Didn't you know?

BOBBY: No, I didn't, I never saw you the last time I was home.

MAG [*simply*]: I saw you one day.

BOBBY: Did you?

MAG: But why did you call him the 'unlikely fella'?

BOBBY: What? Oh ... yeah, well, he used to hang around with Davy

95

Jones ... I mean, Davy Jones and Jimmy Smith ... You wouldn't believe a couple of names like that, honestly, so the gang used to call them the unlikely fellas ... a bit of a joke.

[MAG *laughs dutifully*: 'Oh.']

MAG: Well, he's in the Army now.

BOBBY: Crazy!

MAG: What?

BOBBY: The Yanks say that.

MAG: Just arrived at Lime Street?

BOBBY: Aye, that's right. Eh, Mag, any of the old gang home?

MAG: Like who?

BOBBY: Well, y'know, Charlie, Charlie Modryb ... Jamieson ...

MAG [*flatly*]: Yes, Jamieson's home ... [*eagerly*] and Charlie.

BOBBY: Oh, smashing! I'm going to be home for a couple of months now, taking me ticket, think I've got a pretty good chance.

MAG: Are you doing well then, Bobby?

BOBBY: Oh, I think so, anyway, the old man's pleased and that's all that matters ... [*He pulls himself up.*] Well, y'know what I mean.

MAG: Yeah, I know what you mean.

BOBBY: Eh, how does the old fella look? Is he all right?

MAG: Yes, he's fine ... I think. 'Course [*laughing*] he doesn't talk to me!

BOBBY [*laughing*]: Well, you wouldn't expect him to really, would you?

[*They both laugh.*]

How's your mother, then?

MAG: Still the same.

BOBBY: Aye, they don't change, the old ones.

MAG: Eh! What about you then, Bobby? He must be proud of you, your dad, you being an officer like.

BOBBY: Yeah, I suppose he is ... course, he was a good bosun, y'know. I've sailed with fellas who've sailed with him ... he was a good bosun all right.

MAG: Yeah ... but you're an officer.

BOBBY: Aye.

MAG: D'y'still like going to sea, Bobby?

BOBBY: Not bad.

MAG [*smiling*]: Well, what does that mean?

BOBBY [*after a slight pause*]: Y'see it's all right for a time, going to sea I mean. When I first started, when I was sixteen, well ... I just wanted to be one of the lads. I wanted to be the same as all me mates. There was Charlie going, Jamieson was going, and about five other fellas I knew and they were all going to sea and me father went to sea ... and ... well ... you always want to be like your dad, don't you?

MAG: Do you?

BOBBY: Of course. I thought to myself that it would be wonderful ... and it was in the beginning, it was very interesting and ... y'know, seeing all those places ... I liked it and fine.

MAG: Yes, you must have been everywhere.

BOBBY: Aye ... but sometimes when you get to these places, they're not what you thought they'd be ... cos you don't see that much.

MAG: How d'you mean?

BOBBY: Well, the first thing y'do y'come off the ship and y'always get stuck in some pub down on the ... well ... usually on the dock road, and if you do get into the town, nobody'll talk to you, everybody knows you're a sailor and the policemen look at you as if you're going to do something at any moment. But ... well ... usually, sort of thing, nothing very much happens.

MAG [*after waiting for him to go on*]: Well, what happens then?

BOBBY: Then you're back to sea and all the time you're at sea you're just scraping and painting and standing by your watch.

MAG: Is that all?

BOBBY: Yeah ... and they get lonely, cos ... well ... they're a mixed sort of fellas on a ship and they go their own ways. Y'know you might have one fella, he's very interested in doing a bit of fretwork or something. Well, that's all he's interested in, that's all he cares about, doing his fretwork. Or you might have another fella, he's very serious about navigation and spends all his time studying. Then, of course, there's the fella who does a bit of painting ...

97

y'know, always painting pictures. But I suppose the worst thing on
a ship is when the old man doesn't like you or there's some fella in
the crew you can't stand. Well, you're with him for maybe two
months at a time!

MAG: Has that ever happened to you, Bobby?

BOBBY: Has it? When I was going down to South America we had a
Sparks with us ... and I couldn't stand this fella ... there was some-
thing about him. He was a bloody Catholic ... oh ... I'm sorry,
Mag ...

[*She smiles faintly.*]

[*Going on rapidly*] Y'know, a southern Irishman ... and he used to
get me *down*! I had to sit opposite him when he was eating, and I
wouldn't say he was a bad eater or anything like that, but he had a
way of eating that used to drive me mad! And day after day I sat
opposite him and I knew he didn't like me and I didn't like him and
I thought to meself ... there must be something else in life than
going to sea!

MAG: Well, why do you go on? You haven't got to, Bobby ... or have
you? Why do you go on?

BOBBY: Because I was sixteen when I first went to sea. I went as deck
boy cos me father said it'd knock all the nonsense out of me, then I
sort of liked it, being a kid it was fun ... and then he'd put out all
that money for me gear ... and when he did that ... I had to go on
with it. I mean, I couldn't very well let him down, now could I?

[TEIFION *opens his window and sticks his head out. He is in pyjamas.*]

TEIFION: Look, my mother's a ratepayer and she wants to get some
sleep.

BOBBY [*looking up*]: Hello, skin!

MAG: Hello, Teif.

TEIFION: Oh no, not you two! Eh, Bobby, your father's been hanging round the streets all night, taking it out of every Catholic in
sight because you're late home.

BOBBY: Oh, lummy!

MAG: Is it about the flats?

TEIFION: No, I think it's congenital … but I'm a cynic!

BOBBY: He hasn't changed, eh, Mag!

MAG: No!

[*They grin at each other.*]

TEIFION: Anyway, the male Keegans have been on the rampage as well, it never rains but what it pours! It's stimulating, isn't it?

BOBBY: Well, I don't know about that.

TEIFION: Well, it's a point I'm not prepared to debate. As I always think, a man's got a serious intellectual disadvantage when he hasn't got his boots on … too much freedom of the toes doesn't make for cerebral activity! So why don't you two push off and let Liverpool get some sleep? It's Sunday tomorrow … and in this town that's spiritual cross-country run!

BOBBY [*collecting his gear*]: Aye.

MAG: Aye … I'll be seeing you. Night, Teif, so long, Bobby. [*She goes.*]

BOBBY: See you, Mag.

[*As he moves off he looks up at Teifion.*]

See you tomorrow at the Grapes, Teif?

TEIFION: I'm afraid so. Eh, Bobby, when are you going back?

BOBBY: I've only just got home!

TEIFION: I know, I just thought I'd get you used to the question.

BOBBY [*laughing*]: Yeah … they always do ask you that, don't they?

[*He goes.* TEIFION *watches him and starts to sing to himself.*]

TEIFION [*singing*]: Bobby Laughlin took a notion
 For to cross the Liverpool sea.
 And he left his true love behind him,
 Waiting by the Liverpool Lee.
 First she sighed and then she cried
 And then she broke her heart in two.
 Then she found another sailor,
 Waiting on the Liverpool Loo.

[*He sighs.*] Tomorrow'll be a lovely day if only the local politicians will leave it alone.

CURTAIN

SCENE TWO

Sunday Morning

[*The lights go up, church bells ring loudly, and Sunday morning starts. The newspaper woman and her husband, a blind man, come on to the stage, shouting their papers. Out of his house comes* MR LAUGHLIN. *He crosses to the paper woman.*]

TEIFION: All right. We know, we know.

LAUGHLIN: *News of the World.*

[MR KEEGAN *comes out of his house and crosses to the paper man.*]

KEEGAN: The *News of the World*!

LAUGHLIN: I was first.

[LAUGHLIN *glares at him. The newswoman serves* LAUGHLIN *first, who lordly walks away.* KEEGAN (*loudly*): 'The Catholic Herald!' *and walks away.* TEIFION *comes out of his house, crosses to the newspaper people. He lights a fag and starts to cough. Sound of bugles and kettledrums bursts out.* TEIFION *takes this as a personal attack.*]

TEIFION: Why do the Boy Scouts always choose Sundays! Bugles, bloody bugles everywhere. [*He shouts off to the buglers.*] You're a semi-military organization, probably dominated by the Pope.

KEEGAN: Did you mention the Pope?

TEIFION [*grinning*]: No ... I just said that they were dominated by the Freemasons!

KEEGAN: You've a point there! [*He goes back to his house.*]

TEIFION [*looking after him*]: He's been to early mass, replete he is, from a divine breakfast ... [*To newswoman*] I suppose asking for the *Observer* is esoteric?

NEWSWOMAN: Y'what?

TEIFION: *News of the World*!

[MAG, *her mother* MRS KEEGAN, *and* TIM *enter, and start to cross the stage.*]

TEIFION: 'Morning, Mag. 'Morning, Mrs Keegan. Off to the short 11 o'clock at St Vincent's?

MAG: Hi, Ti.

TEIFION: It's a drag, Mag.

[MRS KEEGAN *ignores him and they exit.*]

TEIFION [*watching them go, singing to himself*]:

> There is a house in Liverpool,
> They call the house of God,
> Oh, they're packing in the Roman Catholics ...
> As tight as peas in a pod ...

CHARLIE: Hello d'ere, me old knock!

TEIFION [*greeting him enthusiastically*]: Charlie is me darling!

[*As he reaches the door of his house,* CHARLIE MODRYB *enters. They do a little dance, singing* 'Charlie Charlie, chuck, chuck, chuck, went to bed with three fat ducks!!!'

MR LAUGHLIN *walks out of his house and past the boys.*]

CHARLIE: 'Morning, Mr Laughlin.

LAUGHLIN: 'Morning, Charlie.

[*He gives Teifion a curt nod as he walks past and off.*]

TEIFION: There he goes, off to church to tell God he's knocked a few more nails in the Catholic coffin. The self-appointed hammer of the Catholic Apostolic Church ... a fife player ... Orange sash-wearer *par excellence* ... and he's kind to puppies too!

[*The sound of the bagpipes and drums starts.*]

CHARLIE [*happily*]: Oh, the Scottish Boys' Brigade.

TEIFION: Honest to God ... this City's full of over-privileged minorities! All we need now is a Chinese funeral! Well, Charlie, thank God the Welsh don't wear kilts!

[*They are now standing outside Teifion's house. Off stage the sound of a woman's voice starts whining in Welsh.*]

TEIFION [*answering her*]: I'm talking to Charlie Modryb!

[*Welsh voice goes on.* TEIFION *listens, then turns to Charlie, smiling.*] How's this for a *non sequitur*? She says 'Modryb's Welsh for Aunt'.

CHARLIE: Aye, I know.

TEIFION: You know! Well ... that means you're Charlie's Aunt!

CHARLIE: Aye, I suppose it does.

TEIFION: Well, you're taking the news pretty well, I must say.

[CHARLIE *leans towards the house and shouts to the woman.*]

CHARLIE: Rwy'n flach ohono.

TEIFION [*amazed*]: Can you speak Welsh?

CHARLIE: Of course.

TEIFION: Isn't it marvellous! I've only known you for twenty-five years and you've never mentioned it before.

CHARLIE: Well, it never came up. Let's get up to the Grapes.

TEIFION: It's a bit early isn't it?

CHARLIE: I've got to meet Jamo first.

TEIFION: I can't stand that phony Irish get.

CHARLIE: Well, that makes it quits, because he can't stand you ... but he's one of the gang.

TEIFION: Oh aye, the sacred hierarchy of the gang!

CHARLIE: Y'what?

TEIFION: I'll just tell the old lady I'm not going to chapel.

CHARLIE: Well, I mean, if it's ...

TEIFION [*cutting in*]: No ... she knows I won't go, it's a game we play, she enjoys her suffering and who am I to deprive her of it! [*He crosses to his door, shouting*] I'm going to the boozer with Charlie!

[*There is a long Welsh whine off.*]

[*Grinning as he cuts in.*] Yeah, I know it'll be the death of me!

[*He closes the door.* CHARLIE *has crossed to the Laughlins' doorway.*]

CHARLIE [*turning*]: I'll give Bobby a shout.

TEIFION: Well, hurry up, his old fella'll be back in a minute.

CHARLIE [*shouting*]: Bobby! Hi, Bob.

[BOBBY *appears at the door.*]

BOBBY: Well, what's up?

CHARLIE: Hi, punch, can you slip out?

BOBBY: Where'll you be?

CHARLIE: Having a reunion drink in the Grapes.

BOBBY [*looking over his shoulder*]: Keep it down!

TEIFION: Look, son, your dad'll have to know you take a drink some day.

BOBBY: Aye, but not on me first day home.

TEIFION: Well, chew a clove.

[MAG *enters at the back of the stage.*]

BOBBY: Is that what you do? Our Joey used to do that. All right then, I'll see you up there in about half an hour. O.K.?

[TEIFION *and* CHARLIE *murmur agreement as* MAG *comes up to them.*]

MAG: Hello, lads.

CHARLIE: Hello, Mag, how are you, kid, how goes it?

MAG: Fine. Hi, Bob. [*She pushes up Teifion's hair.*] How's Curly?

[BOBBY *and* CHARLIE *laugh. At this moment* MR *and* MRS LAUGHLIN *enter the stage and cross to the group outside his door. They are laughing, but freeze when they see him.* MR LAUGHLIN *looks coldly at Mag.*]

TEIFION [*quickly*]: It's all right, she's with me.

[MR LAUGHLIN *ignores him and pushes past Bobby and enters his doorway.* MRS LAUGHLIN *follows.*]

BOBBY: Hey, look, I'll see you later on. O.K.?

CHARLIE: Aye … sure.

TEIFION: Yeah, great.

[*As* BOBBY *turns, he looks at Mag.*]

BOBBY: Sorry, Mag. [*He goes in and closes the door.*]

TEIFION: He's his mother's boy too.

MAG: Ah, chew a brick. See you. [*She goes into her own doorway.*]

CHARLIE: Ta-ra, well.

TEIFION: À bientôt.

CHARLIE: Come 'head, I want me breakfast.

[TEIFION *is still looking after Mag.*]

I know.

TEIFION: What?

CHARLIE: You like her as well.

[*With a burst of laughter and a friendly push,* TEIFION *bounds upstage.*]

TEIFION: Liverpool's full of Celtic Cosmic Purpose … the whole town's feeling its oats.

[*They exit, singing, their arms round each other's shoulders.*]

TEIFION \
CHARLIE / [*singing*]: She's a tiddly ship …
On the ocean she flips
She travels by night and by day.
Cha, cha, cha.

[*Interior of the Laughlins' living-room.* MR *and* MRS LAUGHLIN *are in the room together. He is very angry, and* MRS LAUGHLIN *is trying to pacify him.*]

LAUGHLIN: It was a calculated insult.

MRS LAUGHLIN: Aw, Father, it wasn't …

LAUGHLIN: She was standing there … right on our front step, talking to that Davies fellow … the young slut! I tell you, I'll not have it!

MRS LAUGHLIN: Leave it alone, Father, you might only make things worse.

LAUGHLIN: Oh, I'm not the man to shirk me duty, but be the same token, there's no good in jumping in and raking up old cinders.

MRS LAUGHLIN: Now don't upset yourself.

LAUGHLIN: You're right, it'll only give me the wind. [*She exits as* CARSON *enters.*]

CARSON: The band all ready to play on Monday for the Duchess, Robert?

LAUGHLIN: And that's another thing. Bobby McHugh was bleating about not provoking anybody … wanted to play selections from Gilbert and Sullivan! Well, that Sullivan was a Catholic for a start! He's a good man, Bobby McHugh, but weak, too ready to give in! Well, I said to him, 'Have you got one of the new flats in them buildings?' … cos he wanted one bad, y'know, real bad. [*He laughs.*] That shut him up!

CARSON: It would, it would.

[BOBBY *comes into the room carrying his jacket and shoes, followed by his mother.*]

MRS LAUGHLIN: Where are you going?

BOBBY: For a bit of a walk.

CARSON: Didn't see you in church this day, Bobby.

MRS LAUGHLIN: Well, that was my fault – I let him sleep in this morning.

BOBBY: Hi, Dad, been to church then?

LAUGHLIN [*grimly*]: We were out quick, two hymns and a short sermon. Some English fella, only gave us $7\frac{1}{2}$ minutes. I timed him.

BOBBY: How's the band?

LAUGHLIN: Short on fluters, but we've bought a new Lambeg.

BOBBY: Is that one of them big drums Carson McDerby bashes?

LAUGHLIN: Plays, not bashes! he's a great arm for the Lambeg drum has Carson.

[MRS LAUGHLIN *who has been peering through the window, recoils.*]

MRS LAUGHLIN: Oh God, there's that Randy Murrey lumbering up the entry!

LAUGHLIN: Don't pay him any heed.

MRS LAUGHLIN: Well, he worries me.

LAUGHLIN: There's no harm in Randy, it's just that he looks a bit funny and he has that predicament in his speech. No doubt it's a visitation from the Lord.

BOBBY [*shocked*]: Oh, Dad, you can't say that!

LAUGHLIN: Am I not straight from church! Am I not in my own house! Should I not speak me mind! His father married a Catholic; them's that are of one religion shouldn't be married with the daughter of Rome. It's against God and Man ... so wouldn't the consequences be something terrible like that?

MRS LAUGHLIN [*very quietly*]: I'll get the dinner started.

[*She goes from the room.* BOBBY *is about to try and say something but gives up. He puts his coat down on the table.*]

LAUGHLIN: Are you not wearing your uniform today, Bobby?

MRS LAUGHLIN: He's – he's wearing his mufti.

BOBBY: No, I'm glad to be out of it.

LAUGHLIN: I'd rather hoped you would.

CARSON: Let 'em see you've been doing well.

BOBBY: Aye, I can just hear Charlie and Teifion if I did.

LAUGHLIN: Don't you worry about Davies, he's no respect for him-self, talking to that Keegan girl ... let him stick to his own. Where's your paying-off book?

BOBBY: It's in me coat.

[*He goes to get it but his father forestalls him and without waiting for permission takes it from the inside pocket.* BOBBY *flushes but again he gives in. He starts to busy himself cleaning his shoes.*]

LAUGHLIN [*turning the pages*]: 'A hard-working officer.' Very good, very good.

BOBBY: Oh, they always put that.

LAUGHLIN: They don't unless it's true. Will you get your ticket?

BOBBY: I'll try.

LAUGHLIN: You get it, I want you to get it, understand me. Cos when you've got your tickets, you won't have to stay at sea all your life.

BOBBY [*surprised*]: Eh ... oh ... well, I don't want to stop going to sea oh ...

LAUGHLIN: Y'never know, Bobby! You may be getting married.

MRS LAUGHLIN [*shocked*]: Father.

LAUGHLIN [*turning to her*]: Have you got the dinner to get on with?

MRS LAUGHLIN: Oh aye. [*She goes.*] I've got dinner to get ready.

LAUGHLIN: Sure now, you'd be amazed at Carson McDerby's daughter. D'y'remember what a wee girl she was? For years and years now I've noticed her ... but suddenly she's a grown woman and ... er ... one day I suppose she'll be thinking of getting married. [CARSON *gives a little laugh.* MR LAUGHLIN *dismissing him*] All right, Carson, you can go. [*He exits.*] ... it made me think, if a wee girl like she'd be getting married, I'd ... well ... I'd have to think in terms of maybe you getting married. Make me very happy, y'know, when you marry a Protestant girl. I wouldn't necessarily want you to go home to marry a girl – probably better for you to marry a girl from here, d'y'know, but of good stock, mind, I mean of good stock. It's an important thing. That's what I did with your mother. I could easily have married a girl from Armagh, I could have found a girl easy enough. [*Sly laugh.*] ... I'm not boasting, like ... but ... er ... I was a fine-looking fella.

BOBBY: Oh, I'm sure you were, Dad. I've seen photos when you were a young fella. Oh ... you were very good-looking indeed.

LAUGHLIN: As I've always been taller than you.

BOBBY [*surprised*]: Are you taller than me?

LAUGHLIN [*firmly*]: I'm taller than you, Bobby.

BOBBY: Oh yes, I suppose you are really. I never quite thought about it, y'know. Of course, our Joey ...

LAUGHLIN [*angry*]: I didn't want to talk about Joey!

BOBBY: I'm sorry, Dad, but ... well ... he is me brother.

LAUGHLIN: Wasn't he my son?

BOBBY: Oh, Dad, I wish you didn't feel ... well ... so hard and bitter against Joey ... because ... well ... I often wonder how he's doing.

LAUGHLIN: Well, you needn't wonder how he's doing, Bobby. I know how he's doing. [*Disgusted.*] He's doing fine. He's still married to that woman, and they've got five kids. God in Heaven, and him not twenty-eight! They ruin your stock, Papishas do. By God, they ruined my stock ... I don't speak to them. I passed him on the street the other day with his Papist kids ... I walked on ... and one of them, y'know, was just like your grandfather to look at ... except around the eyes. Funny thing, you can always tell a Papisha by the look they get around the eyes. I don't know what it is ... but they get some sort of a look there. The moment I see that look ... I can tell 'em!

BOBBY: Well, I suppose so. ... Has he got a good job? I mean, has he still got that job?

LAUGHLIN: Aye, he's got that job, he's still working. I suppose he does all right. [*Pause.*] Of course your mother goes round to see him, y'know.

BOBBY: I didn't know that.

LAUGHLIN: Ah, she doesn't know that I know it! [*Pause.*] I suppose it's different with women, your mother was born in Liverpool, she doesn't feel the same way as I do ... she doesn't know what they are like! She doesn't know the way they destroy any decent standard of living a man might have! She doesn't know the way they have no respect for themselves ... she doesn't know what they're really like. Let me tell you, Bobby, they're bad! [*Pauses and looks at Bobby.*] I was worried about you when you took up with that girl when you were still a wee'un, I was worried about you then, Bobby. D'y'know, I got down on my knees and prayed for your saving?

BOBBY [*embarrassed, turns away*]: Oh, Dad, honestly ... I wish you wouldn't talk like that ... it makes me ...

LAUGHLIN [*earnestly*]: Bobby, there are certain things that a man has to say to his son. I'm never a man who's talked to you about ... well ... about anything ... y'know what I mean, Bobby?

BOBBY: No, no, I don't ...

LAUGHLIN: Y'know what I mean ... about women. I just thought that in the ordinary course of events you'd find out about women. But, by God, I mistook it! What with me being away at sea, you never did understand about Papishas! When you took up with that Keegan girl ... I prayed ... and sure, didn't God listen to me? I warn you, Bobby, it's not just for my good, it's for your own good. Y'cannot couple up with them! You mate with a Papisha and you're a damned man! They'll cripple you in every way and you'll never be a free man again. You'll be chained up to yon painted rag of a place, yon Rome! You'll never be a free man again! You'll never be able to stand up to God Save the Queen again!

[MRS LAUGHLIN *enters the room, carrying the meat dish with a joint of uncooked meat on it.*]

MRS LAUGHLIN: I think this joint's going to be a bit ribby ... and it cost more than last week's.

LAUGHLIN: In the name of God, women!

MRS LAUGHLIN [*firmly*]: I've never understood that cooker since it went to shillings. I've sixpences but no shillings.

BOBBY: Here y'are ...

MRS LAUGHLIN: No ... your father'll look after it. [*She gestures for him to go.*

    BOBBY *seizes this opportunity. He is away before anyone can stop him.*]

LAUGHLIN: And mind ... don't be late for dinner!

    [BOBBY, *breathing a sigh of relief, turns to the right and into* MAG, *who is coming out of her front door. They stand looking at each other for a moment.*]

MAG: Hello.

BOBBY: Hello ... where've you been then?

MAG: I'm going to Jones's to get another pint of milk ... the cat knocked ours over. Where are you going?

BOBBY: Up the Grapes, meet the lads, sort of thing.

MAG: Oh.

BOBBY: Well, would you like to walk up there, then, with us?

MAG: All right, I don't mind.

BOBBY: Is it all right?

MAG: Yeah, that's fine.

BOBBY: Well ... let's walk up there then.

MAG: Oh crickey the milk.

    [*They start to walk away from their houses, both looking over their shoulders doubtfully. They catch each other doing this ... and then they grin.*]

BOBBY: How's Davy?

MAG: You what?

BOBBY: Well, come on! Davy! You've just been down to Jones's. You know, the unlikely fellow, Davy Jones!

MAG: Davy? ... Oh, didn't you know, Davy's dead. Fell off a crane three months ago.

BOBBY: Oh, I didn't know ... I'm sorry I spoke ...

MAG: Aye, he's dead. It was quite a shock really. He was at Lairds, do you remember? He went there at sixteen, served his time, then he fell off a crane.

BOBBY: Well ... I didn't know ... Oh Christ! I certainly put me foot into that lot!

MAG: I thought you'd have known.

BOBBY: No, I didn't.

MAG: Well ... stop worrying. Poor Davy's dead and worrying won't bring him back.

BOBBY: But they used to say we looked alike.

MAG [quietly]: Aye, you did.

BOBBY: I went to school with him.

MAG: So did I.

BOBBY [irritated by her apparent calm]: No you didn't, he wasn't a Catholic. He went to Brook Street, you went to St Francis of Assisi's!

MAG: I meant at the same time.

BOBBY [pacified]: Ah, well, that's more like it. Poor old Dave ... Eh, do you fancy going around under the bridge?

MAG: Yes, let's do that.

[As they start to walk, MAG takes Bobby's arm.]

BOBBY [with a slight laugh]: I like the way you did that.

MAG: What?

BOBBY: I like the way you took my arm. It's a funny thing, y'know, about you, Mag ... all my life, that I've known you anyway, you've always been doing the things I like.

MAG: Like what?

BOBBY: Like taking my arm.

MAG: I think you're a bit soft.

BOBBY: No you don't, you know what I mean. There are some people who just do the right thing at the right time ... and you're one of those people.

MAG: Am I?

BOBBY: Of course you are ... you take my arm and I feel good about it ... well, you know what I mean, Mag.

MAG: All right, I know what you mean ... [A pause, she smiles] ... but I don't, you know!

[*They both laugh. A gang of cyclists go past ringing their bells loudly and shouting to each other.* MAG *and* BOBBY *stop to watch them.*]

BOBBY: Look at the kids on their bikes ... I bet they'll get as far as Oglet. Aye, Mag, d'y'remember that time when I was knocking about with you when we were about fifteen?

MAG [*quietly*]: Yes, I remember very well.

BOBBY: Well, d'y'remember when Teifion Davies and meself went over the water to camp for the Whit-week and you came over on the Monday?

MAG: Oh, yes ... of course. I remember, cos there was meself and Phyllis Johnstone came with me.

BOBBY: Aye, that's right. D'y'remember? We had a wonderful time.

MAG: Oh yes! We had a wonderful time, Bobby, didn't we?

BOBBY: I remember we went for a walk in them woods ... and d'y' remember ... [*he gives a little laugh*] ... oh, he's a case, that ruddy Teifion Davies ... d'y'remember, he married us under the trees?

MAG [*slowly*]: Yeah ... I remember. We went right into the centre of the wood together, cos I remember it was all sun ... there was a lot of sun and the leaves were all green.

BOBBY: Yeah ... and then you stuck your face in the water, d'y' remember, cos you said that your face was all hot and you just wanted to put it ... and there was that little stream and you put your face in it.

MAG: I remember ... and when I came out, me face was all wet.

BOBBY [*softly*]: Yeah, and I kissed you and your face was all wet.
[*They look at each other.*]

MAG [*after a moment, almost whispering*]: That was a fine day ... I remember that ... the best day.
[*They look again for a moment.*]

BOBBY [*rousing himself*]: Of course, that was before me old man got to hear about it!

MAG: That was before my mother heard about it and all!

BOBBY: Funny that, wasn't it? We must have been going together for about a year.

MAG: I think it was a bit longer actually, I think it was nearer eighteen months.

BOBBY: God, I remember that night. I went in and had that row with the old man, cos me mother let it slip that you were a Catholic ... and he hit me right across the face. He's a hard man, y'know ... he always found the place to hit – with our Joey it was always across the legs, with me across the face. I'll tell you this, if anyone touches my face now, just puts their hand on it ... I knock it down. I can't stand it. He hit me right across the face with a wet flannel.

MAG: My mother locked me in my room for the whole day, told me it wasn't right. She got the doctor to me. Of course, we were only fifteen and I suppose they didn't want us to think it was serious.

BOBBY [breaking the mood with an abrupt laugh]: Aah, you know what it was!

MAG: Yeah, I do. [Suddenly] Why don't you stop going to sea? There are lots of jobs ashore nowadays, aren't there?

BOBBY: Yes, I suppose there are ... but I made such a fuss about going in the first place ... it's a bit late to turn back now, isn't it? I mean, I haven't got anything else I could do.

MAG: You could be a house painter, you say you're always painting. [She laughs.]

BOBBY: Aye, but I'm used to bossing the fellas that are doing the painting!

MAG [teasing]: Well ... you could learn to be bossed for a change, couldn't you?

BOBBY: Oh ... I don't know about that!

MAG: Anyway, your father gave it up.

BOBBY: Yes, but he got a good job straight away; anyroad, he was married.

MAG: Well, you'll get married one day.

BOBBY: Oh, I don't know about that ... I've never gone around much with girls since I was knocking about ... since I was a kid.

MAG: I see.

BOBBY: And lots of girls don't reckon much to having a sailor for a husband.

MAG: I know.

[*There is a pause while he waits.*]

BOBBY: How do you feel about sailors, Mag? I mean ... what do you think about them as fellas ... if you had to live with one of them, you know, got married to one of them?

MAG: I don't know, Bobby. I've known a lot of sailors, you and Charlie Modryb and Pat Jamieson ... and it seems to me ... well ... all the sailors I've ever known only want a bit of fun.

BOBBY: Well, you know how it is, Mag, a fella gets lonely.

MAG: I know, Bobby, and so do girls.

BOBBY [*quickly*]: Yes, but not in that way.

MAG: No? [*Pause.*] A sailor's a man and not just a sailor ... and I think that if a man loves a woman, he'd want to be with her all the time ... he wouldn't want to go off ... and I'm not sure if ... well ... what you say is true, like, it seems to me that a lot of sailors don't really want to go to sea anyway. But there are other things, aren't there, Bobby? I mean, it's so difficult because most people aren't prepared to do anything about anything, are they?

BOBBY: Aye, I see what you mean.

MAG: Do you? [*Pause.*] Look ... when you love somebody and they love you ... well ... that should be it. But ... I don't know ... [*little laugh of embarrassment*] ... with some fellas it isn't like that and with some girls it isn't like that either. Something can get in the way and it isn't just enough to love. I know that if I loved somebody and they loved me ... I'd marry them and be with 'em all the time and I'd want them to be with me too.

Well, y'know, you don't want to remember love when you're alone, that's sad. But with some people, other things get in the way. They start wanting one thing, something happens and then they just drift ... and you can do nothing with them, no matter how much you love them ... y'know ... they just go on drifting, you can't change 'em, they're the only ones who can ... and they won't change ... will they, Bobby?

BOBBY: Well ... people can't just change because they happen to find out that they're drifting ... or whatever you call it ... you can't just change like that, y'know.

MAG: Yes, you can, Bobby, of course you can ... if you want to ... but first of all you've got to want to ... I mean, it's no good just know-ing you're drifting ... you've got to want to stop, haven't you?

BOBBY: Oh ... I don't know about that. Sometimes you can hurt a lot of people, people who love you if you do just what you want to do.

MAG [gently]: No, no ... if people really love you, they don't stop loving ... they may be hurt ... but in time they'll see you only did what you thought was best. You've got to do what you think's best ... otherwise from then on, it'll all be a waste of time ... you'll always be thinking about what it might have been like if only you'd done the right thing. That's why it isn't really easier to drift. ... As time goes on ... I think it's become harder ... don't you?

BOBBY: I'd better get in to the boys then.

MAG: Yeah ... I suppose you better had.

BOBBY: You wouldn't like to come in for a drink, would you, Mag?

MAG: I don't think I'd better ... the boys might not like it.

BOBBY: Why not?

MAG: Oh nothing ... but they mightn't. Anyway, I promised me mother I wouldn't be late. Goodbye, Bobby, I'm glad I saw you again.

BOBBY: Well ... I'll see you around.

MAG [laughing]: Go on ... over to your mates! Goodbye, Bobby.

BOBBY: Ta-ra well, Mag.

[JAMIESON enters and sees them disappearing. He calls after them.]

JAMIESON: Mag!

[But they don't hear him. MRS KEEGAN and TIM cross the stage from church.]

Oh, hello, Mrs Keegan. I just saw Mag ...

MRS KEEGAN [*hurrying on*]: Yes, she's in the house. [*She then goes indoors.*]

JAMIESON: Ah – for God's sake! [*He stands kicking his toes as* CHARLIE *and* TEIFION *come up behind him.*]

CHARLIE: Hello, Jamo, I didn't recognize you, you look like a blooming Yank!

TEIFION [*taps him on the other shoulder, which makes him start round again; in an American accent*]: Er ... pardon me, friend ... but can you tell me the way to the Catholic Cathedral ... my psychiatrist has let me down again!

JAMIESON [*turning to Charlie*]: I didn't know this fella was going to be home.

TEIFION: And now I am ... you're happy! Give us a kiss!

JAMIESON: Oh ... for God's sake!

CHARLIE [*cutting in*]: Well, let's get in.

JAMIESON [*importantly*]: I was waiting till it was half past before I went over. D'y'know, I can never take a drink before half past twelve.

TEIFION: Why?

[JAMIESON *is nonplussed.*]

CHARLIE [*cuts in again*]: Eh, are you still at the navigation school?

JAMIESON: I am, and d'you know, I thought to meself, if I didn't get me ticket this time, I'd ...

CHARLIE: Why, have you sat it before then?

JAMIESON: Well ... in a way ... yes.

CHARLIE: What d'you mean ... in a way? ... Have you sat it before?

JAMIESON: Charlie, you're too quick a man. Y'see, it was like this. I came back from Canada last trip ... I'd been with a Canadian line, I'd been with them eighteen months, did y'know?

CHARLIE: Aye, I'd heard last night.

JAMIESON: Well, y'see, I couldn't get down to the work. We were stopping in Montreal at the time, and I'm, well, I'm afraid I didn't do as much studying as I'd have liked to, y'see. Well ... I did me three months at the school ... but one thing and another got in the

way and I never seemed to get down to the work. Well ... I failed
me navigation, but ...

TEIFION: Bad at sums, eh?

JAMIESON [*narked*]: Of course, I got past with me seamanship.

CHARLIE: Well, you would.

JAMIESON: The whole thing was a great pity really, because, I mean
... out on the bridge of a ship and I'll do fine enough. Anyway, I had
to take the exam again ... I went down to the office and they were
very understanding about it and very charming about it and they
decided to give me another three months. Well ... I don't know
how it is ... or why it should be, but I don't seem to have passed
again ... I got the news yesterday ...

TEIFION } [*grinning*]: Aye, aye.
CHARLIE }

JAMIESON: The office were rather annoyed about it, they think that I
hadn't worked hard enough. I didn't see Mr O'Higgins ... I had an
interview with Robert McHugh ... that didn't help ... but in the
end he gave me the opportunity of doing something else for them
and waiting on another three months.

CHARLIE: You're a jammy codger, Jamieson!

JAMIESON: Ah yes now, Charlie. [*Innocently.*] Bobby Laughlin's
home, isn't he? I just saw him with Mag.

CHARLIE: Did you?

JAMIESON [*slyly*]: She's hot stuff, that Mag! [*This falls on stony
ground so he continues hastily.*] Well ... as I was saying, they're going
to have me working by ...

TEIFION: Isn't that the job they give the drunks?

JAMIESON [*turning on him*]: It is not! I'm relieving officers who are
going on leave. I'll just work by their watches while the ships are in
port and I'm hoping, with any luck at all, next time I'll be able to
pass ... but the navigation has me worried, y'know, which is really
the pity of it because ... put me on the bridge of a ship and I'll do
fine enough.

TEIFION: Oh yeah ... sure ...

CHARLIE: You sound to me as if you've swallowed the anchor! You want to get a deck under your feet ... and I don't mean the New Brighton Ferry either!

JAMIESON: Ah now, Charlie, don't y'know I can't wait to get back to sea! The last thing I want to do is swallow the anchor, you know that now, don't you, Charlie?

[*During the last speech,* CARSON MCDERBY *and a crony have entered the stage and are crossing to the pub.*]

CHARLIE: Hi, Mr McDerby.

CARSON: Hello, Charlie, Teifion. [*He gives Jamieson a hard straight look then goes into the pub.*]

JAMIESON [*amazed*]: What did I do?

TEIFION: You're breathing, aren't you?

JAMIESON [*mystified*]: Yeah ... sure.

TEIFION: Well, old Carson sees that as a calculated insult!

[TIM KEEGAN *enters with his father and they cross to the pub.*]

JAMIESON: Hallo, Tim ... Mr Keegan.

[OLD KEEGAN *nods and* TIM *smiles, then they both give Charlie and Teifion a straight hard look and go into the pub.*]

In the name of Jay ...

[CHARLIE *and* TEIFION *both burst into laughter.*]

TEIFION: No ... honest ... you've got to laugh. Those lads are all for dragging us back to the Byzantium Empire.

CHARLIE: Well, I'm not going for a start. Come 'head let's get a pint.

[*They cross to the pub as* NEVILLE *and* LESLEY *enter the stage.* CHARLIE *and* JAMIESON *go into the pub.* TEIFION *stands outside for a moment looking at Neville and Lesley with a grin and listening to them talk.*]

NEVILLE: I thought a couple of scoops of ale after a quick knock-up before lunch would be just the job.

LESLEY: Oh, I concur. We've worked up a bit of a sweat, like, as you might say ...

TEIFION [*crossing over to them, speaking in heavy Liverpool accent*]: Hello, Nevoggs. How's your belly for Spots!!

NEVILLE [*shaken*]: Oh, ho, good gracious ... I'm right in thinking you're Tivion Davies?

TEIFION [*leering*]: Yeah ... see you at the Old Boys' Hot Pot Supper! Wack! Tara.

[*He goes into the pub. The boys look after him with obvious distaste.*]

NEVILLE: I'm afraid he won't be welcome.

LESLEY: Was he at Quarry Bank, then?

NEVILLE: Oh, definitely, you wouldn't have known him ... he was always in the A form.

LESLEY: Bit of a swot, eh?

NEVILLE: Definitely, a rotter, had the nerve to appear on the tennis courts wearing his jeans.

LESLEY: Oh, yes, the bohemian type. Is he down South then?

NEVILLE: London, it appears. I met him once when I was at the Albert Hall with the rifle club. I had to choke him off. ... I was with some of the chaps from the office in a public house.

LESLEY: Wine, women, and song, eh!

NEVILLE: Oh definitely, well ... we met Davies and he was saying that it was most enjoyable to hear the old local twang ... but he went too far ... he suggested we all had Liverpool accents ... which is ridiculous ... I mean, nobody would ever know I came from the North.

LESLEY: Oh, of course not! He was a scholarship boy, wasn't he?

NEVILLE: Oh yes, very humble folk ... they lived down here ... and it's a right rough area.

LESLEY: Yes, it's most irritating having to come this way for tennis.

NEVILLE: Well, God knows what it'll be like with those new flats overlooking the courts.

LESLEY: You mean ... derisive shouts?

NEVILLE [*leaning his bike against a wall*]: Worse! In my opinion, we're going to be within bottle-chucking range ... so God help us on Saturday nights when they're all jarred!

LESLEY: Have you put the lock on your bike?

NEVILLE: Hardly. I mean, down here, they'd pinch the lock and leave the bike just to spite you!

[*They go into the pub together.*

[*Inside the pub is full.* TEIFION, CHARLIE, *and* JAMIESON *see* BOBBY *as he enters.*]

TEIFION: Here's the lad! Pints all round!

CHARLIE [*yelling after him*]: Y'mean sodger! It must be wonderful to be Teif ... he's half out before he starts!

JAMIESON: Well ... I don't like that fella.

CHARLIE: Who asked for your opinion for a start?

JAMIESON: I don't care if you asked for it or not, Charlie. I don't like him. Sure ... he doesn't know anything about the sea at all ... but to hear him talk ... well ... and he's always having a go at me. He wants to watch it or he'll get thumped one of these days!

BOBBY: Not by you he won't!

JAMIESON [*backing down*]: I never said me ... but fellas like Tim Keegan won't take any of his old buck for long!

BOBBY: What's Tim Keegan ...

CHARLIE [*cutting in*]: We're talking about Teifion and what's more I'm going to tell you something about Teifion you didn't know, Jamo ... he's a bloody good cricketer, is Teif.

JAMIESON: In the name of God ... what's cricket got to do with it?

CHARLIE: Well, y'see he wouldn't take the game seriously ... used to take the micky out of it.

BOBBY: Yeah ... funny that, cos he'd got a lovely straight bat.

JAMIESON [*amazed at them*]: You don't say!

CHARLIE: Well, what I mean is ... he's more to be pitied than blamed.

JAMIESON [*sneering*]: Is that a fact?

BOBBY: Well, I'm glad he's here.

CHARLIE: But he gives me a laugh, y'know, cos it's dead easy ... look, when he gets up full steam ... chatting away fifteen to the dozen ... wait until he's putting over something really big, something he's really keen on ... then you say ...

BOBBY [*laughing*]: I've seen you do this ... you mean, when you say ...

CHARLIE: Aye, that's it ... when I say 'Have you still got that old dog?' ... or 'Haven't seen your Uncle Ted lately?' ... he goes barmy! Aye ... but it's best when he has a go at the Welsh ... you watch me, I'll get him going ...

JAMIESON: But doesn't he see through it?

CHARLIE: Even if he does, he can't help himself. He's a good kid, but he takes himself too serious, like, and he tries to make out that he doesn't ... so sooner or later ... he always bites.

JAMIESON: But if you've got his number ... you can't still like him?

CHARLIE: I do though ... he's just Welsh and they're like that.

JAMIESON: Well, you're sort of Welsh, Charlie.

CHARLIE: Aye ... sort of.

JAMIESON: Well ...

CHARLIE: Yeah, I'm the same as him. ... I'm older, that's all.

JAMIESON: Yes, but ...

CHARLIE: Aah, forget it. Look, all I care about is having a pint and passing me next medical.

BOBBY: Well, if you stick on that African Fever run much longer I don't think you will!

CHARLIE: Oh God, don't say that ... not even as a joke.

[*There is the sound of a commotion at the bar.*]

HANNAH: He didn't mean that, Tim!

TIM: I heard him!

CARSON: Leave him alone!

TEIFION: All I said was ...

TIM: I heard you!

HANNAH: Take it easy!

CARSON: Picking on the innocent was always their game!

TEIFION: All I said was ...

TIM: You insulted the colour!

CARSON: That's what you say!

KELLY: Break it up.

TEIFION: Don't you stand up for me, Mr McDerby, or I'll be in dead trouble for a start ... and Tim, because I said a preference for green is supposed to indicate homosexuality ... it doesn't mean that all Irish Catholics are bent! Take it easy ... after all, we're all God's children.

[*They all agree and* TEIFION *moves away.*]

[*Sitting down with a sigh of relief.*] And here's one who doesn't feel like collecting his wings yet!

[HANNAH *and* KELLY *follow him into the other part of the pub.*]

HANNAH: Watch it.

KELLY: Take it easy.

HANNAH: You've been away too long.

KELLY: You've forgotten what it's like up here, everybody's very touchy.

TEIFION: Yeah, yeah, all right ... I'll be good.

[*They go.*]

TEIFION [*to the lads*]: Isn't it marvellous, eh! I make a simple Freudian remark and the local aborigines start getting restless. God, I've had a bellyful of the Irish!

JAMIESON: I'm Irish!

BOBBY: Now look here ...

TEIFION: Now don't you two start getting a cob on. I'm probably all wrong but I'd elected you to membership of the human race.

CHARLIE [*grinning and giving the other two a broad wink*]: Aye ... but where do the Welsh fit into all this, Teifion?

TEIFION: Oh, the Welsh have twin obsessions, death and sex! ... and if these two vices ever fuse ... they'll produce the greatest race of necrophiliacs the world has ever seen!

CHARLIE [*wisely*]: Oh ... you're right there ... cos they're all liars!

TEIFION: What do you mean? Honest to God! [*All laugh.*] Oh – very droll!

[MEME *hobbles on to the stage in high heels.*]

MEME: Eh, our Charlie, me mother says you're not to be late and you're not to get squiffed.

CHARLIE: All right ... now push off.

MEME: Can I have a bag of crisps?

CHARLIE: All right ... but then you're going.

JAMIESON: Hello, Meme.

MEME: Hi, Jam.

JAMIESON: God, you're looking great.

MEME: D'y'like me shoes?

JAMIESON: Oh, they're a great improvement. They suit you, y'know; they sort of give you a lift.

CHARLIE [*shortly*]: Aye, they would, they're high heels.

JAMIESON: Ah, now, Charlie, y'know what I mean.

CHARLIE: Aye, I do ... so watch it.

JAMIESON: What?

CHARLIE: You know ... so just watch it.

JAMIESON: Ah ... sure.

CHARLIE: Well ... we'll have less of it.

JAMIESON: But ...

CHARLIE: Have done! [*To Meme*] You push off home.

MEME: Me feet feel numb.

TEIFION: Are your tiny hands frozen and all?

MEME: Y'what?

TEIFION: Well ... you're Mimi, aren't you?

MEME: No, I'm not, I'm Meme.

TEIFION: Well ... it's Mimi, isn't it?

MEME: No ... Meme.

TEIFION: Why?

CHARLIE: Well, when she was a baby she was always saying 'me me' ... so we called her ...

TEIFION
CHARLIE } : ... MeMe!

TEIFION [*laughing*]: Honest to God! Well, what's your real name?

MEME [*to Charlie*]: Don't tell him.

CHARLIE: I'm not going to tell him.

MEME: You will though, won't you, Charlie?

CHARLIE: I've told you, I'm not telling!

MEME: Then I'll tell him. ... [*Pause.*] You won't tell anyone, will you?

TEIFION [*grinning*]: Yeah ... everyone.

MEME: All right, I'll tell you, it's Myfanwy ...

JAMIESON: Ha, ha, 'My fanny'.

MEME: But it's not my fault.

TEIFION: I suppose she speaks Welsh too, Charlie.

CHARLIE: I dunno, you'd better ask her yourself.

TEIFION: Well ... do you, love?

MEME: What?

TEIFION: Speak Welsh?

MEME: Well, it's funny really, cos when I was a little kid ...

CHARLIE: Y'mean last year!

MEME: Oh Charlie! Well, I used to think that there was one way of speaking to me mother and another way of speaking to the kids in the street, and then ... one day I spoke to the kids in the street the way I did to me mother ... and none of them knew what I was talking about ... so then I knew I was speaking Welsh.

TEIFION [*after a pause*]: Well, what happened then?

CHARLIE: If she'd got any sense she'd stop speaking Welsh.

TEIFION: Why?

CHARLIE: To give her brain a rest.

TEIFION: She wouldn't know she was overworking.

CHARLIE: She would now she found she'd got one.

MEME: Yes I would ... so I did.

TEIFION: What?

MEME: Stop speaking Welsh.

[*They all laugh.*]

TEIFION: A whole culture is dying and all you can do is laugh.

[JAMIESON *leering over at Meme.*]

CHARLIE [*shortly*]: Come on you, on your way. [*She goes.*] What are you doing down in London, now, Teif ... apart from not working?

TEIFION: I've been selling TV half-hour scripts. ... I'm a writer now. [*He gives* JAMIESON *a hefty push.*] Did you know that, Jamieson? [JAMIESON *attempts to reply, but* TEIFION *goes straight on.*]

TEIFION: No ... I don't suppose you did ... I can't see that eventuality presenting itself to your eager, alert, tired mind.

JAMIESON [*disgusted*]: Aah ... sure, God ...

TEIFION: Well ... that's me. A writer ... and I've sold three scripts and I know no shame. It's removed me from the realms of the National Assistance Board ... so, I paid me old lady back the fifteen quid I owed her ... I got a return ticket and I'll be back tomorrow.

CHARLIE: Is there any danger of you buying us a round then?

TEIFION: Oh aye, I see the day of the patron's dead. You're a material-ist, Charlie, and a stater of the obvious ... you're the sort of man who can walk up to the Empire State Building and say, 'Isn't it big?'

CHARLIE: Well ... it is!

TEIFION [*bouncing for joy*]: Thank God for you, Charlie ... you're the only sane man in this town!

JAMIESON: Aah ... drink your beer and stop bouncing about, you've spilt half mine already! You're always talking as if you're drawing your last breath ... you're a common man, Davies.

TEIFION: And what are you, Jamieson? You left Ireland when you were ten and you still talk with a Paddy accent! You'll have to come to terms with Liverpool, y'know! You're just another green stumbling-block in the way of racial integration ... but then, that's the trouble with all you Liverpool boys ... no ... Kidneypool boys, there's too much acid in you for liver. You're all ashamed to accept what you are ... you're all so busy being Catholics and Protestants that none of you can take time off to be people ...

CHARLIE [*indignantly*]: Eh!

TEIFION [*grinning and with a friendly gesture*]: Except Charlie and me ... and he hasn't got the courage to kick old Mother Wales in the guts! But you don't worry me ... that's your problem. Listen, I've just been down to London and I've sold three scripts ... this is a recurring point in my conversation, I've sold three scripts ... and

I've got a year's contract. Now, I'm very impressed with this, y'know. The Script Editor said to me 'Come in, Mr Davies'. I was very impressed to hear this said in that nice leather-office-chair voice of his.

CHARLIE: Oh, he was one of those sort of fellas, eh? Well ... get on with it ... did you go in?

TEIFION: With dignity, protecting me rear flank all the way. I sat down and he said 'We're going to give you a year's contract' ... so, for the next year I'm going to slave my guts out at a fair living wage.

BOBBY: I bet they didn't give you an advance.

TEIFION: No, the money's going to be paid to me by the week from Martin's Bank ... and why not Martin's? It's a good old Liverpool firm. ... But apart from that, frankly, I'm finished with Liverpool!

BOBBY: And what's Liverpool done all of a sudden? Aren't we good enough for you all then?

TEIFION: That'll cost you a pint, Bobby! No ... when I was in London I found something out meself ... and the rest of us. I met a couple of Welsh fellas down there, bloody nice fellas, South Walians they were and both Welsh Nationalists ... so listen, Charlie ...

CHARLIE: What are you on about? I can't very well do anything else, can I?

JAMIESON: That's true enough.

TEIFION: These fellas were selling poetry like hot cakes. I wish I had as many hot dinners as they were selling poems. They were selling them to all the American art magazines ... the *Detroit Entre Nous* and the *Des Moines Ariel* ... and both of them were Welsh Nationalists!

JAMIESON: Up the Republic!

TEIFION: And Kevan Barry to you!

[HANNAH *and* KELLY *run in.*]

KELLY: Oh no! Not Kevan Barry! D'y'want a bloody riot on our hands!

HANNAH: We'll have to put the bar on you if you start that caper.

TEIFION: It was merely a quotation.

HANNAH: Well, the next time you're out.

[HANNAH *and* KELLY *retreat, grumbling to each other.*]

TEIFION: See what I mean? It can be pernicious stuff, this nationalism, if you don't put it to work for you.

BOBBY: How's that then?

TEIFION: Well ... it occurred one night when I was in a Scot's house having a few Whitbreads in the teeth of the publican's wife, that I spoke to these fellows in Welsh ... and do you know what ... neither of these lads had more than six words of Welsh between them! And I found out that I was the Welsh cultural boy, that I knew, that I'd read a couple of things and that I could recite half the psalms in Welsh and reams of the New Testament! So I started to exploit my minority where it counts ... in London I mean ... I don't go around talking like I do to you load of slack! No ... what I do is ... [*with a Welsh accent*] ... 'I'm a poor North Walian boy' ... with an accent like this ... believe me, boys, there's money to be made in North Wales ... South Wales is played out, everybody's been up and down those slag heaps long enough! No ... it's the ... 'Me poor father is looking after the sheep on the top of Snowden' bit ... B.B.C. Documentary scripts write themselves before your eyes.

JAMIESON: Hey, Teifion ... let's get down to something important ... how's your sex life? Are you still knocking around with that darkie?

TEIFION: Oh, Jamieson ... a darkie! What kind of a word is that ... I'm disgusted with you ... I'm ashamed of you ... you mean, my 'Chocy bic'! She's a lovely kid and the sheen on her skin is like the blue wave that rolls nightly on deep Galilee ... she's a lovely kid. If this is the black man's era, I'm relying on her to put a word in for me. [*Grabs* JAMIESON.] Come on, Jamo, it's your round, mate!

[*He drags* JAMIESON *protesting to the bar, where* TIM KEEGAN *and* MR KEEGAN *are standing.*]

TEIFION [*to Hannah*]: Four pints.

JAMIESON [*to Tim*]: I saw Mag this morning.

TIM: At mass?

JAMIESON: No ... she was talking to Bobby Laughlin ...

TIM } Y'what!
MR KEEGAN } What's that!

TEIFION: And Charlie Modryb and me! There was no question of compromising your position.

[*The two* KEEGANS *appear mollified.*]

TIM: Well ... that's all right ... but we don't want Bobby Laughlin hanging ...

TEIFION [*cutting in*]: He wasn't! Come 'head, Jamo!

[*They collect their drinks and move off.*]

See what you nearly did!

JAMIESON [*as they rejoin the others*]: All I said was ...

TEIFION [*making a mixing movement with his hands*]: Were you born with a silver spoon in your hand ... or did you have to study it? ... and what's your caper with Mag, Bobby?

BOBBY: Y'what?

TEIFION: Well, don't mess her about. Can't you hear ... [*Pause.*] Well ... that's your dad beating the Protestant drum ... so don't you try playing with your Orange flute past the Keegans' today!

BOBBY: I don't know what you're on about, Teif.

TEIFION [*loudly*]: You don't? Then you're not your father's son. Watch this lad. Poor old Mag ... what it is to be a Catholic. Mag Keegan eats meat on Fridays.

[*At this all hell is let loose in the pub.*]

TIM: What did you say!

MR KEEGAN: I heard him ... he's an Anti-Christ!

CARSON: Shut up. ... Freedom of Speech!

NEVILLE: Was it dirty?

LESLEY: Must have been if Teifion Davies said it!

[HANNAH *and* KELLY *bustle over to Teifion and bundle him out.*]

HANNAH: Out, you ... you're barred.

TEIFION [*protesting*]: What about me pint!

KELLY: I'll post you the money!

[TEIFION *is ejected, the others follow him out.*]

CHARLIE: Now look what you've done!

TEIFION [*angry*]: That settles it! If you can't make a plea for under-standing the dietary strain on the women in this town in a pub ... we'll have to find somewhere where you can.

BOBBY: Aye, I'm fed up with this lot.

JAMIESON: Me too!

CHARLIE: All right ... tonight let's go to the park.

TEIFION: Oh God, yes, it's got to be the park at this time of year. The ladies need to be taught a lesson, and we're the lads to do it.

JAMIESON: By God we are.

CHARLIE: You were at mass then, Jamo?

JAMIESON [*seriously*]: The early second. Oh for God's sake, Charlie! [*The lads laugh.*]

JAMIESON: Did I tell you about the dame I picked up at the 'Mystery'.

CHARLIE: Now, that's an interesting thing, the 'Mystery', Teif.

TEIFION: Oh aye.

JAMIESON: She was built stacked, d'you know.

CHARLIE: They call it the 'Mystery' but it's real name's the 'Waver-tree Playground'.

BOBBY: Yea, funny, isn't it?

JAMIESON [*laughing*]: Her name was Annie.

TEIFION: Why that, Charlie?

CHARLIE: Well, they call it the 'Mystery' because it was a gift, but they don't know who gave it.

TEIFION: Don't they.

CHARLIE [*pleased with himself*]: No, they don't. That's why it's called the 'Mystery'.

TEIFION: Oh, I see, well that's what I want tonight, a mystery. A secret devious game with a girl. Her credit rating does not matter to me, lust will find a way. Black, white, yellow, charcoal, Greek, Russian, or Jewish Orthodox, Methodi, Unitarian, Prod, or Catholic.

[TIM *appears*.]

CHARLIE [*quietly*]: Don't try it, Tim ... there's four of us.

    [TIM *looks at him grimly ... then goes back into the pub. The boys start to move off in the other direction*.]

TEIFION [*as he follows the others*]: God help Mag's Sunday dinner!

    [*They go off stage*.]

    [MAG KEEGAN'S *living-room*.]

MRS KEEGAN: ... and another thing, Margaret, Mrs Molloy tells me that Teresa's giving her five shillings more than you towards her keep.

MAG [*wearily*]: Then she's wrong, Mother.

MRS KEEGAN: Didn't she tell me that herself this forenoon!

MAG: Then she's a liar.

MRS KEEGAN: What!

MAG: Teresa Molloy gives her mother the same as I give you.

MRS KEEGAN: I don't believe you!

MAG: I don't care ... it's true.

MRS KEEGAN: I've known that woman for fifteen years ... she's a good Catholic, I believe her.

MAG [*gently*]: Mother, you've known me all my life ... don't you believe me?

MRS KEEGAN: Have I cause to?

MAG: All right then, don't believe!

MRS KEEGAN: Is it true, Margaret?

MAG: Yes.

MRS KEEGAN: Are you sure now?

MAG: Yes.

MRS KEEGAN [*pausing*]: Aye ... she might just be saying it to be one up on me.

MAG: Aye ... she might.

MRS KEEGAN: I can't think that girl'd give her mother more than you give me ... after all, I've been a good mother to you. ... [*Pause*.] I say, I've been a good mother to you, haven't I, Margaret?

MAG: Yes ... you've been a good mother to me.

MRS KEEGAN: So then why should Teresa Molloy give her mother five shillings more than you give me! That's what I want to know.

MAG: Mother ... I've told you ... she doesn't.

MRS KEEGAN: What makes you so sure?

MAG: ... because we were going down on the bus together and we were both talking and I said, 'How much do you give your mother?' ... and it was the same as I give you!

MRS KEEGAN: Teresa's engaged to be married, isn't she, Margaret?

MAG: Yeah, she's marrying Billy O'Keefe.

MRS KEEGAN: D'y'think they'll be marrying soon?

MAG: I think they're going over to Ireland to get married ... I think he comes from Newry or somewhere.

MRS KEEGAN: Oh ... there's a fine cathedral there.

MAG: Yeah ... well ... he's got a cousin who's a priest, apparently, and they may be able to get married in the cathedral ... I don't really know.

MRS KEEGAN: It'd be fine for a girl to get married in a cathedral, now wouldn't it? Oh, what a splendid marriage. ... Mrs Molloy's a lucky woman.

MAG: Oh, Mother ... don't start again.

MRS KEEGAN: All I said was Mrs Molloy's a lucky woman! Teresa Molloy's never been around with a Protestant fella!

MAG: Teresa Molloy's never been ... a fat lot you know about it! She certainly has!

MRS KEEGAN: What did you say?

MAG: I said she certainly has.

MRS KEEGAN: D'y'know something ... d'y'know something, Margaret?

MAG: I'm not telling you, Mother, so you needn't go on about it. ... I'm not going to tell you.

MRS KEEGAN: D'y ... now ... now, wait a minute, Margaret ... do you mean to tell me that Teresa Molloy has been around with a Protestant fella? Now ... now, who is it ... tell me, who is it? Come on, out with it ... tell me!

MAG: Mother, I'm not going to tell you! It's got nothing ... look, you'll only go and tell Mrs Molloy and then ... it's all over now, it's a long time ago. Now she's going around with Billy O'Keefe and they're going to get married ... well, that's all right ... it doesn't matter, Mother!

MRS KEEGAN: It does matter, it matters to me!

MAG: Honestly, Mother, you want to know everything!

MRS KEEGAN: Well, why would I not? Here's that woman just told me a lie about money! I'd like to face her up with something!

MAG: Oh ... Mother ... you shouldn't want to go about doing that sort of thing!

MRS KEEGAN: Are you telling your mother the right way to behave? Are you telling your mother how to behave?

MAG: No ... I'm not telling you how to behave. I'm sorry, I've said too much already! [*She goes into the back.*]

MRS KEEGAN [*grumbling after her*]: You haven't said enough! Who was this Protestant fella that she was going around with?

[*There is a sound and she turns to look.*]

Is that you?

TIM: Yes, it's us.

[*They are slightly tipsy, that is, heavy from beer, not drunk.*]

Well, I'm disgusted and that's flat!

KEEGAN: Leave it alone, will you ...

MRS KEEGAN: What's the matter with you, Timothy?

TIM: I've heard something ...

KEEGAN: You don't know for sure ...

TIM [*overriding him*]: ... today ... and I'm ashamed of me own sister!

MRS KEEGAN [*hoping for the worst*]: What is it ... heart of Christ ... what have you heard?

TIM: In a common beer house, I've heard my sister's name bandied about by every Protestant lout in the district. She was seen walking with Bobby Bloody Laughlin!

KEEGAN: Don't swear in front of your mother.

MRS KEEGAN [*brushing him aside*]: Whisha! [*To Tim*] ... Is this true? [*But* MRS KEEGAN *has crossed to the kitchen door.*] Margaret ... come in here!

KEEGAN: Oh, leave it, Mary.

MAG: What's up?

MRS KEEGAN: Yes ... there is something up, Margaret Keegan!

KEEGAN: You don't know ...

MRS KEEGAN: Shut up, Eugene! I knew I should never have let her go and work in the hat shop!

MAG: The hat shop? What have I done now?

MRS KEEGAN: Your brother, Tim, says it's all over the public house that you've been seen talking to Bobby Laughlin ...

MAG: Well, I ...

MRS KEEGAN: Now I thought that had all been scotched. ... I thought that was all over and done with!

MAG: Now, wait a minute ...

MRS KEEGAN: I thought that it had all been stopped.

MAG: Will you shut up and listen ...

TIM: Don't tell your mother to shut up or I'll ...

MAG [*turning on him*]: You'll what ... go on, you'll what! Look, Mother, I only met him by accident, I just happened to be ...

MRS KEEGAN: Don't you give me any of your 'onlys' and your 'justs'! Facts are facts! I thought I told you then that there was no way round this, your man is a Protestant man ... and him with a father the leader in the Orange Band! Are you out of your mind! Oh God, what a daughter to have brought into the world!

MAG: All I did was to link his arm to the corner ...

TIM: You what! I'll kill him!

MRS KEEGAN: Arm in arm is it! ... and taking pleasure in it as well!

MAG: Oh, Dad ...

MR KEEGAN: You've overstepped the mark now, my girl ...

MRS KEEGAN: Right. I've tried, your father and your brother have tried ... so now it's up to the priest. I'll go to Father Curren. I'll have him round to you, maybe that'll bring you to your senses!

MAG [*very quiet*]: Do you mean that ... you'd go to the priest about me? ... your own daughter?

MRS KEEGAN: Yes!

MAG: Right! [*She turns and leaves the room, her mother following her.*]

MRS KEEGAN: And where do you think you're going?

MAG: Out.

MRS KEEGAN: What do you mean?

MAG: What I said ... out!

MRS KEEGAN [*frightened*]: Margaret ... you're not going to meet that fella, are you?

MAG: No, Mother.

MRS KEEGAN: Now tell me you're not going to meet him!

MAG: I need a bit of fresh air.

MRS KEEGAN: Margaret ... will you promise me now, Margaret ... I'm sorry I said that about getting the priest ... I shouldn't have said it ... it wasn't right ... God help me and save me ... it probably wasn't right.

MAG: All right.

MRS KEEGAN: Oh God, Margaret, I'll pray for you ... but please ... give me your word you won't ...

MAG [*suddenly very angry*]: Mother – I'm going out! Will you understand that ... I'm going just out! Now ... do you understand? That's all there is to it. ... I'm going for a walk! I'm a big girl now. ... I'm going for a walk! [*She leaves the house quickly.*]

CURTAIN

ACT TWO

The scene is the same as in Act One. It is seven o'clock in the evening of the same day. CHARLIE MODRYB *and* PAT JAMIESON *are facing the audience. They are looking out at the river.*

CHARLIE: Jamo ... now listen. Stand on your toes ... yes, that's right ... stand right up on your toes and look down the street. No ... no ... don't just look down to the *end* of the street, for God's sake!

JAMIESON: Ah, sure; well, what am I supposed to do! What am I about?

CHARLIE: Now, look ... stand on your toes and look right down past the allotments and across the river. For God's sake, look up! Look up at the mountains! D'y'see the mountains ... up there!

JAMIESON: Is it the Welsh mountains I've got to look at?

CHARLIE: I don't know. I can't understand you sometimes, Jamo ... you've got no feeling for scenery. Well ... go on ... look at it! See the way the sun is moving across very clear, isn't it? I remember when we were kids we used to go out on our bikes, we used to go on the ferry then go along the Chester road ... anyway ... we'd get up there and we'd be on the top of Moel Vamau. [*They both look.*] Y'know, they used to say ... 'If you can see across the river in the morning in the summer, that's not a good sign. But if you can't, if it's all haze like ... y'know, misty ... then it's going to be a lovely day' ... [*He gives a little laugh.*] Eh ... look at that super little cloud ... look ... it's going right across ... and it'll be dark where that cloud is now and yet we can see the sun on either side. [*He pauses.*] Well ... that's Moel Vamau.

JAMIESON: Aah ... so it's Moel Vamau. I ... I didn't quite know what I'm looking at ...

CHARLIE [*breaking in*]: Oh, I don't suppose you do. [*Pauses.*] Sometimes, when I'm out in Africa I think about it ... cos it gets very hot out there, y'know. ... Oh God, it gets very hot indeed! But Moel Vamau's always cool.

JAMIESON [*off on his own tack*]: I never think about scenery ... you're right, y'know ... I never think about it at all. I'm always thinking about ... er ... well ... some café or some sophisticated American bar that you'd got into. ... Or I'm thinking about big shops, the big shops in Montreal. I love those big shops. D'y'know, I'd like to work in one of them big stores there ... because, well ... It's a funny thing ... but ... over in Canada [*he gives a little laugh*] they think I speak very nicely ... the people ... they're always saying what a charming voice I have. I was walking down those ... those long alleyways between the counters, d'y'know, they're vast, they're very big ... and I was walking along there and I happened to say ... there was a man standing there and I said, 'Excuse me, could you tell me where the tie counter is? I'd like to know' ... and then this man, a Canadian fella he was, he said to me, 'Well, gee, you speak very nicely,' and I said, 'that's very nice of you to say so ...' and he said, 'Er ... you're a sailor, aren't you?' ... and I said I was. Well, naturally enough, y'see, I was in me uniform at the time ... and he said, 'Well, you're a sailor ...'

CHARLIE [*breaking in*]: Oh well, all right ... go on ... he said you were a sailor! It'd be written all over you with your uniform on, wouldn't it! Well ... what was he trying to do ... was he one of those bent fellas?

JAMIESON [*very pained at this*]: Ah no ... he was not one of those bent fellas! Sure, he was just a nice man passing the time of day! Anyway ... he suggested to me that I ... er ... I'm a British citizen and I can stay in Canada ... that I could get a good job in one of them big stores.

CHARLIE: D'y'mean to say that you'd like to stand around in a monkey suit all day having soft bloody sailors come up to you and ask you where the tie counter is? Honestly, Jamo ... I don't get you! You've got some funny ideas ... that's no life for a man!

JAMIESON: Where the hell is Bobby ... what's keeping him?

CHARLIE: Oh, I suppose he's got to make up some excuse to get out, y'know what his dad's like.

JAMIESON: I've never had anything to do with them Ulster fellows. [*Pause.*] Did you see him with Mag Keegan this morning?

CHARLIE: No.

JAMIESON: I did! [*He gives a sly laugh.*] She's hot stuff, that Mag!

CHARLIE: Ah aye.

JAMIESON: You ought to know ... you knocked about with her that time you were home for Christmas.

CHARLIE: She's all right, Mag.

JAMIESON: She likes sailors ... By God, she likes the sailors.

CHARLIE: Since when was Teifion a sailor?

JAMIESON: D'y'mean she went with Teifion?

CHARLIE: Of course she did, and with Jimmy Smith and with ...

JAMIESON [*breaking in*]: I didn't know that! Well ... she must have gone the whole hog with Teifion Davies ... I'd never have believed ...

[TEIFION *has come on to the stage and heard the last speech.*]

TEIFION: What's occurring, did I hear my name?

CHARLIE: Hi, skin!

TEIFION: Hi ... [*He waits.*] Well, come on, what were you saying about me?

CHARLIE [*grinning*]: Why ... have we got you worried?

TEIFION: Oh, for God's sake ...

JAMIESON: We were talking about Mag.

CHARLIE: *You* were talking about Mag, all I said was ...

JAMIESON: I didn't realize you *knew* her ... you know what I mean ...

TEIFION: Why ... did you think you were the only one, you egomaniac?

JAMIESON: Me and Charlie, you and Jimmy Smith, Bobby ...

TEIFION: Not Bobby.

JAMIESON: Aah ... go on!

TEIFION: Nothing happened with Bobby ... he's special.

JAMIESON: Well, special or not ... she was always on about him, to me.

CHARLIE: Same here ... I think she likes him.

JAMIESON: Well, with her that can only mean one thing ... sure she's got a taste for it!

TEIFION: Oh, Jamieson!

CHARLIE: Shurrup, will you! Y'don't talk about her like that! She's not a bag, y'know!

JAMIESON [*hastily*]: Oh no ... of course ... no ... Watch it now, here's Bobby.

[BOBBY *enters and crosses to the boys.*]

TEIFION: Hi, Bob.

CHARLIE: What kept you?

BOBBY: Honest to God, I thought the old fella'd never stop ... he's been on about those bloody flats [*indicating*] all the afternoon. You know he put in for one.

CHARLIE: What happened?

BOBBY: Turned down.

JAMIESON: That's a pity, Bobby, because they're beautiful flats, d'y'know, central heating and all that.

BOBBY: Why, have you been in them?

JAMIESON: My mother's getting one ... we're moving in ...

BOBBY: Wait a minute ... are you telling me that your mother's got a flat?

JAMIESON: Of course ... why?

BOBBY: Oh ... nothing.

JAMIESON: They're lovely big bedrooms, d'y'know.

BOBBY: Aye ... I've heard. [*He turns to Teifion.*] Isn't it marvellous, eh, Teif?

TEIFION: What's that then?

BOBBY: Jamo's old lady's got one of the new flats.

TEIFION: Oh, aye.

JAMIESON: And why not ... what d'y'mean?

BOBBY: Nothing ... what I said, nothing, it's just funny, that's all ... my old man was turned down, that's all.

JAMIESON: Aah, for God's sake, Bobby ...

BOBBY [*cutting over*]: Oh yeah, it's all right, it's just funny, y'know ... funny.

JAMIESON: I don't see what's funny about it?

BOBBY: No ... I don't suppose you would!

JAMIESON: Sure ... she's been on the list for seventeen years!

TEIFION: Be reasonable, Bobby ... Jamo's old lady was even on a list to get on the list!

BOBBY [*raising his voice*]: This isn't a joke, y'know ... all I said was it's very funny!

JAMIESON [*raising his voice*]: And all I said was ... what's funny about it?

TEIFION: Now look here, you two. ... I'm fed up to the back teeth with this! I've come to the Park to get away from all this nonsense. I'm just standing on my sacred rights to behave like a 'happy idiot', I just want a few jars and to mix it with a girl. I can't do it in the pubs or on the streets ... so I'm going to do it in the park ... and you two aren't going to stop me either.

[TEIFION *glares at* JAMIESON *and* BOBBY *and they glare back.*]

CHARLIE [*firmly*]: Teifion ... look across the river.

TEIFION [*surprised*]: Eh?

CHARLIE: Bobby, look across the river, both of you at Moel Vamau.

[BOBBY *and* TEIFION *do so in amazement.*]

CHARLIE: Can you see anything?

TEIFION: Of course.

CHARLIE [*excited*]: What?

TEIFION: Sheep? Bloody sheep?

[*The boys all laugh and are mates again.*]

BOBBY: Let's go into the park.

JAMIESON: The pub first, eh?

CHARLIE: Not tonight; son, you wouldn't get me in a pub, not for a big clock ... tonight I've got two half-bottles of the real stuff ... out of bond!

TEIFION: Charlie ... I'm warming to you!

[*The boys start to move off in the direction of the park.*]

CHARLIE: You are a mean get, Teif!

TEIFION: What d'y'mean? Maybe I have got a reluctance to part with a penny if it'll keep me going for a day longer. I'm determined to survive!

BOBBY [*grinning*]: Yeah ... you always were!

TEIFION: It's easy go but as far as I'm concerned ... it's never been easy come!

[*He sees a tin at his feet and starts to kick it gently.*]

BOBBY: God ... I'm looking forward to seeing a good match. ... I haven't seen a game for nearly a year.

JAMIESON: They don't play it much in Canada.

BOBBY: It must be a fair old time since you've seen a game, Charlie?

CHARLIE: What you don't understand is ... they play it out there, they really do ... all the black fellas with fuzzy hair. Oh, it's very funny, really ... because I went to watch a match, they're bloomin' marvellous footballers, y'know, kicking the ball all over the place ... but they don't wear boots!

BOBBY: Are you trying to tell me they don't wear boots?

CHARLIE: They don't wear boots.

JAMIESON: Yeah, I've heard that, d'y'know, I've heard that before, that they don't wear boots ... sure they must have strong toes.

CHARLIE: You're telling me they've got strong toes! Ah ... they kick it! [*Shouting.*] Ooh ... get in there ... you want to see them! Honest, it's fantastic!

[TEIFION *starts to kick the tin in earnest towards Bobby.*]

Pass it over!

BOBBY [*kicking it to him*]: Here y'are then!

JAMIESON [*intercepting*]: Down the wing!

TEIFION: And up again! [*Charging.*]

BOBBY [*yelling*]: Centre, Jamo, centre!

[BOBBY *passes and* JAMIESON *and* TEIFION *face each other, the tin at Teifion's feet.* TEIFION *charges Jamieson, who sulks at being hurt.*]

CHARLIE [*eager*]: Gerron with it! Give him his titty-bottle, Teif.

TEIFION: Come on, Jamo. You're like a big soft girl.

[JAMIESON *feints to the left and* TEIFION *dodges to the right and away.*]

TEIFION [*laughing*]: Gerron ... I've played with Bobby before!

CHARLIE [*neatly taking it away from him*]: Aye up there!

JAMIESON [*accepting a pass from Charlie*]: Up the side!

BOBBY: For Christ's sake, Jamo ... You're not playing against the Pope's Eleven now, y'know!

[JAMIESON *stops in mid-play and looks at Bobby, taking in what he has said ... Then he turns and deliberately kicks the tin hard far away into the distance. The other three look at him in astonishment ... it is no longer a game.*]

BOBBY [*hotly*]: Well ... what was that in aid of?

JAMIESON: I just felt like a good kick!

BOBBY: Well, I'm not going after it for a start. [*He walks away from Jamieson, muttering under his breath.*] Bloody idiot, you'd think he'd have more bloody sense!

[JAMIESON *is stubborn and erect.* CHARLIE *turns to Bobby.* TEIFION *is still looking at Jamieson.*]

TEIFION: Pax Vo-bloody-biscum!

[*He begins to whistle 'The Orange Sash' and* BOBBY, *grinning, joins in ... the three lads parade up and down before* JAMIESON, *miming instruments and singing ... at the end of the song, they all laugh.*]

JAMIESON: Sure, you're easily amused!

CHARLIE: Ger out of it, Jamo ... it's only a joke!

JAMIESON [*indicating Bobby*]: Not for that fella it isn't!

BOBBY [*genuine*]: Oh, come off it, Jamo ... of course it is.

JAMIESON: Oh yeah, a great joke ... well ... I'm not laughing!

BOBBY [*dismissing the whole incident*]: Well, that's your look-out, son!

JAMIESON: You want to watch it or you'll maybe laugh on the other side of your face!

BOBBY: What was that?

CHARLIE: Forget it.

BOBBY: No ... you tell me to watch it, did you?

TEIFION: Bobby ... don't be daft.

JAMIESON: Aye ... daft's the word. Oh, Catholics are great jokes to your man ... even the women.

BOBBY: What's he on about now?

JAMIESON: We may be funny but that doesn't stop you messing about with Catholic girls.

BOBBY [*very quiet*]: What's that?

JAMIESON [*moving to Bobby*]: Mag Keegan. If Tim Keegan ...

CHARLIE ⎫ Shut up!
TEIFION ⎭ Knock it off!

[BOBBY *moves forward.*]

BOBBY: I'll have your guts for garters!

[*But* CHARLIE *and* TEIFION *get between them.*]

TEIFION: Don't be a bigger fool than you've got to be, Jamo!

JAMIESON: Oh ... it's all right for you and Charlie ... but you heard him before about my mother getting a flat!

BOBBY: What's your mother got to do with Mag, you bloody madman! Aah ... I won't even waste my time on you!

[*He turns away angrily and walks upstage,* CHARLIE *hurrying after him.*]

CHARLIE: Bobby, come back ... now don't be so daft ...

[JAMIESON *turns angrily in the other direction, and stalks off.*]

JAMIESON: God ... these Billy Boys are proud of themselves! Did you hear him!

TEIFION [*following him*]: Keep your wig on!

[BOBBY *and* CHARLIE ... TEIFION *and* JAMIESON *argue and harangue together as they walk about the stage.*

141

NEVILLE *and* LESLEY *walk on to the stage, wheeling their bikes, completely unaware of the row that is taking place.*]

NEVILLE: Well, with him being a Londoner, I just laughed! [*He gives a little chuckle.*] ... I was tickled! 'Racial prejudice in Liverpool,' I said, 'I can't imagine where you come by these ideas!'

LESLEY: Oh, it's just another of those popular misconceptions people from the South have about Liverpool.

NEVILLE: Oh, definitely. I pointed out to him that we'd had coloured people in this city for the past seven hundred years without any trouble.

LESLEY: Oh yes, cos they came here, breaking their journey on the way to the American slave markets, didn't they?

NEVILLE: Children of the sun.

LESLEY: Y'what?

NEVILLE: Children of the sun. [*Pause.*] Darkies!

LESLEY: Well ... that's incontrovertible for a start!

NEVILLE: Anyroad ... he was flabbergasted! 'No!' I said, 'there's no racial bigotry up here, I can assure you of that!'

[BOBBY *walks downstage in front of them arguing with* CHARLIE.]

BOBBY: The trouble with Micks is ... they're all as thick as two short planks! [*He turns on* CHARLIE *angrily.*] I knew that something would go wrong tonight! I saw two nuns on the way up here and that's bad luck for a start!

[*He turns and walks away angrily,* CHARLIE *trotting after him, muttering reassurances.*]

LESLEY [*giving them only a passing glance*]: All the same, Neville, I hope you made it clear that there was a certain danger if you went around shouting 'To Hell with the Pope!'

[JAMIESON *walks downstage arguing with* TEIFION.]

JAMIESON [*exploding*]: I tell you ... they all believe in artificial insemination! God ... they'd take the pleasure out of anything! [*He rounds on Teifion.*] ... It's all flesh and no bloody spirituality with them fellas!

[*He walks away upstage,* TEIFION *following, trying to ease things.*]

NEVILLE [*sees them, does a double-take*]: Oh well … [*Then turns back to Lesley.*] Oh no, I didn't mention it. … I was more concerned with disabusing these more popular fallacies.

LESLEY: Yes … they do have some funny ideas, these Londoners … they get it from the television.

NEVILLE: Oh, definitely.

[*They start to wheel their bikes across the stage and are confronted by the two groups of angry faces, glowering at each other.*]

NEVILLE: Gentlemen … your close proximity to the tennis courts is no place for a barney. … I suggest you adjourn to the furry glen … it's more secluded there!

[*This is too much for the lads, they all burst into laughter … this drives* NEVILLE *and* LESLEY *away … then* BOBBY *and* JAMIESON *look at each other sheepishly.*]

BOBBY [*awkwardly*]: Look, Jamo …

JAMIESON [*sheepishly*]: Well, Bobby …

TEIFION: Oh, for God's sake … go on … kiss and make up and be done!

[*Good humoured now, they cuff each other in a friendly way; then* CHARLIE *takes out the two bottles.*]

CHARLIE: Here … have a swig of this.

JAMIESON [*drinking*]: Oh, that's better.

BOBBY: Oh … that's the real stuff, eh?

CHARLIE: Here … pass us the bottle, Jamo. Don't just open your throat … give it here. [*He swallows loudly.*] … eh … that's marvellous! Y'know, I'd rather drink this stuff than go to a boozer and have umpteen pints. Knocking around in the park, having a few drinks … what d'y'say to that, Teif? Eh … Teif … are you with us?

TEIFION: Am I with you? I don't know if I am with you … why should I be with you? Yesterday I was walking down Fleet Street, I had me ticket but I had serious doubts if Liverpool even existed … and now I'm beginning to wonder if London's still there.

CHARLIE: What's he on about?

TEIFION: Listen. Sometimes, when I'm in London, I get lonely for this city cos when I try to tell them about it, that you lot up here *care* about things, mad things, wicked things, silly things, so much so, that you want to hit each other because you're so sure you're right, they won't believe me! Everyone down there is tolerant and withdrawn to the point of religious excess but if a fella's a pacifist up here, he'll beat the living beejesus out of anyone to prove it ... and never doubt himself once! [*Declaiming aloud and walking about.*] Oh Liverpool, you great Muck Heap of Intolerance and Certainty, beating out life to such an extent that it even frightens *me*! Honest to God, the power of your life must be indestructible! Charlie, if someone said right now, 'They've dropped the bomb ...'

CHARLIE: What bomb?

TEIFION: *Their* bomb ... 'they've dropped it right on New York, right on Paris, right on Liverpool' we'd still go on walking along this Monkey Rack and the girls'd be walking along. I think that if we were all obliterated ... if that bomb went off and we weren't here any more, something of us'll still go on walking along after four girls and if we're lucky we'll get hold their hands, and if we're lucky, we'll get to tickle them in the middle of it all, we'll get down to the whole business somewhere in the middle of the park hiding in the brown grass. It makes you think, doesn't it? It makes you think wonderful thoughts, makes it all go exploding round in your brain, it makes it for me ... for somewhere, when I think about this park, it's all a flash and a wiggle of girls' legs. Nylon stockings and swelling sticky-out pettys ... that's what it is for me and fellas ... [*He starts to walk up and down.*] Liverpool fellas, walking up and down, y'can always tell a Liverpool fella by the strut and his shoulders going from side to side with a 'Well, hello der, like, and how are 'y!' ... and all those songs ...

    [*Singing:*] Mother, scrub my head with brickdust,
              Soothe my hair with lemonade,
              If my head continues burning,
              Go and fetch the fire brigade ...

[*He finishes on a flourish.*] Here ... give us a drink! [*He takes a big swig from the bottle.*]

[JAMIESON *hurries over to him, speaking rapidly and anxiously.*]

JAMIESON: Oh God ... are you going to be off now! Listen ... I want to say this to you! It's a very embarrassing thing to be walking along the road with you! Either you're not saying a bloody word ... or you're running and skipping about like a bloody madman!

[TEIFION *takes another big drink from the bottle.*]

JAMIESON: Can you ... can you not control yourself, there's a way of drinking, you know ...

[CHARLIE *and* BOBBY *murmur agreement.*]

[*Going on*] ... drink, just to get it inside you and feel good d'y'know, get possession of yourself and ... [*He mimes being a gentleman*] ... maybe say a few words to your friends and if you see a nice girl, y'might say ... 'hello dear!' d'y'know and y'might click with her ... but with you around ... what happens? ... Either the three of them want you ... or they run away!

TEIFION [*grinning*]: I don't care, Jamieson! You can't destroy me tonight! You can't make me feel unhappy ... because I'm ... Walking down the Monkey Rack. Look for a girl to put on her back!

CHARLIE: Will you shurrup, Teif! Will you shurrup! I mean ... I know you're enjoying yourself, son ... but ... I mean, ease off.

JAMIESON: You don't want to go shouting things like that out. ... We want to do all right tonight ... to pick up a couple of girls.

TEIFION: Well ... let's get back to Jamieson's favourite subject ... the sexual stakes. ... I'd like to point out to you gentlemen friends of mine that there's a certain aspect of life that is passing you by. ... I mean, Liverpool here is about fifty years behind the times. ... But out in London ... now ... on the sloping hills of Notting Gate, the girls are hunting. They are hunting singly, doubly, and in packs! Young ladies of South Kensington and Kensington Gore are out looking for likely lads like you and me. Oh ... all you have to do is show them those horny hands of yours which have become rough and hard because you do a hard day's work ... not because you wanted to ... but because you had to! Well ... the girls like that ... it gives them the frissons every time they touch your hands ...

JAMIESON: Oh it does, definitely.

BOBBY: What's that then?

TEIFION: I'll tell you ... you're rough trade. Look ... I've got a friend in London, a West Indian writer, a Latin scholar. ... He teaches in a school in Clerkenwell and his life is made a misery because these young ladies ... these middle-class darlings ... are out for him! So, I tell you, he's a worn-out man ... a shadow of his former self ... cos, believe me, men, when you're coming up for the fourth time in the stroking stakes ... it's not as easy as all that! The lasses are out for it ... they'll romp you home and between the sheets before you can say, aye ... yes ... or no!

JAMIESON: Has this ever happened to you, Teif?

TEIFION: I'll tell you. I was taken along the other night to a party, and, y'know, it was one of them posh parties ...

JAMIESON: How could you tell?

TEIFION: Because I had to wear me suit ... and when I was at this party there were three lovely girls there ... they were crackers! They were beautiful! Well, in the ordinary course of events, being a human being, like [he laughs] ... Well, I like to take the aggressive part in riding the Cock Horse to Banbury Cross. ... But these young ladies ... they wouldn't have it! One of them suggested she drove me home in her car ... another one said she only lived around the corner and would I like to come in for a cup of coffee ... and the third ... the third pointed out to me that it was very charming and very romantic to walk along the embankment at 3 o'clock in the morning! I tell you lads, the girls are out! The middle classes have thrown down the gauntlet ... and the gauntlet happens to be a rather expensive silk glove which the ladies want us to pick up. ... Personally I don't want to pick it up! But, I tell you boys ... you're wasting your time around this drum because the drum is tight around Knightsbridge ... the girls are out ... the secretaries of the secretaries of the British Council are looking for likely lads!

JAMIESON [*mouth opens, after a pause*]: My God is it really like that ... London, I mean.

TEIFION [*sitting down on the grass*]: It's lying, sprawled like a sleeping whore ... waiting for a lad like you ... or you ... or even you ... to wake her up with a prod!

JAMIESON: God, Montreal's like that too! [*Pauses.*] I'll tell you what we'll do ... we'll split up ... the four of us'll never meet four girls ... and anything less'll lead to me ... I mean to one of us being nosed out.

CHARLIE: Well, Teif and I'll have another drink and you two walk down as far as the bandstand. If you don't find anything ... meet us back here. All right, Bobby?

BOBBY: Aye ... I suppose so.

JAMIESON [*eager*]: Yeah ... Come on, Bobby, the place is teeming with them ... we're bound to find it ...

[*They start to move away.*]

BOBBY: Eh, Jamo, what were you saying about Mag before?

JAMIESON: Don't worry about Mag.

BOBBY: No ... no. I just wondered what you were saying about her.

[*They move out of sight.*]

TEIFION: Oh ... that's Jamo!

CHARLIE: Well ... at least you got 'em off religion!

TEIFION: Eh?

CHARLIE: All that chat about women.

TEIFION: Oh aye ... but up here everyone confuses sex with religion.

CHARLIE: Well, you got Jamo thinking through his pants. ... Ah, y'know him, a couple of drinks and he's got to have his bit of nasty.

TEIFION [*after a slight pause*]: I can't think whatever Mag saw in him.

CHARLIE: Aye, but it was only for a couple of days. Anyroad, you know him, Teif, he can't stand 'em afterwards and he always talks about it ... and I can't stand that.

TEIFION: Does Bobby know?

CHARLIE: I shouldn't think so ... anyway it doesn't mean anything, she's always been daft about Bobby.

TEIFION [*slowly*]: Yeah, of course, she uses his mates to be near him.

CHARLIE [*touchy*]: I dare say you're right.

TEIFION: Of course I'm right.

CHARLIE: She's all right, is Mag ... she's all right.

TEIFION: Give us a drink.

CHARLIE [*drinking first*]: Good old Mag.

TEIFION [*drinking*]: Good old Mag.

[*The two lads sit quietly having a drink.*]

Charlie ... I want you to tell me something, I want you to tell me ... now tell it me true, Charlie, what do you do for women when you're at sea?

CHARLIE: Y'mean, when I'm at sea? Well ... I don't do anything for women, do I ... I mean, I'm not on a passenger boat, y'know!

TEIFION: No, you know what I mean, what happens?

CHARLIE: Oh ... well, I suppose it's always a bit of a risk, really ... y'know what I mean ... but what I find is, if you go to a place regular, you might ... well, you might be lucky enough to pick up with a girl ... I mean, meet the same girl every time ... but, other than that, y'might have a brass ...

TEIFION: Y'mean, go with a tart?

CHARLIE: Yeah, that's right ... with a prostitute.

TEIFION: Well? [*He waits.*] What's it like?

CHARLIE: Oh, it's not much fun, but ... I'll tell you ... you usually have a skinful, y'know, and you want to get rid of something ... it's as if y'had ... well ... you know how it is ... something on your mind and you want to get rid of it. So ... you go up ... and it's usually a cubicle that's clean ... and a bed that's clean ... and, well ... the whole thing's over in a matter of minutes and you pay your money and you're on your way and you feel a bit of a fool. But ... er ... it's different ... well ... in Africa y'can do what I do ... usually go with the same girl every time.

TEIFION: She's a black girl, is she?

CHARLIE: Oh ... I don't know about that ... she used to be black!

TEIFION: What d'y'mean, she used ...

CHARLIE: Well ... it's a funny thing ... she used to be black but every trip she gets a shade lighter! D'y'know ... she's coming up for lemon colour at the moment ... and at any time now I'm afraid her eyes are going to turn from brown to blue! [*They both laugh.*] Oh, y'know what I mean. [*Pause.*] No, there are other things beside women, Teif ... I mean, for me ... sometimes it's just like eating a piece of bread and butter. Y'see, I don't go a bundle on it all the time. ... I suppose I will a bit later on. The way I look at it is that when I know what I'm at ... I'll get married.

TEIFION: Charlie ... you amaze me! You just sit there and say when you know what you're at ... you'll get married!

CHARLIE: That's right. [*He laughs.*] Honestly, Teif, whenever I talk to you, I have the problem of trying to make you understand what I'm like. I'm the sort of fella that decides one day that he's going to do something ... and Teif ... I do it ... it's as easy as that and as simple as that. I don't have to tear myself up the way you do, y'know, tear yourself around, running up and down and shouting and screaming and carrying on. ... If you could just learn, y'know, to take it easy, it'd be all right ... but you can't, can you? You just run up and down. [*Pause.*] Anyway ... I'm going out to New Zealand in a couple of years.

TEIFION: Have you ever been there before?

CHARLIE: No ... I've never been there ... but I'm going.

TEIFION: Why?

CHARLIE: I don't know. But I've always fancied New Zealand.

TEIFION: Well, good luck. [*He sees* MAG.] Hello there, me old Mag.

CHARLIE: Hi, girl.

MAG: Just the two of you?

TEIFION: Yes, just Charlie and me, we get on well cos we both stayed at school till we were sixteen. In the ordinary course of events that last year at school plays hell with the working-class caste system, but with Charlie and me it produced a cultural united front that's got the Welsh B.B.C. dead worried.

CHARLIE: You know what? ... Shirrup!

MAG: Why are you two on a double? Where's ...

TEIFION: Bobby ...

MAG: ... and Jamo?

TEIFION: *Touché.*

MAG: Aye, all of that.

CHARLIE: Are you going to join us, love?

MAG: I hadn't thought.

CHARLIE: You ought to watch yourself. There's lots of sailors about.

MAG: Yeah and *I* know what sailors are.

TEIFION: Aye, you're a right glutton for nautical punishment.

MAG: I'm off then.

TEIFION: Should I come with you?

MAG [*looking at him with a pause*]: I don't think so.

TEIFION: No, I suppose not.

CHARLIE: How about me?

MAG: I'm a lucky girl really, aren't I?

TEIFION [*offhand*]: Bobby went down to the bandstand.

MAG: Y'what?

TEIFION: Bobby, he went down to the bandstand.

MAG [*starting to go*]: Well, I might see him then, mightn't I?
    [*She exits.*]

TEIFION: Oh, that bloody Bobby!
    [JAMIESON *hurries in to them.*]

JAMIESON: Hey, now ... you two! I've just seen two beautiful girls ... and they're on their own ... two beautiful girls! Just walking on the far side over there ... so ... mm ... which one of you's it going to be? Are one of you coming with me? Is it to be you, Teifion ... or is it to be you, Charlie?

CHARLIE: Eh ... what d'y'mean? Oh ... I see ... there's only the two of them ... I see. Well ... er ... well ... d'y'fancy them, Teif?

TEIFION [*laughing*]: God ... I don't know, I haven't seen them, Charlie ... I don't know! I mean ... I'd rather like to see ... I have to view the property first! It's rather like the livestock market here, isn't it?

CHARLIE [*after pause*]: Well ... what about it, Teif? D'y'fancy it or would you rather stay here and have a drink with me?

JAMIESON [*cross and frustrated*]: Aah ... now, sure, look what's happened! Two soldiers are talking to them. [*He snarls.*] Aah ... there it is, y'see! It's gone! Well ... God Almighty! You've got to take action if y'want to get anything! You've got to go up and get it!

CHARLIE [*dryly*]: It's a pity you don't feel that way about getting your ticket, isn't it, really?

JAMIESON: Sure that wasn't called for at all, Charlie.

[MEME *trips on to the stage wearing very brief tennis shorts and a tight sweater, swinging her racket.*]

MEME: Is that you, our Charlie?

[*The boys all stare at her in stunned silence, gloating.*]

TEIFION: Remember this night, kid, cos it'll never be the same again.

CHARLIE: Does your mother know you're out?

MEME: I'm going to play tennis.

TEIFION: That's plausible.

JAMIESON: Aren't you dressed for it! [*Letching over her.*] Sure you've got the right gear on?

CHARLIE: Well, what do you want?

MEME: A shilling for an hour on the courts.

[*They all hand out a pocketful of change and offer it to her.*]

MEME: I'll take it from Teifion.

TEIFION: Oh, aye, playing favourites, now?

MEME: Yes.

[*She takes the money and flaunts off the stage, the boys watching.* CHARLIE *attempts to give the money back to Teifion.*]

TEIFION: No.

CHARLIE: You take it.

TEIFION [*does so reluctantly*]: Charlie, you'll have to do something about that sister of yours.

CHARLIE: Like what?

TEIFION: Well, I suppose a change in the law is out of the question.

CHARLIE: Y'what?

TEIFION: She needs protecting.

JAMIESON: By God she does!

CHARLIE: Aye, from you lot!

TEIFION: No, from her own bio-chemistry. [*Grinning.*] Charlie, d'y'think she'll wait for me?

CHARLIE: Well, she reckons she's going to.

TEIFION: You're kidding.

CHARLIE: No, she told our mam this morning.

TEIFION: Then she must mean it!

CHARLIE: Congratulations, son ... you're engaged.

[*They both laugh.*]

JAMIESON [*pauses*]: God ... I must say I'd like to be in Montreal this night.

TEIFION: Tell me, Jamo, what's Montreal like? Y'know ... is it pretty good?

JAMIESON: Oh, God ... is Montreal good! [*Pauses.*] D'y'know ... it's a French-speaking town, y'know ... French ... the second largest French-speaking town in the world ... that's what they tell me anyway ... and ... er ... I can 'parle' a little bit, y'know ... and as they're Frenchie, they don't mind ... well ... they know I'm a Catholic. ...

[CHARLIE *and* TEIFION *look at each other quizzically.*]

JAMIESON: Well ... they know I'm not an Englishman ...

TEIFION: Oh ... they're quick, Charlie.

JAMIESON: Well ... they don't go a bundle on the English. ... I get on very well and I'm in the cafés, y'know, and they've some terrible saucy shows there! [*He chuckles.*]

CHARLIE: I'll tell you something ...

JAMIESON [*cutting over*]: The girls don't wear a thing! No, not a thing. Ah ... it's easy enough to pick them up too! Hmm ... lovely! Oh ... I love Montreal, it's a great town. Y'know, they drink wine and it's all sort of ... café like and it goes on late.

CHARLIE: I'll tell you someth ...

JAMIESON [*cutting in*]: Y'can be walking along and picking up girls or going to one of them cabarets and watching the dancing ... and there's one place ...

CHARLIE: I'll tell you somethin ...

JAMIESON [*cutting over*]: Oooh ... well ... of course, there are some very curious happenings going on there! And every night the places are full and the girls are dancing ... ye know ... and with bare breasts! I tell you, Teifion ... they've got bare breasts! I ... Oh ... it's wonderful to watch! I enjoy it ... I enjoy ...

CHARLIE: I'll tell you something else to Montreal ...

JAMIESON: And down here ...

CHARLIE: If I can get a word in edgewise ... Teif, if you really want to know. They have a tramway system that goes right through Montreal ... but you have to get off the tram that you're on because in one half of the town the width of the rails, y'know, the gauge, it's narrower than the other! Well, now, what do you think of that?

JAMIESON [*narked*]: God ... what are you telling him about the width of the rails for ... and I'm telling him about the good time he can have!

TEIFION [*laughing*]: Charlie ... I'm indebted to you! From now on my knowledge has been increased and I'm not fooling, Charlie. ... I've learnt something tonight ... there are two gauges to the tram tracks in Montreal ... I'm an increased man, Charlie. By God ... give us ... [*little laugh*] Give us another drink, son.

CHARLIE: Open the other bottle, Jamo ... where's Bobby? Did he find a girl then?

JAMIESON: No, he didn't.

CHARLIE: Well, where is he then? ... did you split up?

JAMIESON: Yes.

CHARLIE: What's up?

JAMIESON: Aah ... nothing.

CHARLIE: Come on, what's up?

JAMIESON: I left him when we got as far as the café.

CHARLIE: Why?

JAMIESON: I never thought that Bobby had no sense of humour ... I always thought he could take a joke.

CHARLIE: Bobby ... of course he's got a sense of humour ... what's the matter with you?

JAMIESON: I tell you he hasn't!

TEIFION: Of course, it'd depend on the joke ... there's the odd blind spot in all of us.

JAMIESON: I said something to him about Mag Keegan.

TEIFION: Oh, for Christ's sake.

CHARLIE: Aye, aye!

JAMIESON: No, sure, he didn't get it the first time ... so ... as it was too good to waste and wouldn't keep ... I explained.

CHARLIE: Did you mention *me*?

JAMIESON: No.

TEIFION: Did you mention *me*?

JAMIESON: No ... I didn't mention either of you ... I just asked him if he remembered something about her.

TEIFION: I see ... you like to share your points of reference with your mates.

CHARLIE [*exasperated*]: You are a bloody fool, Jamieson! Your brains rattle around in your head like a pea in a drum! [*Rises.*] Come on ... let's go and find him.

JAMIESON: Aah ... forget him ... let him grow up!

CHARLIE: Grow up! You're the one who wants to try that! You behave like a bloomin' bridge boy half the time! Come on ... let's go and find him, for God's sake!

TEIFION: Have I your permission to look after the bottle, Charlie?

CHARLIE: Aye ... but go easy.

TEIFION: That's the story of your life, Charlie.

CHARLIE: What?

TEIFION: 'Go easy.'

JAMIESON: Come on, Charlie.

CHARLIE: Coming ... anyway ... go easy, for Christ's sake!

[*The two boys go off and leave Teifion alone. He takes a swig from the bottle and cuddles it like a baby, he waltzes about the stage singing softly ... 'Ar lan y mor'. A tennis ball bounces gently on the stage.* TEIFION *picks it up and after a second* NEVILLE *runs on.*]

NEVILLE [*apologetically*]: Pardon me ... but ... could we have our ball back, please?

[TEIFION *looks at the ball seriously for a moment, then throws it back to him.*]

Ta. [*He turns to go.*]

TEIFION: Neville ... what church do *you* go to?

NEVILLE: Oh ... I'm an agnostic ... open to conviction, sort of thing.

[*He exits.* TEIFION *takes another drink then sings.*]

TEIFION: I wish I had a coil of
    Orange Rope.
    I wish I had a coil of
    Orange Rope.
    If I had a coil of
    Orange Rope.
    I'd make a noose and
    hang the ...

[*He gives a little laugh.*] Mag ... [*Singing softly*]
    Oh, Dirty Maggie May,
    They have taken her away
    No more down Canning Place she'll roam,
    Oh ... the judge he guilty found her,
    For robbing a homeward bounder,

Margaret ... Maggie.

[MAG *walks on to the stage.* ... TEIFION *sees her and says softly* 'Mag'.]

MAG: Hello, Teif.

TEIFION: How are you doing, kid?

MAG: All right.

TEIFION: You look tired.

MAG: Do I?

TEIFION: And very beautiful.

MAG: Ah ... chew a brick. ... Where are all the lads?

TEIFION: If you want Bobby, he's around somewhere. [*Pauses.*] I should be very angry with you ... have you any idea of the insult it is to have been used as a dream substitute?

MAG: You are a baby, Teif.

TEIFION: Well, you're not the doctor to smack me into life, you can't make me cry.

MAG: I don't want to.

TEIFION: I admire female selfishness ... they won't even share their misery with you.

MAG: Aren't you funny? You want to live off everyone else, you don't want to share, you want it all for yourself ... to see what happens.

TEIFION: You see me as a sort of emotional voyeur, is that it?

MAG: You're only using them long words to show off, aren't you?

TEIFION: God, you must hate me, Mag.

MAG: No, you soft thing, I've always thought that about you ... I rather like you ... but I just know about you, that's all.

TEIFION: Would you like a drink?

MAG [*pausing slightly*]: Yes, I think I would.

[*She takes the bottle and drinks.* BOBBY *enters by himself. He is quiet and not his usual self.*]

BOBBY: Aye, aye ... what's all this?

MAG: Just the lads, having a spot of fun.

BOBBY: Is it private, or can anyone join in?

TEIFION: Pull up a sod and sit down.

BOBBY [*sitting down*]: Pass us the bottle, Mag.

MAG: Here y're.

BOBBY: It's a nice night.

MAG: It's sort of full, isn't it?

BOBBY: How d'y'mean?

MAG: Oh, I don't know ... all round you, everywhere ... it's full and makes you hold your breath.

TEIFION: On nights like this, when I was a kid, I used to get out of bed and look through the window and see the people whose voices I could hear laughing away at me.

BOBBY: Go on, they were laughing at each other.

MAG: No, because they were with each other.

TEIFION: There's an awful lot of 'being with each other' going on in this park tonight.

BOBBY [*pause first*]: Am I smaller than my old man?

TEIFION: That's the sixty-four-dollar question, son ... why?

BOBBY: Oh ... just something he said.

MAG: What's the matter with you, Bobby?

BOBBY: I dunno, he holds himself straighter than me but I think I'm taller.

TEIFION: Of course you are! [*Looks closely at Bobby.*] Can you blow the flute, Bob?

BOBBY: No ... never could. Our Joey could though.

TEIFION: Robert ... a word in your ear ... in the day of the Nuclear Warhead, it's a bit of a liberty to ask a fella who's suffering from hydrogen burns if he's a Catholic or a Protestant! ... before you tell him you can't help him!

BOBBY: Knock it off, Teif!

TEIFION: All right ... if somebody shouted 'Scouse!' in the King's Road, Chelsea, would you turn round?

BOBBY: Of course I would.

TEIFION: What I mean is, your dad has got nothing to do with the price of contemporary tea, shake him off.

BOBBY: Well, what do you say, Mag?

MAG: The sky's all pink. 'Red sky at night sailor's delight, Red sky in the morning, mariner's warning.' Isn't it lovely, Bob?

BOBBY: Yes, it is. Can you hear the band playing over there? Gosh ... it's a nice night.

TEIFION [*rising*]: Y'know, I've got hopes of you two, I really have. [*To Bobby urgently.*] It's going to be all right, isn't it, Bobby?

 [BOBBY *looks at him puzzled.*]

MAG: Weren't you going, Teif?

TEIFION: Yeah. I mustn't crowd my luck! I'll look for the lads, I might even find them. [*He walks away.*]

BOBBY: Hello, Mag.

MAG: Hello, Bobby.

 [*They kiss.*]

BOBBY: Oh, God ... Mag ... it's been a long time, it's been such a long time, I ... I missed you, I've missed you so much, Mag, I never realized how much, just how much, I have missed you.

MAG: How d'y'mean, Bobby?

BOBBY: I just didn't think that the thing that was missing all the time was you ... I ... I ... there was something wrong, I know for years there's been something wrong ... it must have been you, Mag, it must have been you, mustn't it?

MAG: I know I've missed you, Bobby. Every time I've seen you in all those years ... it's been awful all over again. Sometimes I've seen you in the street ... and I've cried in the street.

BOBBY [*embarrassed*]: Oh, Mag ... I wouldn't like you to say that, y'know ... [*Pause.*] Is it true though ... I mean ... y'cried, did you?

MAG: I've cried so often about you, Bobby Laughlin, that I think the Mersey must be a bit deeper.

 [*They both laugh.*]

BOBBY: Oh, Mag, you're a lovely kid, you are. I always thought you were the loveliest kid I ever knew.

MAG: Did y', Bobby?

BOBBY [*laughs*]: I never know what's going on in the back there.

MAG: The back of where?

BOBBY: In the back of your eyes.

MAG [*softly*]: Bobby.

    [*They kiss.*]

BOBBY: Oh God, Mag, you're a woman, you're bloody marvellous, y'know. [*Pause.*] Y'kiss well.

MAG: That's because of you, Bobby.

BOBBY: Aye. [*He stretches himself and lies full out on the grass.*] God, it's a night, Mag. ... It's wonderful. I could sit here with you for ever and ever ... but somebody'll come along or the sun'll come up or something. But it all seems so safe here, doesn't it? Just you and me sitting in the park.

MAG: Bobby.

BOBBY: What, Mag?

MAG: What's the matter with you?

BOBBY: Oh ... nothing ... I was ... I was ... oh, something got me down.

MAG: Somebody say something to you or something?

BOBBY: Aye ... somebody said something to me ...

MAG: Well ... what did they say?

BOBBY [*pausing*]: Oh ... it was Jamo ... he said something about you.

MAG [*pausing*]: What did he say, Bobby?

BOBBY [*pausing*]: He just sort of said ... he'd knocked about with you for a bit.

MAG: Well ... that's true in a way, Bobby, but I don't think it's true in the way you think it is.

BOBBY: He ... er ... he seemed to think he'd been very friendly with you.

MAG: Oh ... you know fellas, Bobby.

BOBBY: No, Mag ... tell me about fellas ... no, I don't know fellas. ... You mean that everything he said is just talk ... is that what you mean?

MAG: Well ... I don't know what he did say. Bob, all I know is I've never had any feeling about Jamo. I went around with him for a few days just to hear if he'd any news of you ... he's a big kid ... just like Charlie and Teifion.

BOBBY: Have you been around with Charlie and Teif too?

MAG: For a bit.

BOBBY [*ruefully*]: Well ... I don't know, er ... in between all those fellas like ... [*little laugh*] ... all me mates! What about this thinking of me? Y'know, me mates you were going around with ... why?

MAG [*pausing*]: Well ... I suppose it isn't easy to tell you, Bobby ... you were away and I never saw you for a long time ... it's been a long ...

BOBBY [*brusquely cutting in*]: I know ... it's been a long time ... yes ... all right, all right ... well ... I was away ... [*Demanding.*] Come on.

MAG: Yes ... well ... you were away and I'd meet Jamo or Charlie or Teifion and ... Well ... I'd go out with them for a bit ...

BOBBY: Aye ... and Jimmy Smith!

MAG: Yes ... yes ... and Davy Jones ...

BOBBY: Davy Jones!

MAG: Lots of fellas you know I've been around with.

BOBBY: You've been doing a bit of a Paul Jones, haven't you?

MAG: Wait just a minute. Well ... what was I supposed to do? Just sit around and wait until maybe one day you'd walk past and see me again? But I always thought about you ... and I've always remembered you.

BOBBY: Have you! [*Pause.*] Look, Mag, I was very angry before with Jamo because of something he'd said. ... Because ... you see ... I know Jamo! Oh, I know Charlie and I know Teif too; they're all right in some ways ... but I know Jamo, I know his sort of fellas, and I know Jimmy Smith too, the sort of fellas they are ... I know why they go around with girls ... so ... so what have you got to say about it?

MAG: Bobby Laughlin, I've waited to see you and to talk to you *alone* like this and be kissed by you for the past five years and we're having a row!

BOBBY: Aye ... that's what it seems like!

MAG: Oh, for heaven's sake!

BOBBY [*pause*]: Well ... I don't want to row with you, Mag, because you're lovely and you're y'know ... you're pretty ... and I'd rather just kiss you.

MAG [*after a moment*]: Bobby ... do you love me?

BOBBY: Oh ... er ... well ... yes ... yes ... in a way. Yes, yes, I do love you.

MAG [*very quietly*]: Bobby, can I tell you something? You're just like Jamo at this moment.

BOBBY: What does that mean?

MAG: Well, he didn't like it when I talked about you, y'see, he didn't like it at all ... but he had to stop rowing with me cos I had something he wanted and that's what happened with you a minute ago. You've got the right ideas about the things I've done, but you saw it in the wrong way. You want to have a row with me ... but if you do, you think you'll spoil your chances. Well, I've waited for you so long, I should be able to play the game you want ... take you at any price as long as I can get you. ... But I can't do it.

BOBBY [*angrily*]: Oh, don't go on like that! I'm not interested in Jamo and the rest of them. ... It's you now.

MAG: Aye ... now ... on the grass. I'll settle for that as long as you understand I know what you're about.

BOBBY: Well, for God's sake! [*He jumps to his feet.*] Isn't it wonderful, isn't it bloody marvellous! You're making out I'm in the wrong! I'm not the one who's gone around saying he's cried and waited for bloody years!

MAG [*getting up*]: Why are you swearing?

BOBBY: Let's understand each other, Mag. You've heard me swearing before and a lot more as well ... so, for Christ's sake don't start to pull that stuff on me! All I know is I'm the laughing-stock of all my mates. They've all had you but me! [*Pause.*] Oh ... I'm sorry, Mag, I didn't mean that ... honest.

MAG: Y'did, y'know.

BOBBY: I didn't ... I was just angry, who wouldn't be?

MAG: Well, you can go now ... go away and as far as I'm concerned ... You were just a waste of time.

BOBBY: Well ... don't worry ... I did all right without you and your sort for long enough. I made a big mistake ... any decent pape wouldn't look twice at me ... I should have known you weren't much in the first place ... and anyone who'd go around with Jamo ...

MAG [cutting in]: Wait a minute! You owe me too much to get away with that! I just won't have it! I've told you something tonight that I've never told anybody before ... but I can see that I made my mistake in being honest with you, telling you the truth, the way things really are ... you don't want the truth, you just want fairy stories and if you can't get them you behave like a spoilt child.

BOBBY: It's you that believes in fairy tales ... talking about love and crying and waiting while all the time you've been having it off ... Oh why don't you push off!

MAG: I loved only you.

BOBBY: You what! [He bursts into laughter.] Don't make me laugh! God ... what a slag you turned out to be.

[MAG stares at him for a moment and then walks away.

BOBBY stands looking after her ... alone, defiant. He picks up the bottle and takes a stiff swig with a shudder. He looks about angrily. He is all alone. His misery is disturbed by noises off, then across the stage march CARSON MCDERBY, and a MAN. MCDERBY has his large Lambeg drum; he is beating it loudly and shouting as he crosses the stage.]

CARSON: Keep the Coggers out of the flats! Keep the Coggers out of the flats! Rally at the bandstand. ... All true sons of Billy rally at the bandstand! We'll show them.

[BOBBY grabs the MAN.]

BOBBY: What's to do?

MAN [as he goes]: The boys of the lodge are going to demonstrate against the flats.

[*As* BOBBY *crosses back to the centre of the stage,* MR KEEGAN, TIM, *and his* CRONIES *enter from another side.*]

MR KEEGAN: They shall not pass! Remember '98?

TIM: We'll scrag 'em. [*Over his shoulder to Bobby.*] I'll see you later, Bobby Laughlin!

   [CHARLIE *and* TEIFION *appear at the rear of the procession.* TEIFION *sees Bobby.*]

TEIFION: Well, thank God you haven't gone mad! [*He looks off as the sound of an angry roar starts.*] Have you sent Mag home?

BOBBY: No ... I haven't sent the *cow* home! Don't care where she is.

CHARLIE: What's up with you then?

BOBBY: Nothing's up with *me* ... oh no ... but come on, you two, what about Mag? Come on, what about her?

   [TEIFION *and* CHARLIE *just look at him.*]

   [*Snarling.*] Well, I'll tell you about her. She's a whore, a bloody red-neck whore and you both know it. My old man was right, he knows about them, he knows about them, knows about everything.

TEIFION: What's your old man got to do with Mag? She's a young girl, he's an old bigot and it's too late to change him. Anywhere else he'd be a joke but up here he's taken seriously cos so many other fools think the same way.

BOBBY: Listen, Teifion Davies, that cow's made a fool of me, and that Jamo ... he's a Catholic too.

TEIFION: Yes? Well, what about Charlie and me?

BOBBY: Aye, you're a couple of sly Welsh bastards!

CHARLIE: Oh, for God's sake.

TEIFION: Did your father teach you that too?

BOBBY: My old man's right, he must be, he's never made a mistake in his life! [*Irrationally.*] They ruin your stock, look at our Joey, five bloody kids!

CHARLIE: You're drunk! You're talking like a bloomin' Orangeman!

BOBBY: Well ... what's the matter with that? I am one, aren't I, and it's a damned sight easier to be one and all.

TEIFION: Ah, now we're at it! 'It's easier to be one!' Well, don't kid yourself, son, you'll have to work at it, you'll have to learn to believe all sorts of nonsense that you know couldn't be true.

BOBBY [*sneering*]: Oh, you think you're clever, don't you! You think you know it all!

TEIFION: No, I don't, but I'm damned sure your father doesn't either.

BOBBY: She's slept around, hasn't she? Well, that's enough for me!

TEIFION: If you're parcelling out moral blame, son, you can start with your old man, he's made Mag what she is.

[MR LAUGHLIN *enters the stage and sees his son.*]

MR LAUGHLIN: Good boy, Bobby, I was looking for you. Come on, we're away down to the rally.

TEIFION [*furious, grabbing hold of Mr Laughlin*]: Listen, Mr Laughlin, there's a kid called Mag Keegan who did your son the honour of going crazy about him, calf-loving him to distraction ... and she still does love him, but because you stopped them even talking to each other, she's had to make do with second-bests like me, Charlie, and ... Well, you've lost one son, isn't that enough?

[MR LAUGHLIN *tries to break away from his grip.*]

MR LAUGHLIN: How dare you molest me, you damned thing, you!

TEIFION: I'm only trying to rape you into humanity!

MR LAUGHLIN [*breaking away*]: Come on, Bobby. We'll need all we can muster.

TEIFION: No, Bobby, don't you go with him. He's trying to live your life for you! If you go now, he's got you for ever.

BOBBY [*weakly*]: I don't know.

MR LAUGHLIN [*commandingly*]: You'll come with me ...

BOBBY [*hesitating*]: Well ...

TEIFION: Ah, go on, you weak bastard! You don't deserve a woman like Mag and that's why you never had her.

[BOBBY *is so incensed by this he hits Teifion on the chest and knocks him over.*]

[*Ruefully, on the ground.*] Bobby, I'm a Protestant too, y'know.

BOBBY [*helping him up*]: Oh God, Teifion, I'm ... I didn't mean ...

MR LAUGHLIN [*dancing with delight*]: Hit him again, Bobby ... give him good.

BOBBY: No, Dad, I've made a big enough fool of myself for one night. Sorry, Teif. [*Starts to go.*]

MR LAUGHLIN [*shouting after him*]: Joey!

TEIFION: You what?

MR LAUGHLIN: Ya, damn thing.

[*He glowers off to the rally.*]

TEIFION: Well ... at least I've reduced you to an honourable neutrality. [*Little laugh.*] Oh – I'm sorry, Bob, I didn't realize that you – were pressed so hard. [*Pause.*] You know what I think, Bobby? I think you're coming up for a decision. I've high hopes for you, cos – the moment you want to belt somebody – to smash them and shut them up, it means that the voice inside you is speaking very clearly.

[*There is a pause while* BOBBY *watches Teifion as he gets up and brushes himself down.*]

Bobby – go and look for Mag. Why don't you? After all – you've only got one life to lose ...

[BOBBY *stares at Teifion and then comes to a firm decision. He turns and runs off stage in the direction in which Mag left.*]

CHARLIE: Are you all right then, Teif?

TEIFION: Aye – I think so.

CHARLIE: It'll be all right, Teif, ye needn't worry. No harm's been done.

[TEIFION *looks at Charlie in wonder. He speaks ironically and, as he goes on, he gathers momentum to Charlie's growing dismay.*]

TEIFION: No harm's been done? No, you're right, Charlie, come to think of it, no harm's been done at all. Because if you take the long view of things, Bobby's never going to catch up with Mag. Oh no, boy, I can see Bobby – sliding along the lane back to his dad. He'll fumble in his pocket, get out a clove, chew it a bit and get it round his tongue. After that he'll start to sing 'just to keep up his spirits'. And d'ye know what he'll sing?

CHARLIE: No, I don't.

TEIFION: 'The Orange sash me father wore.' Oh, he's a good boy for his dad our Bob is! Oh, he'll study through tomorrow and all the rest of the hot days that are coming up for a hot July. And, comes August, every week-end he'll be off on the bike and across to Wales and with a bit of luck, and Bobby's the boy for luck, he'll find the girl campers from Bolton, waiting for him, ready to drop their morals specially for a week. Well, it's Wakes Week! And after dissipating his strength all the way through August, he'll be in a suitable frame of mind to buckle down to the exams in September and by the time these exams are over it'll be October and he'll be away and life'll go on and on. Good old Bob! October boy! The seas boy! Back to the free-easy riding sea. Anywhere – just to escape from Mag. Oh, she's a demander is Mag. They're all demanders! And anyway, it'll be all right for Mag cos – no harm's been done there, ye know. No! She can lose herself in plates and spoonfuls of scouse. She can get away from her mother's nagging through the heat of July with the beads of sweat on her upper lip out in the kitchen. [*Pause.*] But in August she's got the Holy Voyage and her mother's demands will be drowned by the busy gnats of Ireland. The slabs of Soda bread washed down with Orange-coloured tea. Yes – she'll live through September. Her sex is resilient!

CHARLIE [*getting worried*]: Now, steady on!

TEIFION: And, by God, this town is resilient! I'm not worried for Mag. October may be a bad month for her but Mag's not a suicide girl. Despair is outside our Mag. Despair is outside this town, because this town is like an indiarubber ball and it makes us all indiarubber! Throw us on the ground and we'll bounce back! And, Charlie, with any luck at all, tomorrow I'll get on that train, clutching in my hot sticky hand a second-class ticket and brazen me way past Crewe in a first-class seat [*triumphantly*] and ye can drop me off at Sloane Street any time at all, son, any time at all. No harm's been done, Charlie, no harm at all.

He gazes out at the audience, viewing the vision he has conjured up as the

CURTAIN FALLS

JOHN WHITING

Marching Song

MARCHING SONG

First produced at the Prince of Wales Theatre, Cardiff, on 8 February 1954, and at the St Martin's Theatre, London, on 8 April 1954. It was presented by Tennent Productions Ltd with the following cast:

HARRY LANCASTER	Hartley Power
DIDO MORGEN	Penelope Munday
MATTHEW SANGOSSE	Robert Sansom
FATHER ANSELM	Philip Burton
CATHERINE DE TROYES	Diana Wynyard
RUPERT FORSTER	Robert Flemyng
JOHN CADMUS	Ernest Thesiger
BRUNO HURST	Michael David

Directed by FRITH BANBURY

The action of the play takes place in a room of Catherine de Troyes's house set on the heights above a capital city in Europe.

ACT ONE: Late evening, moving to night.
ACT TWO: The next day. Night.
ACT THREE: Later the same night, moving to dawn.

ACT ONE

The scene is a room in CATHERINE DE TROYES's *house set on the heights above a capital city in Europe. The time is the present: it is late evening moving to night.*

The house, of which the room is representative, was designed by a great German architect of the nineteen-thirties. Built into the hillside which ranges high above the city lying to the south, it transcends the mere purpose of a dwelling-place.

The room is a shell caught within a web of glass and steel. It is dominated by the sky. Entrances to the room: a wide circular stairway leading down to the main door of the house. A second entrance: a gallery leading to an apartment of rooms above which stand alone. This is the highest point of the house.

A third entrance: from a balcony of considerable size – a main feature of the room and of the house – projecting like a finger towards the city (or an arrow, perhaps, set within the bow of the room). The house is built of stone, glass, and steel. Within the room there is an impression of air and space – an impression of delicacy, almost fragility, yet the place is a fortress in strength and position. A warmth is given to the room by the use of wood and fabrics in the decoration and furnishing. In the spare decoration of the room there is a plinth surmounted by an antique bronze helmet.

It is the late evening of a spring day. The great expanse of sky above the room retains a savage brilliance, but within the room shadows have begun to form. The lights have not yet been put up.

> [HARRY LANCASTER *stands in the centre of the room. He is in the act of getting out of a heavy sheepskin coat which is half-off his shoulders.*]

HARRY: You! [*He is shouting to a man who is standing on the balcony with his back to the room.*] I'm speaking to you! [*The man does not turn.*]

All right, then. To hell with you! [*The man is motionless, silent.*] To hell, sweetheart, with you. [HARRY *throws the coat over a chair and speaks to another person.*] I said just now that my youth must be considered past – done with. Know why? Because – [*He turns to find himself alone in the room. After a moment he goes to the circular stairway and calls down.*] Come on up! Don't be scared. Come on up! [*He backs from the stairway keeping in sight and speaking to the ascending person.*] My youth – done with. For why? Because I want you for my workmate, believe me. And believe me truly last fall I'd have wanted you for my playmate. Last fall – six months ago – I was young and loving. Now, I can only say – welcome.

[DIDO MORGEN, *a young girl, has come up the stairway and now stands within the room.*]

Welcome! Look – but look kindly – on these grey hairs. Trust this ancient head. Will you?

DIDO: Yes.

HARRY: That's the girl.

DIDO: Who's in this place?

HARRY: Relax. They're friends here.

[DIDO *silently points to the man on the balcony.*]

You're right. A stranger. Tourist, maybe. [*He shouts again to the man.*] Have a drink! [*The man is silent.*] Not an American, any-way.

DIDO: You are.

HARRY: I was made unhappy there so I came over to Europe. I'm unhappy here too – so I guess it's the condition of the man. Let's not blame places, shall we?

DIDO: A long way to come just to stay unhappy.

HARRY: And let's not talk around the point. My misery is my dearest possession – for God's sake leave me that. You're not one of those women who think men should be made happy, are you?

DIDO: No. But if you don't want to be made happy why did you pick me up and bring me here?

HARRY: I want to give you a job. Why do you clip your hair?

DIDO: Keep it clean. Cleanliness before wantonness, you know. What sort of job?

HARRY: How long have you lived down in the city?

DIDO: All my life. Nearly twenty years.

HARRY: The day you were born there was music and laughter – and maybe they let off fireworks.

DIDO: It was a very obscure birth.

HARRY: But twenty years ago there was music and laughter every day. I know. I was there.

DIDO: Laughing with the best of them.

HARRY: Sure. I was young and the place was – well – [*He sings and pantomimes an old waltz song*] – but you won't remember.

DIDO: No, I don't remember. What were you doing here then – besides laughing and letting off fireworks?

HARRY: I was making a film – a movie – something I've done all my life. That's what's known as my job. I was young then – do I talk too much about my age? I had money and people said I was – well, they said I was all right. They said Harry Lancaster was all right.

DIDO: That's you.

HARRY: That's me. I'm back again.

DIDO: Welcome!

HARRY: But I'm not young – I've no money – nobody remembers me and the old songs have all gone, but here I am and I'm making a new picture. Twenty years ago I made the picture of my youth. I'll show it to you. Only one copy left. I keep it with me against the dead days. Like an old actor's yellow press-clippings. Baby, look up to me – I once did this!

DIDO: And the new picture?

HARRY: The magazines'll call it the film of my maturity. Let's leave it at that.

DIDO: What do I do?

HARRY: I don't know yet.

DIDO: What sort of picture is this, for God's sake?

HARRY: You'll see.

DIDO: Where do you make it?

HARRY: On the streets – around. I can't pay you. I know! I said I could – well, I can't. Want to go? I can feed you, keep you happy by telling you stories of the old days, give you somewhere to sleep, maybe make you laugh. That's all. But it's better, surely, than sitting on bar stools and drinking beer and eating broken biscuits out of your pocket.

DIDO: Where? All this eating and sleeping, I mean.

HARRY: Here. Kate won't mind.

DIDO: Kate? Let's play fair.

HARRY: Catherine de Troyes. This is her house. I knew her 'way back. When I came over some six months ago I sort of moved in here. Kate's putting up the money for this new picture – enough for the truck, the cameras and film, and a half-witted assistant.

DIDO: Can she afford it?

HARRY: Look around you and ask that again.

DIDO: I like money.

HARRY: She was born to it.

DIDO: What's more, she's kept it. I couldn't live here. I'd get lost.

HARRY: That was the idea.

DIDO: To get lost?

HARRY: Kate was in love. The house was built for Kate to get lost in with her man.

DIDO: And they were happy. Say they were happy.

HARRY: For a time. Then he went away. Kate stayed on.

DIDO: In this place? What's that? [*She points to the bronze helmet.*]

HARRY: It belonged to a man called Forster. A soldier. It's an old helmet.

DIDO: Rupert Forster. He fought this last war.

HARRY: It's he who has left Kate alone. He was a terrible man. I mean that. He – I don't know.

DIDO: Well, never mind. He's dead.

HARRY: What?

DIDO: I said, never mind. He's dead.

HARRY: No, no, he's not that. But they caught up with him. They shut him up in prison. There's still something, you know, that catches up with men like that. Even now, in this world, there's something says, No! this is enough. That's what happened to Forster. He got his arse kicked so hard in that last fight they daren't even bring him back. I guess they'll let him die up there in the camp in the mountains.

DIDO: You're glad.

HARRY: I'm not sorry. I knew him back in the old days with Kate. When I was making the first picture the Government lent me some soldiers for a couple of scenes. He was the young officer commanding them. I liked him then. But in the preliminaries for war, in the war itself – I don't know what happened to him. Men should be humble, I guess.

DIDO: And that helmet's all that's left for Kate. What's she like?

HARRY: You'll see her. She's beautiful. Rupert was beautiful too. They were both beautiful – in the old days.

DIDO: So was the first picture.

HARRY: So was the first picture. So was the world.

DIDO: In the old days.

[*They laugh. From the well of the circular stairway* FATHER ANSELM *calls.*]

ANSELM: May we come up?

DIDO: Who's that?

HARRY: It's all right. Mustn't be scared. Look, I'll show you. [*He leads her to the stairway, and together they look down.*] See! Nothing to frighten you, is there? [*He calls.*] Come on up, boys. [HARRY *and* DIDO *move from the stairs.*] Be nice to them.

DIDO: Who are they?

HARRY: Ssh!

[FATHER ANSELM, *an elderly priest, and* MATTHEW SANGOSSE *come up the stairway and into the room. They wear coats and carry hats.*]

Hullo, Father. Hullo, Doc.

ANSELM: Are we disturbing you, Harry?

HARRY: I'm doing nothing. [*To Dido*] This is Father Anselm, and this is the Doctor.

MATTHEW: My name is Sangosse.

HARRY: Have you got another name?

DIDO: Morgen.

HARRY: This is Dido Morgen. Where've you boys been?

ANSELM: For a walk.

MATTHEW: It's a strange feeling walking down there now that all the foreign soldiers have gone. You can miss something you dislike, I suppose.

HARRY: Do you know, it hadn't struck me they'd gone. But then you're a native. I'm not. Anyway, you had a good walk.

MATTHEW: We went as far as the monument and back.

HARRY: That must've taken you quite a time.

MATTHEW: Two hours.

ANSELM: Catherine sent us.

HARRY: Sent you? I've only just got back. Been out all day in the truck. So I don't know about things. Tell me, boys, what goes on?

ANSELM: Goes on, Harry?

HARRY: Yes. You were sent out for a walk. Sent out. And look – [*He points to the man on the balcony.*]

MATTHEW: Who is it?

HARRY: You don't know, either.

MATTHEW [*to the man*]: Excuse me, what are you doing out there?
[*The man does not answer.*]

HARRY: Was he there when you went out?

MATTHEW: No.

HARRY: Hell! Where's Kate? What is all this? Go find her. Tell her somebody's trying to break up the happy home.

ANSELM: Coming, Matthew?

HARRY: That's my boys.

[*FATHER ANSELM and MATTHEW go out.*]
Question is: good or bad?

DIDO: News?

HARRY: I don't want my quiet life disturbed. I'm happy. Looked after.

DIDO: Are there servants here?

HARRY: Plenty. Kate keeps them under cover. Like kids of an earlier generation – but better! – they're neither seen nor heard.

DIDO: But we kids of this generation – say me! – when do we eat?

HARRY: Hungry?

DIDO: Yes.

HARRY: Keep going. [*From his breast pocket he takes a bar of chocolate, which he throws to* DIDO, *who catches it.*]

DIDO: It's soft.

HARRY: From the warmth of my heart. You're too young to know – but that's the last part of you to die. The coldness creeps around your more private parts, but that public organ, your heart, just won't go out. [*He attempts to kiss her but she pushes him away and laughs with her mouth full of chocolate.*] You'll make yourself sick.

DIDO: I don't care.

[CATHERINE DE TROYES *comes from the upper room. She wears a dressing-robe.*]

HARRY: Don't care, eh?

DIDO: No. Don't care.

HARRY: Give him – [*the man*] – a bit.

DIDO: No.

HARRY: Gi'me a bit.

DIDO: No!

HARRY: Poor Harry! Gi'm li'l bit choc'late.

DIDO: No. No choc'late f'Harry. Eat't all m'self. [*She has stuffed the remaining chocolate into her mouth.*]

[HARRY *appeals to the man on the balcony.*]

HARRY: She's ate up – right up. Now, an't that nasty – plain nasty? No choc'late f'you'n'me – s'none f'working men like you'n'me. Though what in hell your work is – standing there! – God knows.

CATHERINE: He's my new guardian angel, Harry. Don't abuse him. And how very interesting to hear that you look upon yourself as a working man.

HARRY: Why not? I've been out on the truck since early morning.

CATHERINE [to Dido]: He gives himself away every time. Have you found that?

HARRY: Sleeping! You should be ashamed.

[CATHERINE has come down into the room, and again speaks to Dido.]

CATHERINE: He'll manage to put you in the wrong, too, when you come to play your part. I take it you are one of his troupe, or whatever it is he makes his pictures with.

[DIDO wipes her mouth with the back of her hand.]

HARRY: This, incidentally – indeed, quite by the way – is Dido Morgen.

CATHERINE: I'm Catherine de Troyes. How do you do?

HARRY: Miss Morgen will be staying here. [There is silence.] For a few days. She is temporarily part of my troupe, as you'll have it. Just for a few days.

CATHERINE [to Dido]: Americans possess two endearing qualities. Their innocence which delights me – and their feeling for hospitality which often inconveniences me. But of course you must stay, Miss Morgen. For tonight, at least. Did you come up those stairs on your way here?

[DIDO nods her head.]

Well, now go down them, and instead of turning through the main door – which will take you out into the world – turn the other way. There you'll find someone to attend you. Have you any night things with you?

HARRY: No, she hasn't.

CATHERINE: It can be arranged. [There is silence. DIDO has not moved.] Have you understood what I've said?

HARRY: Go on, honey. I'll be around to see you soon. We'll talk about the picture.

[DIDO *wanders to the stairway and begins to go down. Before she is out of sight or hearing* CATHERINE *speaks.*]

CATHERINE: Like a puppy. Where did you find it?

HARRY: In a bar.

CATHERINE: What do you want it for?

[DIDO *has gone.*]

HARRY: I've told you. For the picture. She's fine. Right out of that stinking city.

CATHERINE: Like the filthy old man we had up last month. What was he? Christ down on his luck, wasn't he? He came out of that stinking city. But he wasn't right after all.

HARRY: There was nothing back of his eyes. That's what I'm looking for to photograph. The something back of their eyes.

CATHERINE: And this girl has it?

HARRY: Maybe. I don't know yet.

CATHERINE: When will you know? When you've tried to sleep with her?

HARRY: That's not fair, Kate.

CATHERINE: What is fair, Harry? You, living here on my weakness and indulging your notions at my expense. Is that fair? I don't think it is.

HARRY: Go on – give. I'm expecting the worst.

CATHERINE: Here it comes. I'm afraid there'll be no more money for the film.

HARRY: No more money. What've I done?

CATHERINE: Nothing. That's the point. You should have made up your poor muddled mind before this, and finished the picture. Finished it while I was prepared to pay for your ridiculous antics.

HARRY: My ridiculous antics.

CATHERINE: I've gone beyond such amusements, Harry. I don't want – I shan't need you about any more.

HARRY: Suddenly seen sense, you have.

CATHERINE: You admit it? That however much money and time I

give you, the film will never be made? You know, don't you, that
all the business of getting the faces, finding the places – the right
faces and the right places to photograph at the right time – it was
nothing more than a putting off because you've nothing to say any
more. You see and you feel the misery – say down there in the city –
but you can't do anything about it. You can't even represent it by
your old love, the camera, on a screen. You're not big enough,
Harry.

HARRY: Maybe not. But you knew what I wanted to do.

CATHERINE: Yes, I knew.

HARRY: That I wanted to go back of their faces.

CATHERINE: Yes.

HARRY: Back of their faces – those godawful masks – and get whatever it is.

CATHERINE: Yes, that.

HARRY: And keep in on film. That hope, that something –

CATHERINE: At the back of their eyes. But it's in everyone, Harry.
You don't have to look for it. It's in me. But the failure to see is in
you.

HARRY: Sure. So – no more money.

CATHERINE: No.

HARRY: No money – no picture. What about Poppa and the Doc?

CATHERINE: They must go too.

HARRY: No picture, no sweetness from the little white pills, no God
any more. You've found something.

CATHERINE: Yes. You talk about it. You talk about love an awful
lot, Harry. But do you understand what you say, I wonder?

HARRY: I talk to myself in a language I understand, if that's what you
mean.

CATHERINE: I was a young woman when Rupert left to fight nine
years ago, and through the two years' absence at war and the seven
years of his imprisonment I've had to live on my kind of love. You
don't understand, do you?

HARRY: I've never understood.

CATHERINE: You like me, Harry, because you're sorry for me. That's safe, isn't it? Because I'm one of your old tramps or funny little girls with my heart in the wrong place. Because I'm alone. But, Harry, you can stop being sorry for me. I'm not alone any longer.

HARRY: He's back.

CATHERINE: Yes. Rupert's back.

HARRY: Up there? [*He points to the upper room.*]

CATHERINE: He's sleeping. Very tired. Long journey.

HARRY: You've been up there with him.

CATHERINE: Yes. With him.

HARRY: You knew he was coming back today.

CATHERINE: This morning. They sent me a message.

HARRY: That's why you sent Poppa and Doc out for a walk.

CATHERINE: I wanted to meet him alone.

HARRY: You've muddled them. They don't know what goes on. I didn't either for that matter.

CATHERINE: I'll explain to them. Soon enough.

HARRY: And show them the door.

CATHERINE: Well, am I expected to have you three old things around my neck for the rest of my life?

HARRY: So Forster's back.

CATHERINE: Yes. And Harry – Harry, he's going to be free!

HARRY: Are they unlocking all the cages at the zoo today as well? Free. My, my! [*He points suddenly to the man on the balcony. It is darker and the man is barely visible.*]

CATHERINE: That man? He was sent with Rupert to guard him. There are two more below. They'll only be with us for a little while. Just so long as the country needs to get used to the idea of Rupert being free. All great men must be guarded in these days.

HARRY: Sure, sure.

CATHERINE: Well, got everything straight now?

HARRY: I guess so. Was there a need to be quite so harsh? I suppose there was. I'd never get out of anywhere nowadays without being pushed out. There's one thing I'd like you to know – not important to you but important to me. It's in you, Kate, that my lamented youth resides. You're the person who represents all that I wanted to be and believed I could be when we first knew each other in the old days. I translated everything – ambition, talent, all values – into your person. I suppose – in my own way, a way you despise – I love you. Don't put up the lights for a minute! [*It is very dark within the room.*]

CATHERINE: Dry your tears. I'm not looking.

HARRY: It's just that I hate saying goodbye.

CATHERINE: The party's over, Harry.

[FATHER ANSELM *and* MATTHEW SANGOSSE *have come into the room.*]

MATTHEW: Catherine?

CATHERINE: Yes, my dears. I'm here.

MATTHEW: May I put on the light?

CATHERINE: Not for a moment. We must allow Harry to recover himself.

HARRY: Also, I'd imagine, we must give you time to think of something you can say to these boys.

ANSELM: Are you upset about something, Harry?

HARRY: Poppa, we're all three of us going to be upset together in a minute. Go ahead, Kate.

CATHERINE: You tell them, Harry.

HARRY: Well, I'm damned!

CATHERINE: Go on. Tell them.

HARRY: Poppa, Doc – we're fired. We're out, boys. On our ears.

MATTHEW: Out?

HARRY: The life we've had here, bringing in our several ways comfort to this lady, is finished. An incident has occurred.

ANSELM: Have you quarrelled with Harry, Catherine?

HARRY: No, no. It's all quite friendly. Just this: we're being told to leave, boys. Find other quarters. As simple as that. Go fasten your suckers, you suckers, on somebody else. But don't forget we have done her some small service. That's why the light's out; to spare her blushes.

[CATHERINE *does not speak.* HARRY *continues, very softly.*]

If you listen very hard both of you, you'll hear the sounds of war. Coriolan – Coriolan. You'll hear the soft stumbling tread of returning men. Men out of order and out of heart. There's no trumpet left will call them to attention. There's no drum can fit the broken rhythm of their march. But they are come back – they have come home.

[RUPERT FORSTER *calls quietly from the gallery before the door of the upper room.*]

RUPERT: Catherine!

[*The lights go up in the room.* CATHERINE – *she has her hand on the light switch – and the three men look up at* RUPERT. *He speaks to Catherine.*]

You left me alone. You promised not to do that.

CATHERINE: I was coming back.

RUPERT: Shall I come down? I'm quite awake now. [*He comes down into the room.*] Good evening, gentlemen. I overheard – forgive me! – the lament spoken by one of you. Coriolan, may I remind you, was a tyrant. But yes, I've come back.

CATHERINE: Have you had a good rest?

RUPERT: How long have I been asleep?

CATHERINE: Only two hours or so.

RUPERT: It must have been the darkness that woke me. It can, you know.

CATHERINE: Are those the only clothes you have?

RUPERT: I borrowed them from my servant. I'm no longer allowed to wear uniform.

HARRY: Too bad!

[CATHERINE *speaks to Matthew and Father Anselm.*]

CATHERINE: This is Rupert Forster, Father Anselm and Doctor Matthew Sangosse.

[*They shake hands as* CATHERINE *turns to* HARRY, *who speaks.*]

HARRY: Remember me, sir?

[RUPERT *stares at him without recognition.*]

CATHERINE: It's Harry Lancaster, darling.

HARRY: Well, if my face doesn't mean anything to him it's scarcely likely my name will.

RUPERT: You must forgive me. I've been away.

HARRY: I know.

RUPERT: Away for a long time. I can't recall –

HARRY: Ever having seen me before in your life. I know.

RUPERT: Won't you help me?

HARRY: It was a long time ago. And it doesn't matter.

CATHERINE: You met Harry when he was making a film here. Remember?

HARRY: Years ago.

RUPERT: God! Yes, of course. I'm so sorry. What are you doing here now?

HARRY: I was making another picture of your beautiful city. It was to be a sequel to the first picture you remember so well. It was to show how all the pretty little girls of the first picture have become cellar drabs. How the dirty finger of time has pushed in all their sweet little cheeks. It was to show how all the fine young men in their uniforms of the first picture have – well, it was to show that they aren't around any longer.

RUPERT: It sounds most entertaining.

HARRY: Yes, it's the sort of thing would make you laugh a lot.

RUPERT: And you were going to film it in the city.

HARRY: Yes. There – or in somebody's armpit.

CATHERINE: Harry, do you think you should so neglect your girl?

HARRY: My girl? You want us to get out at once?

CATHERINE: Of course not. Stay, at least, tonight.

HARRY: Many, many thanks. [*He has moved to the stairway. He looks down.*] I promised her lots.

CATHERINE: Fulfil your promises.

HARRY: For one thing I told her she was among friends. [*He goes down the stairs.*]

CATHERINE: I thought we'd have dinner later.

RUPERT: Yes, I'm a little –

CATHERINE: What?

RUPERT: I'm a little confused. What is it? Early evening?

CATHERINE [*laughing*]: Yes, darling. Later, then.

RUPERT: Remember I've been on a prison diet.

CATHERINE: What was it like?

RUPERT: Not bad. Everything had onions in it.

CATHERINE: Everything?

RUPERT: Even the shaving water.

[FATHER ANSELM *and* MATTHEW *have been speaking together.* FATHER ANSELM *now comes forward.*]

ANSELM: I'm speaking for myself and Matthew.

CATHERINE: What's that?

ANSELM: When do you want us to leave, Catherine?

MATTHEW: No arrangements have been made, of course.

CATHERINE: Have you anywhere to go?

ANSELM: We shall stay together. Matthew has a sister living in the country. He thinks it probable she'd welcome us.

MATTHEW: I'll telephone her tomorrow.

CATHERINE: Very well.

MATTHEW: For tonight we'll go to our rooms. Unless you need us for anything.

CATHERINE: No, I shan't need you.

ANSELM: Your prayers, later.

CATHERINE: Not tonight.

[FATHER ANSELM *and* MATTHEW *go out.*]

RUPERT: Why are they here?

CATHERINE: To look after me. To keep me well and safe until you came back.

RUPERT: But why those men? So shabby, so at odds with the world.

CATHERINE: Are they shabby? I suppose they are. I've never noticed. They needed somewhere to live after the war. And I needed friends.

RUPERT: Friends?

CATHERINE: No, that's not the word, is it? I needed someone to notice that I was here and that I was human. You've been away a long time, Rupert.

RUPERT: They're not what I'd have expected to find with you. And the American – I don't remember him at all. I said I did, but it's not true. Faces and names, you know, they just disappear. Not one thing about him remains.

CATHERINE: He's changed since the old days. He was amusing then, I think. But he's been home and seems to have picked up the national failing: he sees everyone as a distorted reflection of himself. He feels he should straighten out the image. So he questions strangers on their misfortune. It doesn't amuse him to have a woman now unless she's down on her luck. There's a girl in this house at the moment. Brought her back this afternoon. She's to be in the film, he says. Ach! he's pathetic. He doesn't even take them into his bed any more – only into his great big American heart. He came over six months ago, penniless, and asked me to put him up.

RUPERT: You took them all in because you were sorry for them.

CATHERINE: Not exactly. Darling, you make the place sound like a charity lodging-house. They're none of them quite as bad as that, you know. Father and the Doctor do their jobs professionally, and Harry once made very good films.

RUPERT: So they've filled your life for the past seven years in place of the others I remember.

CATHERINE: The others?

RUPERT: The men who dressed your hair and painted your face, designed your clothes and fitted your shoes. Those are the people I remember with you.

CATHERINE: When they sent you away to prison and I was left alone I did a very natural thing – I got down on my knees. But the words that had been there since childhood weren't there any longer. I just couldn't say them. It was Father Anselm who in his own muddled way gave me back the words. We started from the beginning – it was 'say after me' all over again. As for the Doctor, he's easy to explain. I was not able to sleep – not for a long time – and he had magic in his boxes and bottles.

RUPERT: Now you've told them they must go. You feel you can do without them.

CATHERINE: Of course. You're back, Rupert. Why should I need anything more?

RUPERT: Catherine – [*In silence he measures, in a number of paces, a certain distance across the room*] – that, square, was the exact measurement of my room at the camp. I was sent to that place direct from the freedom of a battlefield. I occupied it for seven years. That little space could have been my childhood nursery, my cadet's room at the military academy, my old battlefields, this room in this house with you – indeed, it could have been any of my particular heavens or hells. Imagination could have made it so. And I could have been any man I wished to be. A free man, if I liked. I chose that the room should be a brick and steel cell in a prison camp in the mountains and that I should be its occupant. A man called Forster.

CATHERINE: You're accusing me. I don't understand why.

RUPERT: I'm not accusing you. You told me of your life during my absence. I'm telling you of my life at that time. Nothing more. There's no accusation.

CATHERINE: I've got into the habit of imagining things.

RUPERT: Yes.

CATHERINE: You're trying to tell me something.

RUPERT: How I lived at the camp. My room was entered twice a day by my servant – the first time to clean the room, the second time to attend me, the prisoner. I left the room once a day for exercise – alone. I was permitted to walk to the boundary of the compound and return at once. I was allowed to look at the sky. The camp commandant visited me once a week, but as a gesture of faith didn't enter the room. That procedure was followed exactly for the first two years. Now, tell me from that description, Catherine, is that the man you remember?

CATHERINE: Of course not. Never imprisoned – never! No, I think of you as –

RUPERT: Let me go on. In the third year the conditions in the camp altered. I was given more food and a change of bedding. The comforts multiplied. One day I was sent a message saying that if I wanted a woman a young girl could be obtained from the village below the camp. The message came by a junior officer, who assured me that the child would be bathed and deloused before being sent to my room. I refused the offer.

CATHERINE: Because you loved me.

RUPERT: It had nothing to do with love.

CATHERINE: Because you remembered me.

RUPERT: You don't understand, Catherine. I didn't think of you in that place. I didn't think of you at all. If I'd done so, it would have become a place of freedom. In fact, it was a prison.

CATHERINE: Some men would have tried to get out if only by imagination – by memory –

RUPERT: Some men dream away their lives without having to be put behind bars. I'm not one of them.

CATHERINE: You talk like this because we made love only a little while ago. You were always cruel afterwards.

RUPERT: That demand hasn't changed, certainly. I refused the girl at the camp – but not you.

CATHERINE: There is a difference. Take a risk and think back for a moment. You'll remember, I love you.

RUPERT: You love the man your loneliness has created, perhaps.

CATHERINE: Then tell me: what are you now?

RUPERT: A defeated soldier who is allowed to live only to further his disgrace.

CATHERINE: All right! I'll accept that.

[*Then, from all the speakers of a public address system which covers the city, a man's voice speaks.*]

ANNOUNCER: The time is twenty hours. The time is twenty hours. It is now – officially – night.

[*A bell is struck.*]

RUPERT: What is it?

CATHERINE: It comes from the public address system all over the city.

RUPERT: What are they – amplifiers?

CATHERINE: Yes. Rupert, kill your pride – kill it!

RUPERT: Who put up those things?

CATHERINE: John Cadmus. To speak to the people. There are speakers in every street – even all over the hillside in the trees. They make announcements.

RUPERT: Has John Cadmus been here?

CATHERINE: Yes. Very often.

RUPERT: Why?

CATHERINE: I asked him to come the first time. It was a few days after your arrest when he was recalled as Chancellor at the time of the defeat. I asked him to use his authority to have you released. He said it was impossible. The second time he came here without invitation. We sat in this room and talked. I can't remember what about – not about you. After that he came here at irregular intervals but very frequently.

RUPERT: What you're saying, in effect, is that you formed some kind of friendship with him after that first meeting.

CATHERINE: He was kind and often amusing. Sometimes he gave me small gifts. For instance, the last time he brought a string quartet which played Beethoven for three hours. I went to sleep in front of them.

RUPERT: Why didn't you ask him about me? He got a weekly report on my behaviour.

CATHERINE: I didn't want a weekly report on you – to hear of you growing older and sadder and more and more hopeless.

RUPERT: Why not? If it was true.

CATHERINE: I want to know you as you were! If they've changed

you I don't know what I shall do. O God! I remember you, Rupert.
But do you remember me – do you remember me?

[HARRY LANCASTER *has come a little way up the stairs.*]

HARRY: Forgive.

CATHERINE: What is it?

HARRY: There's been a message.

CATHERINE: Well?

HARRY: Over the telephone.

CATHERINE: Yes?

HARRY: The Chancellor is on his way here to see General Forster. His
arrival is imminent. Poppa's waiting to receive him at the door.

CATHERINE: All right, Harry. Thank you. What does he want,
Rupert?

HARRY: Affairs of State, maybe. Ssh!

CATHERINE: Go away, Harry. [*He remains.*] Tonight. Why must he
come tonight? [*She begins to move to the upper room.*]

RUPERT: Where are you going?

CATHERINE: I must dress. Were you expecting him tonight?

RUPERT: No. Were you?

HARRY: There's one you're going to have to tell yourself, Katie. Tell
him he's like the rest of us boys – just not welcome here any more.
All right! I didn't speak – I'm not here.

[CATHERINE *goes into the upper room.*]

This can hardly be the return you imagined in your youth, General.

RUPERT: What's that?

HARRY: I say, when you were a young man you must've thought the
return from war to your native city would be very different.

RUPERT: In what way?

HARRY: Oh, come now. Where is the triumphal drive through the
streets, the heroic music, the garland of war? Where is the howling
mob upping its sweaty nightcaps? Where are the young virgins
casting themselves in front of your jeep?

RUPERT: You're a romantic, Mr Lancaster. I suppose all entertainers
are that.

HARRY: I wonder what it is the world finds so unfunny about you? In my part of professional entertainer you interest me. Suppose I put you in a cage like a wild beast, would they pay their pennies to come and look at you? I doubt that. I doubt it very much.

RUPERT: Please leave me alone.

HARRY: Tell me, sir, is your release unconditional? If so, who is our constant companion?

RUPERT: I'm told he's to protect me from annoyance.

HARRY: Then he's not doing his job, is he? Why don't you call him to order?

RUPERT: I've no authority to do that.

HARRY: Authority. That's an interesting word. Are you sure you don't mean power?

RUPERT: No, Mr Lancaster, I mean authority. I have power. Power to throw you down those stairs, for instance. That remains.

HARRY: Would you resort to violence, General?

RUPERT: You're a small man.

HARRY: Has that anything to do with it?

RUPERT: The use of power? Of course, you fool!

[*From below the stairs* DIDO *calls:* Harry!]

You're being called.

HARRY: All right, honey. I'm talking to what looks like a man. They tell me he's something more, but he looks like a man. I guess the failure to see is in me. Eh, Kate?

[CATHERINE *has come from the upper room. She is dressed. She does not answer Harry.*]

CATHERINE: Is this an amusing dress, Rupert?

HARRY: Even if you think it is, General, you're not supposed to laugh. I once made that mistake. [*He goes down the stair.*]

CATHERINE: There's one good thing about this visit of John Cadmus. We shall know your exact position. What have they told you?

RUPERT: Nothing. What have they told you?

CATHERINE: There was a message this morning giving me the time of your arrival.

RUPERT: Is that all?

CATHERINE: What do you mean?

RUPERT: I thought you must know something more.

CATHERINE: It was enough. To know you were coming back was enough.

[FATHER ANSELM *appears on the stairway.*]

Yes?

ANSELM: The Chancellor is here.

CATHERINE: All right. Bring him up.

[FATHER ANSELM *goes down the stairway.*]

When did you see him last?

RUPERT: Seven years ago. On my way to the camp. Catherine, we really know nothing of what's happening.

CATHERINE: He'll tell us. We'll just let him talk himself out of the house. We'll be alone together soon, and then we can find our way. We've wandered off the road for a while, that's all. It's only to be expected.

[JOHN CADMUS, *assisted by* FATHER ANSELM, *comes up the stairs. He is a man of great age, physically and spiritually wasted by many years spent in the exercise of power.*]

CADMUS: After such a climb as that I always expect to find myself in heaven. [*To Catherine*] Angel! [*He kisses her.*] Somewhere to sit. [CATHERINE *takes him to a chair, and he sits.*] Hullo, Forster.

CATHERINE: Would you like something to drink?

CADMUS: Yes, I would. I'd like my usual warm milk.

CATHERINE [*to Father Anselm*]: Get it.

[FATHER ANSELM *goes down the stairs.*]

CADMUS: As a temporal power, Catherine, you speak with unusual authority to the spiritual. You must attend one of the tea parties I give for my princes of the church.

CATHERINE: They'd eat out of my hand.

CADMUS: As long as there was something in it. Otherwise they'd bite. A good journey, Forster?

RUPERT: Yes, sir.

CADMUS: Did we provide transport suitable to your position?

RUPERT: Three cars, six guards, and an aide.

CADMUS: Excellent. And they brought you safely to this place.

RUPERT: They did. The guards are still here. I say, the guards have stayed on. I was told they are for my protection.

CADMUS: Forster, we all go in mortal danger. Can we even trust the guards? The whisper of ambition is in their hearts without a doubt. Who is to guard the guards? That's an old question which has never been answered.

RUPERT: What am I to understand by it?

CATHERINE: Wait. He never asks questions he can't answer.

CADMUS: Ah! it's possible to breathe up here. Down in the city the smell of corruption becomes insufferable. The stench of the spilt guts of the world is always in the nose. D'you know, Forster, twice in a lifetime I've been brought from retreat to stand over the murdered body of our country. They turn to me. The misfortune of being the father-image. I'm known as Daddy Cadmus now. Did I say I'd like some hot milk?

CATHERINE: It's coming.

CADMUS: You'd imagine the aftermath of war to be depressing, wouldn't you? Not a bit of it. Defeat has resulted in a splendid get-together. At least, socially. The difficulty is to keep them apart. The birth-rate is astounding. Politically we are split exactly down the middle, and however I play the submissive female part we remain distressingly infertile. A few weeks ago it was thought the body-politic might produce a tiny policy, but it was only wind. Seven years married too. But my problems of administration don't interest you.

RUPERT: They might, but I'm out of touch.

CADMUS: Has my gadget spoken to you yet? The amplifiers, I mean.

RUPERT: They announced the time.

CADMUS: They can do better than that. When I'm faced with excitement in the city – they riot, you know – those things pour out music and it works like a charm. The angry fellows have their grievances washed away by the memory of what has been or the thought of what might be. The way to prevent revolt is to stop men living in the present time. Given a sad song they drift off with their wives and sweethearts and resolve their misery in quite the oldest way. That, of course, gives rise to another problem already mentioned. But the human milk supply luckily remains constant.

[FATHER ANSELM *comes up the stairway. He carries a tray on which there is a flask of milk, a drinking glass and a bowl of sugar.*]

From the cow, I hope.

ANSELM: Quite fresh, sir.

CADMUS: Pour it out. Three spoons of sugar.

[FATHER ANSELM *serves the milk.*]

I find a grave distaste for all food now. For instance, this innocent-looking liquid on which I'm compelled to live is actually the glandular secretion of a dying animal. But then, if we were to look too closely at any of our main supports, we'd – [*He stops speaking for a moment and tastes the milk.*] What would happen, Forster? You've had plenty of time to think about such things. Let's have your opinion.

RUPERT: I'm afraid I can't share your obvious horror of material existence.

CADMUS: You can't? That's a pity.

RUPERT: Why a pity?

CADMUS: I'll tell you. [*To* FATHER ANSELM] Thank you.

[FATHER ANSELM *goes down the stairs.*]

Catherine, would you like to leave us?

CATHERINE: No.

CADMUS: Very well. First of all, Forster, I can take no credit for fetching you out of prison today. If I had my way you'd remain shut up for the rest of your life.

RUPERT: That's very interesting. Who am I to thank for this – freedom?

CADMUS: Freedom? You're back here for a purpose. It's three shots a penny at you now, Forster. But I'm confusing you. You may or may not know that modern government is based not on theory or even practical policy but on emotion. This country has been compelled to accept that system of government from the conquerors. It is known as democratic. It means that I have an opposition party. This, of course, is a great novelty. My opposition party is liberal minded, and they have all the savagery possessed by good men. They say it is love but they bare their teeth when pronouncing the word. It is these men who have brought you back.

RUPERT: Why?

CADMUS: We're now an autonomous state again. The occupying forces were withdrawn some weeks ago. For seven years we've been able to refer our major problems to foreigners. Now, once again, as in the war, we're on our own. We have to make up our minds about bigger things than the city drainage. One of these bigger things, my opposition tells me, is to find out who was responsible for this country losing the war. There has to be a man, Forster. Something they can stretch out and touch, which breathes and reasons and answers questions. They can't put Bad Luck in the dock, Forster, but they can put you there.

RUPERT: I'm to stand some kind of trial?

CADMUS: That's the intention. It's to be a big show. It'll take place in the Parliament House. Your accuser is the State and its People. The charge will be treason arising from cowardice in the face of the enemy. Your behaviour during that last battle in the East appears to give certain grounds for such an accusation.

RUPERT: Do you expect me to defend myself – to you, here and now?

CADMUS: No.

RUPERT: You said – I think – that you would not have brought me back.

CADMUS: I did say that. But these men who've asked for your return have the country behind them. So, you see, I can't refuse to have you brought to trial. It would look, you must admit, as if I defended your behaviour. And I can't do that. It seems on the face of it a reasonable request.

RUPERT: My section of the Eastern front was comparatively small. Too small, I should've thought, to have merited consideration as a factor of absolute defeat.

CADMUS: That has nothing to do with it. You're a man. More, you're Rupert Forster. These good men must give the country something worth having. Something the butcher, the baker, and the candlestick-maker – in their guilty sickness – can recognize as the cause of defeat and disgrace. Those ordinary people want to go out into the world and say, I wasn't responsible for the war starting or for the war ending in defeat: it was that man Forster. He was tried, you know, and found guilty. That's why the people of this country will back the group of men who oppose me. You are about to be taken into the great mouth of that modern monster, the Demagogue.

RUPERT: The result of the trial is a foregone conclusion, then.

CADMUS: Not at all. If it takes place I shall do everything to ensure that it's fairly conducted.

RUPERT: What do you mean, if it takes place?

CADMUS: Catherine, a social fact of some importance to you. I can allow no one to leave this house for thirty-six hours or so. No one, that is, except myself. And I must go straightaway. [*He rises.*] I had luncheon with the actor, Constant, today. I asked him how he would go about telling a man that it was necessary, indeed imperative, that he should kill himself.

RUPERT: What did he say?

CADMUS: He said drama was, of course, inherent in such a situation for the essence of drama is the dilemma of the central heroic figure. He was very interesting about that.

RUPERT: Did he advise you further?

CADMUS: Yes.

RUPERT: May we not be told?

CADMUS: Certainly. Constant went on to say that if he was to play such a scene in the theatre the prosaic details would be sufficient.

RUPERT: Will you not tell me those details?

CADMUS: I was about to do so. The time: within thirty-six hours. That is, by dawn of the day after tomorrow.

RUPERT: The place?

CADMUS: Within this house, secretly. The means – [*He has taken a jewelled box from his pocket.*] I have removed the dismal original package. Look upon this box as a gift, Forster. The substance within, I'm told, is also used for extracting gold from its ore. A factor which, applied philosophically, may be of comfort to you.

[RUPERT *takes the box.*]

CATHERINE: You don't take it seriously. You're smiling.

RUPERT: Am I? Why didn't you get her out of the room, Cadmus?

CADMUS: He takes it seriously, Catherine, and you must bring yourself to believe it is right.

CATHERINE: Right!

CADMUS: The thing to do. You must bring yourself to believe it is necessary.

CATHERINE: But why, John, why?

CADMUS: Because I cannot allow this trial to take place. I love this country, Catherine, and I believe that given a few years I can make it again seem worthy of a place in Europe. But not if I have this trial forced on me. The mud that is thrown won't only hit Forster. It will stick to every man, woman, and child of this nation. That is why I will not allow the trial to take place. That is why Forster must kill himself.

CATHERINE: You've no authority to give such an order.

CADMUS: It wasn't an order. It was a request. I thought that was understood.

RUPERT: Perfectly.

CATHERINE: A request. Is that all? Can we do anything else for you?

CADMUS: Nothing. Will someone help me down? I've a horror of falling nowadays.

CATHERINE: You're not to touch him, Rupert! You've done the wrong thing, John. He's safe with me.

CADMUS: Any complete protection – even one of love, Catherine – is also an effective prison. Yes, he's safe with you.

[*He takes Rupert's arm and they go down the stairs.* CATHERINE *remains alone until* RUPERT *returns.*]

CATHERINE: Can you ask for a man's life as simply as you'd ask for his advice?

RUPERT: Yes, you can. I've done it. With many lives.

CATHERINE: You were their commander.

RUPERT: Yet the final decision remained with each man. We never really command. We only – like Cadmus – request.

CATHERINE: And you were obeyed. Why is John so sure that you'll obey him?

RUPERT [*standing beside the bronze helmet*]: I found this helmet beneath the tracks of my carrier in battle. I picked it up and a skull rattled inside. After hundreds of years he'd come to the surface, and we were still fighting over the same ground. Nothing had been gained since the day he'd fallen. I was attempting with my armoured vehicle only to do what he'd tried to do with his armoured head and his antique sword. His end on that field was death, mine was disgrace. But I was left as surely and eternally in that clay-cold earth as was this comrade-in-arms of mine. Our intentions must now be effected by another man in another time: it no longer rests in us. They've taken away the means of achievement, my soldiers. I can't stretch out to the future because I've nothing to use. Cadmus knows that. When I was young I could see far into the future and that makes a man alive. When he cannot see – as at this moment – then a man may as well grant such a request. Cadmus knows I'll do what he asks because there is no future action for me. He knows there is nothing here – nothing anywhere to detain me.

CATHERINE: I am here.

RUPERT: I'm no longer in love with you, Catherine. Such things need to be said. When they are true and the time has come, such things need to be said.

CATHERINE: You have a great regard for the truth. I knew the truth all through today – but I pretended that you still loved me. Couldn't you have done that? Truth of your kind is for the very young – not for me.

RUPERT: Did you want me to lie?

CATHERINE: It would've been for such a short time. John said within thirty-six hours.

RUPERT: I gave you the truth in the past.

CATHERINE: Now you give it to John Cadmus.

RUPERT: I loved you, Catherine.

CATHERINE: In the past. What do you want?

[*She speaks to* DIDO, *who has come a little way up the stairs.*]

DIDO: Can I come up here? My honour is imperilled.

CATHERINE: What does that mean? Harry?

DIDO: Yes. He talked about God, social injustice – he cried a little there – war and love of mankind. What he meant, of course, was love of his own kind. I want to go home.

CATHERINE: And they won't let you out.

DIDO: The men at the door said I stay. So here I am.

RUPERT: I'm sorry. It's my fault.

DIDO: You're General Forster, aren't you? My experiences with soldiers have so far been unfortunate. [*She holds out the palm of her hand.*] That scar was a mortar shell fragment in the street fighting when I was a baby. [*She touches her face.*] This, a broken bottle in bar-room fighting when I was somewhat older.

RUPERT: I hope our acquaintance – however short – will be more peaceful.

DIDO: I thought you were dead, but Harry said you were up here. You know, he doesn't like you.

RUPERT: I know. What's your name?

DIDO: It doesn't matter.

CATHERINE: Yes, it does. She's called Dido.

DIDO: Please don't laugh. Blame my father. He was an archaeologist. Always grubbing in the past. Disgusting occupation. I say, am I bothering you?

CATHERINE: No.

DIDO: Well, with those men on the door it looks as if I'll be here for a time.

CURTAIN

ACT TWO

The scene is the same. The time: the following day. It is night.

The room is in darkness. A small film projector has been set up, and is in action with a film showing on the screen.

> [*Before the screen in the darkness sit* RUPERT, CATHERINE, DIDO, FATHER ANSELM, *and* MATTHEW SANGOSSE. HARRY *is standing by the projector as operator. The film is in its final sequence. It ends.*]

HARRY: Will somebody put up the lights?

> [*The lights of the room are put on by* MATTHEW. RUPERT *and* DIDO *are shown to be sitting together –* DIDO *on the floor with her head resting against Rupert's knees.* CATHERINE, *turned away from the screen, is observing them as she must have been in the darkness.*]

That's all, everybody.

ANSELM: Thank you, Harry. It was most enjoyable.

HARRY: It's all right, Poppa. Anything I can do to make our enforced stay in this house tolerable – just call on me.

ANSELM: I thought the girl was rather like you, Miss Morgen.

HARRY: You're being spoken to, honey.

RUPERT: She's asleep.

HARRY: Well, I'm damned!

> [FATHER ANSELM *laughs.*]

CATHERINE: Wake her, Rupert.

> [RUPERT *ruffles Dido's hair.*]

RUPERT: Wake up.

DIDO: What?

RUPERT: Wake up! The show's over. Do you want to be locked in?

DIDO: God! Sorry, everybody. Sorry, Harry.

HARRY: It's all right.

DIDO: Did I miss much of it?

HARRY: I don't know. Did you?

DIDO: From what I saw of it I'd say it was funny and old. The women! Did they ever look like that? Did they ever behave like that?

HARRY: They did. Just twenty years ago.

DIDO: The young ones look sort of muddy – and don't they grin a lot? Was there so much to laugh about in those days? [*She suddenly looks round at the others.*] I suppose all of you were young at that time.

HARRY: Yes. Yes, we were. Around that time.

DIDO: So that's your masterpiece, Harry.

HARRY: It is. You must see it some time.

CATHERINE: Shall we go down to supper? It's ready.

HARRY: Let's do that. There's always eating left for us. I must clear up this junk first.

CATHERINE: Come along, Father – and Matthew.

RUPERT [*to Harry*]: I'll help you with this.

HARRY: I can manage. All right, pack up the screen, please.

[CATHERINE, *with* MATTHEW *and* FATHER ANSELM, *goes below.* HARRY *begins to dismantle the projector and* RUPERT *the screen.* DIDO *stands beside Rupert.*]

I'll not bother to rewind.

RUPERT: What's that?

HARRY: The film. I'm not bothering – oh, forget it. From all the sense it made tonight I might just as well run it backwards next time. Not that there'll be a next time.

DIDO: How long since you last showed it?

HARRY: Long time. Maybe ten years. I don't know.

DIDO: Why did you show it tonight?

HARRY: I thought – wrongly, of course – that it might relax the tension for a couple of hours. I thought it'd give Kate something to look at besides you two. You'll forgive me asking this: what the hell are you up to?

RUPERT: Where do you want this? [*He refers to the cinema screen.*]

HARRY: I'll take it down with me. For God's sake, Forster, couldn't you have kept this sort of thing until we were all let out of this place? I know you've been shut up for seven years, but you could surely have waited a while longer. Until you could have got this – this girl out of here. Away from Kate.

RUPERT: Anything else I can do? With this stuff, I mean.

HARRY: Not a thing. Do you think since you came back last night you've been playing fair?

RUPERT: Fair?

HARRY: Look. I'll try to explain. Don't you think it would have been better to pretend for a while? Pretend with Kate that everything is just as it has been. Christ, man, you're breaking her heart! Is that simple enough for you?

RUPERT: There! Everything packed. You can go down.

HARRY: All right. But just tell me this: how much longer are we going to be shut up here?

RUPERT: Not much longer.

HARRY: What's the reason for it anyway? I suppose we're the only people to know you're back and they don't want the news to leak. What are they going to do – suddenly release you into an unsuspecting world as the latest saviour? If so, I take cover. Who's the enemy going to be this time? Or haven't you decided yet?

RUPERT: I have to act on my decisions, Lancaster. Unlike you I don't make up my mind and regard it as an end in itself.

HARRY: Me! I'm just an old dreamy-eyes. But I don't murder.

RUPERT: When you have you'll find it simpler to tell the innocent from the guilty.

HARRY: You'll go to hell, Forster.

RUPERT: That, too? You go to supper.

DIDO: Harry, I'm sorry – sincerely sorry – that I went to sleep during your picture.

HARRY: The difficulty with you, sweetheart – and with him – is that you're honest about yourself. I'm sorry, but I've lost the talent for doing that sort of thing.

RUPERT: Can you carry all that?

[HARRY *is laden with cinema equipment.*]

HARRY: Sure. I'll tell Kate you're on your way. [*He goes down the stairs.*]

RUPERT: It's sad.

DIDO: Harry?

RUPERT: He has an affectionate nature which overrules his moral judgement. Because of what he believes he must censure me for being what I am – and you for accepting me – but he comes near to liking us. That conflict can upset a man.

DIDO: Surely that was a damned bad film.

RUPERT: I thought so.

DIDO: He told me you commanded the soldiers in it.

RUPERT: I believe I did. It was in my comic-opera days. We'd no other use for the army then.

DIDO: You found a better use for it later.

RUPERT: It was put to its proper use.

DIDO: All right. I don't need convincing.

RUPERT: I'm sorry. Anyway, that's all over.

DIDO: So what are you going to do? Live in retirement? Say, a house in the country, your feet up of an evening, early to bed. You'll be healthy all right, but I've doubts as to your wealth and wisdom. What else? You'll be able to walk round your estate in the morning and again in the evening. If you get very bored perhaps you could shoot a small animal every so often. Do I make the prospect sound attractive?

RUPERT: No.

DIDO: I wasn't trying to. As an alternative you might make it up with Catherine, stay on here, and – as Harry suggested – pretend.

RUPERT: I'm not good at that.

DIDO: No good at pretending! Then I'd say your future is about as bright as a blind man's holiday.

RUPERT: You're very encouraging. What about you?

DIDO: People like me don't think about the future. We don't matter, you see. If we survive – that's good. If we go out – well, there's not much harm done. Mind, if somebody tries to put us out before we think it's time we fight. What for? Just to stay alive to see one more day end, have one more hot bath, be made love to once more, hear one more tune we've heard before and got fond of. This is apt to make us a nuisance about the place, but you people are getting better at making bigger gadgets to end all that.

RUPERT: In a little while they'll let you out of here. What will you do?

DIDO: Go back where I came from. Pick up where I left off. You're the problem. You can't pick up where you left off. Have you got any friends who might start a nice new war for you to fight?

RUPERT: There seems to be difficulty in financing such a project at the moment.

DIDO: We might start a subscription fund.

RUPERT: Do you think Harry would give something?

DIDO: You know, he might – just to get you out of here. That man's got principles, but he can sometimes step over them. Ought we to go down?

RUPERT: Not yet.

DIDO: I don't want to go down. I'm out of my depth with Catherine. I suppose I should be out of my depth with you.

RUPERT: Aren't you?

DIDO: No. And it's obvious to everybody. But Catherine – she's in a hell of a position. Do you know, we've talked to each other all day. Couldn't you try talking to her for a while? It's not easy, I suppose, but surely there's something left between you. There must be. It'd be too horrible if there wasn't even kindness left. Won't you try?

RUPERT: Why do you think I've spent my time with you today?

DIDO: Well, Harry's not your sort – nor are the boys. Catherine – difficult. That leaves me. You had no choice.

RUPERT: I could've shut myself up – alone.

DIDO: Yes, you could have done that. Look! I know I'm young but may I give you a bit of advice?

RUPERT: If you want to.

DIDO: You're about to make some kind of confession to me. Well, don't do it. I don't want to hear.

RUPERT: Very well.

DIDO: I don't want to get mixed up. I don't want to have any influence on what you think or do or say. I'm free, and I want to stay like that. It's been very nice and interesting talking to you, but now I must be getting back.

RUPERT: To what? Somebody down in the city? Are you in love?

DIDO: That's the point. I'm not. I've told you, I'm free and I want to stay free.

RUPERT: What's the danger here?

DIDO: Oh, don't be such a bloody fool! You are.

[RUPERT *laughs*.]

It's not funny! Think of Catherine. For seven years she's been shut up in her love for you. Everything she has done – everything she has thought and believed has been decided by that love. Was it worth it? I don't think so. She may get free again in time – she's brave, you can see that – but life's too short, too damned short for these stretches of hard labour.

RUPERT: I'm convinced.

DIDO: You are? Good. Start work to get me out of here.

[CATHERINE *comes up the stairway*.]

CATHERINE: Aren't you coming down to have some food?

RUPERT: I'm not hungry.

CATHERINE: Can't you persuade him, Miss Morgen?

[DIDO *shakes her head*.]

RUPERT: Is the telephone down there?

CATHERINE: Yes.

RUPERT: I want to speak to Cadmus. There's no reason to keep this girl here another night. I'm going to ask Cadmus to let her go home. [*He goes down the stairs*.]

CATHERINE: Do you want to go?

DIDO: Yes, please.

CATHERINE: Where will you make for?

DIDO: Back to my room.

CATHERINE: What's it like?

DIDO: My room? Oh, it's fine. It belongs just to me. I don't have to share it as you share this place.

CATHERINE: Where is it?

DIDO: In a part you wouldn't know. The house looks over – or rather, leans over – the river. I couldn't be more strange to you if I came from the moon, could I?

CATHERINE [she smiles]: No. My manner towards you last night when you arrived with Harry wasn't welcoming. I'm sorry.

DIDO: I understand.

CATHERINE: I suppose you do. Harry tell you about Rupert and me?

DIDO: In a way.

CATHERINE: Rupert's had a very bad time and he's desperately uncertain of the future. We mustn't blame him for what he does. You won't do that, will you?

DIDO: No, I won't blame him.

CATHERINE: He likes you very much so won't you stay on?

DIDO: No.

CATHERINE: For tonight, at least.

DIDO: No. I want to go home.

CATHERINE: Is there something urgent calling you back?

DIDO: No. I just want to get out of here.

CATHERINE: Please stay. For my sake.

DIDO: For you?

CATHERINE: Yes.

DIDO: I'll stay for you.

CATHERINE: You funny girl. Do you make a habit of the unexpected? Anyway, thank you. Would you like a change of clothes? You've been in those since you arrived.

DIDO: I haven't got any others.

CATHERINE: Well, you didn't come prepared to stay. What can we do? I know. My maid has some very pretty things. Run along and see her. I'm sure she'll help us.

DIDO: I don't want to.

CATHERINE: Now don't be silly. She dresses very well.

DIDO: Where do I find her?

CATHERINE: She'll be in her room.

[HARRY *has come from below. He has a glass of wine in his hand.*]

And whilst you're there get her to comb your hair.

HARRY: Excuse me, miss, but you're beautiful. You should be in pictures.

[DIDO *passes Harry and goes down the stairs.*]

Is Forster calling off the watch-dogs?

CATHERINE: What do you mean?

HARRY: He's on the telephone down there. He asked me to get the number. Didn't want to give his sacred name.

CATHERINE: He's speaking to Cadmus about something. Harry, why did you tell that girl about the break between Rupert and me?

HARRY: Dear Kate, I didn't tell her. Not in so many words. It's been pretty obvious to everybody that – well, that –

CATHERINE: That he's not come home to me. Yes, I suppose so.

HARRY: You're putting up a good fight, Kate. I'm proud of you.

CATHERINE: It's not that he doesn't want to love me any more. It's really that in losing everything he lost me.

HARRY: Yes, that's the way it is. Kate, answer me two questions.

CATHERINE: What are they?

HARRY: One – why did Cadmus come here last night?

CATHERINE: To welcome Rupert back.

HARRY: Two – what big fish are you expecting to catch with my little girl friend as bait? You're not going to answer that, are you?

CATHERINE: No.

HARRY: Here's an alternative. What are you fighting to keep?

CATHERINE: Nothing for myself. That surprises you, doesn't it? You've always thought me possessive. It's not altogether true. I don't like waste. There are some things worth keeping because they're rare and fine. Not for yourself. I suppose it's like having children. They're never yours – as a possession – but they're worth having and sending out to be themselves. That's me at this moment. I'm not fighting to keep something, Harry, but I am fighting to save something.

HARRY: To save something from going to waste?

CATHERINE: Just that.

[HARRY *looks into his wine-glass.*]

HARRY: Empty. Yet if I bring this and the bottle below into union it will breed kindness in me. So down I go.

CATHERINE: Don't get too kind, Harry.

HARRY: Oh, Poppa and Doc asked me to say that they've gone to bed. [HARRY *and* RUPERT *meet on the stairs.*] If you don't want to keep on meeting me like this, Forster, you'd better do something about getting us all out of here.

RUPERT: Are you coming down?

HARRY: I am. [*He goes down the stairs.*]

[RUPERT *comes up into the room.*]

CATHERINE: Did you speak to Cadmus?

RUPERT: He's not at the Chancellery, but he's expected back within an hour. I left a message.

CATHERINE: The girl's staying.

RUPERT: What?

CATHERINE: I asked her to stay. For a little longer. That's what you wanted, isn't it? Rupert, it's not a sign of weakness to have someone with you through these hours. Why be afraid of showing that you're human? It's a failing the rest of us admit. Why not you? There have been times in the past when I've been able to comfort you. I don't remember them as moments of weakness.

RUPERT: Catherine, I didn't want it to end like this with you. Believe that. But I had to tell you.

CATHERINE: I know that, now.

RUPERT: I hate lying. Anyway, I'm no good at it.

CATHERINE: I wanted you to love me – not merely be faithful to me. That was before. Now I only want you to live.

RUPERT: Why try to save me? I'm useless now. I've been tamed by long captivity.

CATHERINE: That's not true. You've just forgotten how to fight, I think. And you're mistaking the enemy.

RUPERT: I don't think so.

CATHERINE: The real enemy is the darkness you hope to bring on yourself tomorrow morning.

RUPERT: There's a word for it.

CATHERINE: I know. I know from the past seven years. There was the early morning when I didn't want to wake, the sound of my footsteps going about this house, the end of each year. At those times I longed to stop fighting. But I believed it would be wrong to give in. Sinful, if you like.

RUPERT: In my profession death can never be a moral problem. You were always brave, Catherine.

CATHERINE: You've never thought of your absence in that way, have you?

RUPERT: No. No, I've not.

CATHERINE: Don't let it influence you. Live for yourself. Face this trial. How can they condemn you?

RUPERT: Very easily. I failed in what I set out to do.

CATHERINE: They'll not sentence you.

RUPERT: Perhaps not. Then I'll have to live. Where's the girl?

CATHERINE: Have you told her? About John's visit last night and the trial.

RUPERT: Of course not. Why should she be involved?

CATHERINE: Yet you want her to stay. You watch her. You wait for her to speak. What do you hope to hear?

RUPERT: I don't know.

CATHERINE: Something that can never come from me. So I asked her to stay. She may casually – without any thought at all – help you.

RUPERT: I think it's unlikely.

CATHERINE: You have to trust someone at this time. I'll leave it to the girl.

[DIDO *has come up the stairs and into the room. She is now in a simple dress and her hair has recently been brushed and combed.*]

DIDO: Be careful. I'm here.

CATHERINE: So you are. [*To Rupert*] What did you arrange on the telephone?

RUPERT: That Cadmus should call me when he got back.

DIDO: Is that about me?

RUPERT: For permission to leave this place.

DIDO: I always came and went as I pleased before I met you people. Anyway, I thought you wanted me to stay.

CATHERINE: I do.

DIDO: Well, I'm still here, so what's the fuss about? Are you going?

[CATHERINE *has moved to the stairs.*]

Do you want me to come with you?

CATHERINE: No. Stay. [*She goes down the stairs.*]

DIDO: Well, I'm back. Looking different, but don't let that put you off. What were we talking about?

RUPERT: I can't remember. What have you done to yourself?

DIDO: She thought I was looking grubby. I probably was. No pride, that's what's wrong with me.

RUPERT: It's very late. Don't you want to go to bed?

DIDO: No. If I do I'll have just got in when there'll be a very small knock on the door, and then a very small American voice will ask to come in. Whatever I say, in it will come. It'll want to know if I'm all right and it'll move about the room for a while – somehow getting near to the bed. When I feel its breath I'll say, Go to hell! and off it will go – hurt. At least, that's what happened last night. I'll stay up. What's going to be left to me? By Catherine. I overheard. 'I'll leave it to the girl.' That's what she said.

RUPERT: You mustn't bother your head about it.

DIDO: It's not my head that's bothered – it's my heart. I like her, you see. I'm sorry for her too.

RUPERT: Save your pity.

DIDO: What did you say?

RUPERT: I said, save your pity.

DIDO: For you?

RUPERT: I don't need it.

DIDO: Who is there left? Harry. He'd love it. But not tonight. What's the matter?

RUPERT: A little while ago you said it would be horrible if there was nothing left between Catherine and me. Well, there is that. I don't care to hear her pitied.

DIDO: Sorry. Forgive me asking this, but I've a conventional mind: why didn't you marry her?

RUPERT: Because of my job. I was always away. She's not the sort of person who could've lived the life.

DIDO: That's not a reason. That's an excuse. Tell me the reason, please.

RUPERT: Very well. It was unwise to commit myself to another. Not from a sense of independence. Nothing so simple. One of my predecessors in war, an Irishman, once said: 'All the business of war, and indeed all the business of life, is to endeavour to find out what you don't know by what you do.' And he went on: 'That's what I called "guessing what was at the other side of the hill".' That's how he put it, and that has been my job – to guess what was at the far side of the hill. Towards the end my sense for doing that was highly developed, but only because I kept myself free. Were I committed I saw the other side of the hill with eyes not entirely my own. Do you understand?

DIDO: Let me tell you something before you go on. I'm not frightened of you.

RUPERT: Why did you decide to stay?

DIDO: Because of Catherine. I don't have to help or comfort many of my friends, you know, because none of us have much to lose. But people like Catherine, who've had a lot and lost it – well, that's new to me. And she was so damned proud when she asked me to stay. People are too often humble. She was fighting like hell at that moment. Suddenly I felt – well, this is as good a point as any for me to stop running away. I'm on the edge of a trap, but it can't be helped.

RUPERT: A trap? Do you mean a conspiracy?

DIDO: No, I mean a trap. The thing you catch wild animals in. Look! Now, look here. You kept yourself free because of your job. Well, I kept myself free because I'm not strong enough, good enough, or wise enough to have another living, loving person with me. But the trap's always there. You – I've only to discover something about you – you've only to tell me something and I'm caught.

RUPERT: Tell you what?

DIDO: How do I know until I hear it? What was it shut the trap on Catherine all these years?

RUPERT: You think I'm preparing the same for you?

DIDO: Nobody – not even the proudest person – knows when their cry for help goes out. It may not even be spoken by you. When I was a kid there was a boy and he went to the war. He came back from the fighting earlier than was expected. I went to meet him at the East Railway Station, and it was there the trap was sprung. He'd come back without his eyes. I cut myself loose from that one easily enough, but as I get older it's more difficult. Everywhere I go there are the unhappy and the aimless waiting for me to put out my hand and walk into that trap made of human arms. Ach! this loving business.

[HARRY *has appeared on the stairs. He carries a glass of whisky which he is careful not to spill.*]

DIDO: What do you want?

HARRY: Just to know if you're all right.

DIDO: How do I look?

HARRY: Different. You tired?

DIDO: So I look tired.

HARRY: I didn't say so. You going to bed?

DIDO: Not yet.

HARRY: You're all right.

DIDO: Yes.

HARRY: Sorry about this, but I feel responsible – bringing you here.

DIDO: Don't get that on your conscience as well, Harry.

HARRY: You're all right, then.

DIDO: I'm all right. [*In silence she stares at Harry. He goes down the stairs.*] Why do I do it? He means it kindly. Always has. He picked me up last night in that bar because he thought I was down on my luck. But he was really looking for somebody to do him a good turn. And you, Rupert. Catherine kept herself and this place for you in all kindness. You refused it. What's the matter with us? What are we afraid of losing? You know, we must think very highly of ourselves to keep ourselves so free.

RUPERT: You're young. You won't be free for long. You'll have to commit yourself and love because you're a woman.

DIDO: It's an easy excuse for weakness. You kept free for years. What's the secret? Being a man?

RUPERT: That and having an objective.

DIDO: Something you fought for in that war of yours.

RUPERT: Yes.

DIDO: They said it was for your country and for people like me.

RUPERT: It was for myself. Not for Cadmus or country or you, but myself. To impose myself.

DIDO: They say that's wrong. They say we should live, suffer, and finally die for others.

RUPERT: Yes, that's what they say.

DIDO: You don't believe it's true. Well, what do you believe?

RUPERT: The night before that last battle I still believed that I could reach a point of achievement never before known to a man. The way I chose was conquest by war. Some men need an art to fulfil themselves. Saints need a religion. I had to pursue a triumph of arms. The greatest the world has ever known. By that I believed I could become myself, the man I was intended to be.

DIDO: But whatever you believed, you were caught like everybody. You were caught in that battle.

RUPERT: Not by man. No man could have trapped me at that time.

DIDO: You were caught. I heard about it, don't forget. The papers were full of it. The radio chattered day after day.

RUPERT: Did anyone defend me?

DIDO: Not that I remember. But I was young – seven years ago I was about fourteen.

RUPERT: Just the age to have been there. It might have been you.

DIDO: Seven years ago.

RUPERT: It was a fine morning. The action was a small one along the main route of advance. It would never have found its way into the history books. The town lay in the bend of a river. I intended to take the place by a *coup de main*. The main enemy forces had evacuated the town and were in prepared positions on the far side of the river. My intention was to go in at dawn and take the town at my leisure through the day, but at dusk, with the full weight of my force, to establish two bridgeheads over the river and attempt a crossing that night: on the supposition that the enemy would expect a break between the attack on the town and the river crossing. You understand? It was to be a very beautiful battle, having an elegance difficult to achieve with the use of armoured forces. I was satisfied with the preparations, and at dawn the attack went in. I led in my command tank. We were not delayed by infantry movements as the infantrymen were on the flanks moving with us and not intended to engage, but to save themselves for the river-crossing at night. On reaching the town I halted my force preparatory to its dispersal for street by street occupation. My own tank was halted beside a small church. I got down and walked the length of the street ahead alone. The place was deserted and there was no indication of the roads being mined. It seemed safe to proceed. I went back to my tank and climbed in. I had picked up the microphone of my transmitting set – I was using open communication – and I was about to give the order to continue the advance

215

when the church door opened. I was shocked by the noise in the silence, and I turned. A little boy had come from the church and was standing on the steps. He put his hand to his mouth – oh, as if to put in a sweet – but it was a whistle he held. He blew the whistle and at once the children were upon us. Hundreds of them. They came from the church, from the houses in the street and from far off down the street itself. They rolled like a wave towards us, screaming and shouting, some armed with sticks, some carrying flags. Reaching us they beat themselves against the sides of our tanks. I saw my commanders and their crews laughing at them, cheering them on, encouraging them in their attempts to scramble over the armour. We might have been liberators and not an attacking force. Was I the only man to see the danger? We were virtually immobilized, for they were everywhere, even beneath our tracks. The laughter of my men became louder. Our concentration was broken. The attack – timed by seconds to co-ordination – was flinging itself to pieces. My central armoured force was the governing factor of movement. Delay it and the two infantry groups became as ineffective as naked men. The boy who had come first from the church had clambered on to my tank. He was black-haired and black-eyed and he carried a wooden sword which he swung above his head. He shouted something which I didn't understand, and then spat at me. That was no provocation for what I did: I had already decided. I stretched out and drew his head to my shoulder like a lover, and shot him in the mouth. I took him by the hair of his shattered head and held him up for my men to see. They understood. The shooting began. They also used knives to cut them free from the armour. The note of the children's cry changed and was in mercy drowned as the motors started up and we moved forward.

DIDO: They say four hundred were found dead.

RUPERT: Four hundred. Do they say that? I'd no idea.

DIDO: What was the place?

RUPERT: It was a children's colony, I was told later. They were of all nationalities. Some of the enemy, some of our own, herded together by the shuttle of armies. You always get such things in modern war. Nobody's discovered what they were about that morning. Was it a reckless imitation of their fathers and older brothers? Were they put up to it by unscrupulous commanders? Or had those children reached a point from which there is no further retreat and a stand – against whatever odds – must at last be made?

DIDO: They say you're a coward, you know.

RUPERT: I know.

DIDO: It's not true. What is true, then?

[CATHERINE *and* JOHN CADMUS *come into the room by way of the* *stairs.* CADMUS *is in evening dress.*]

CADMUS: I got your message, Forster. Forgive the fancy dress but I didn't wait to change.

RUPERT: I was prepared to speak to you on the telephone.

CADMUS: Impossible. I never hold two-way conversations on that instrument. It allows for great ambiguity of meaning. Who is this?

CATHERINE: Miss Morgen. A friend of Harry Lancaster.

CADMUS: How do you do? What have you been talking to Forster about, Miss Morgen, until this late hour? Has he been telling you stories of his battles? He's a great fellow. We shan't see his like again. But we must thank the Lord we're not a couple of his soldiers. They tell me he has them drilled until the blood boils in their tails.

DIDO: Has he got any soldiers now?

CADMUS: Not at the moment. But he will have – he will have. Glorious legions at his command fighting for a nobler cause than we can give him.

DIDO: You mean when he's dead.

CADMUS: Yes, I did mean that. Who are you?

DIDO: Dido Morgen. Don't bother! I know who you are.

CADMUS: There is an old-fashioned idea that extreme youth and, if I may say so, beauty –

DIDO: I'm not beautiful.

CADMUS: No, you're not. I'm so sorry. Never mind. Perhaps you're clever instead. Are you?

DIDO: No.

CADMUS: Oh, dear! Neither beautiful nor clever. You're kind-hearted, that's what it is. That's the gift God gave you. To understand your fellow beings.

DIDO: That's it.

CADMUS: Catherine – Forster, will one of you disengage me from this conversation, please?

DIDO: I'll go.

CADMUS: No, don't go. Catherine, would you do a little errand for me?

CATHERINE: What is it you want?

CADMUS: You haven't forgiven me, I see.

CATHERINE: What do you want me to do for you?

CADMUS: Go to the car, outside at the door, and ask the driver for my benzedrine tablets. I shall want to take one in about five minutes.

CATHERINE: Very well. In about five minutes.

CADMUS: It's very good of you.

[CATHERINE *goes down the stairs.*]

Even at my age we play the game. She sees through that device to get her away for a while, and from the first I know she'll see through it. Yet we observe the convention. You, Miss Morgen, wouldn't do that, would you?

DIDO: No.

CADMUS: Then you're made of the same stuff as revolutionaries. Unlike poor Catherine. So intensely vulnerable by her love of life. I detest vulnerable people, don't you?

DIDO: I like her very much.

CADMUS: Oh, you've mistaken me. I was speaking generally. I love Catherine. Surely everyone does. I mean, rather, that I find it difficult to like people for whom I feel pity.

DIDO: Yes, that's true. So do I.

CADMUS: Good! A point of agreement. I am pleased!

DIDO: Are you?

CADMUS: Do you like Forster?

DIDO: Kind of.

CADMUS: Then you can't be sorry for him.

DIDO: Should I be? Look! I don't know anything. All right? I'm the girl you see on the edge of the crowd at a street accident. It's got nothing to do with me. I just happened to be there. I don't want to be a witness. All right?

CADMUS: What did you want to speak to me about, Forster?

RUPERT: Miss Morgen. Is it necessary for her to be shut up here? She came with Lancaster and it seems senseless for her to be virtually imprisoned. She can have no influence on your plans.

CADMUS: No influence. She can have no influence, you say.

RUPERT: None. May she go home?

CADMUS: Certainly.

DIDO: Thank you very much.

CADMUS: At once, if she wishes.

DIDO: We just wanted your permission. Liberty consists of doing what you want to do when you want to do it. That's in the books. I don't want to go yet. But it's good to know I can leave when I wish.

CADMUS: My car will take you back. Don't you think it would be wise to go at once?

DIDO: No, I don't.

CADMUS: Go away! I want to speak to Forster alone.

DIDO [she laughs]: No conventional excuses for me. Go away, he says.

CADMUS: And I mean it. Also keep Catherine below for a time. I'm sure you've something in common to talk about.

DIDO: Yes, we have. [She goes down the stairs.]

CADMUS: Who is she?

RUPERT: Lancaster picked her up yesterday and brought her here.

CADMUS: Yes, but who is she?

RUPERT: One of the people you govern.

CADMUS: Forgive my astonishment. Are there many like that, I wonder? Is it a volcano I'm sitting on and not, as I'd supposed, a dung-hill?

RUPERT: It might be wise to reconsider your position in such a light.

CADMUS: What does that mean? Can it mean your own position?

RUPERT: Certainly it can mean that.

CADMUS: That's very interesting. But there's not much time, Forster, for a detailed reconsideration. When I saw you last night you were content with my proposal. You're not content now?

RUPERT: No, sir.

CADMUS: Why not, damn you?

RUPERT: What are you going to do if I don't use this stuff? [*He has taken the jewelled box from his pocket.*]

CADMUS: What can I do?

RUPERT: There's always assassination.

CADMUS: Don't be so tiresome. From the facts I gave you last night you must know that's impossible. There's only one course I can take: to produce you for trial. I'm asking you to make yourself unavailable. Something's occurred which makes you unwilling to do that, if I understand you correctly, but I'm now only asking you to make up your mind, Forster.

RUPERT: Where do I go if I'm still alive and kicking after dawn this morning?

CADMUS: You'll be taken to the military prison in the city. The place the soldiers laughingly call Arcady. I shall make a statement that you are there and that you are to be tried. The process of law will be set in motion. As the trial proceeds you'll be forgotten, and all we shall be aware of will be the rotting corpse of the country covered by the ordure of our recent history.

RUPERT: You're appealing to me as a patriot. I find that odd.

CADMUS: I'm doing nothing of the kind. I'm asking you to make up your mind. Decide.

RUPERT: My last positive action – by my decision – was the murder of that child seven years ago. From that moment I not only relinquished command of my army, but also of myself. For the seven years in prison I lived by other men's decisions regarding my habits, my actions, and my thoughts. I did what I was told. Nothing more. I was content it should be like that. Soldiers, you know, are forced to action by their decisions. There's no getting out of it for men in my job. No going back and saying I didn't mean it, when in my hand I'm holding the casualty list for thousands. You'll forgive my contempt for men who think they've fulfilled their obligations by expressing an opinion.

CADMUS: My God, Forster, you're talking like the romantic 'man of action' which all the intellectuals are in love with nowadays.

RUPERT: I'm talking as myself, not as any man's conception of me.

CADMUS: Go on.

RUPERT: I found freedom only in the years of fighting. I waited for that war, Cadmus. I wanted it with physical desire. It came, and I was released into action. In the years of preparation before the war – ach! my life was a formality. Because a man is seen in a crowd it must never be thought that he is of the crowd.

CADMUS: What you're telling me is that solitariness – aloneness, if you like – cannot be imposed. In your case imprisonment was never a punishment. Have I got that straight?

RUPERT: Do you believe absolute imprisonment to exist?

CADMUS: Yours seemed very efficient. At least, it was intended to be so.

RUPERT: Absolute. With no line of communication.

CADMUS: Put it that way if you like.

RUPERT: An army's line of communication is both its strength and its weakness. It stretches back sometimes broad and firm, sometimes fine and worn to base. It is not a steady supply. It pulses like a human vein according to need. Yet it must always be kept open. It must always be kept alive. In war I have struck so far forward that the line back has been stretched until it is invisible to all eyes but mine. For it is not always a thing you can mark on a map – you can't neatly signpost it for everyone to follow. You can only feel it in your belly like homesickness. It is what makes an isolated group fight its way out of an apparently impossible situation. Faith that there's a way back.

CADMUS: Yes. I understand you.

RUPERT: A man is an army, a striking offensive force. Each one of us has the line of communication stretching out. With some of us it is weak and with some of us it is strong according to our courage. The line goes back to other people, places, and ideas. From you and Catherine back into the past: from myself and the girl out to the immediate happening. But we all call it by the same name, don't we, Cadmus? Love. And as long as that line remains open we have to live.

CADMUS: How did you manage to keep contact in prison? There are classic examples, of course. Did you adopt a mouse?

RUPERT: No, it was not a mouse. It was a human voice. On the hills behind the camp there was a goat-herd. At dusk he greeted the night and at dawn the day with song. I've no idea what he sang – some prayer, I suppose. I tried to take it down phonetically but I failed. It must have been in some local dialect. I don't know. Early on I tried to resist it. I felt it was an intrusion. However, I was compelled to accept him. I came to be fond of him – like a man with a plain wife – and I ended by understanding that you can't shut out the human voice – especially when it's expressing itself in an act of faith. The pulse became stronger. I continued to live.

CADMUS: I thought I knew exactly who would be in this house today. Catherine, the doctor, the priest, and that clown of an American. I was safe with them. Not one of them would touch the sensibilities of a man such as yourself. But this girl – I'd not counted on her being here. She is now the sentimental singer of your goat-song, I suppose.

RUPERT: Yes.

CADMUS: Very well. You'll be taken down within six hours. I shall send for you.

RUPERT: What are my chances?

CADMUS: Reasonable. Of getting away with your life. You won't save anything else.

RUPERT: I go within six hours, you say.

CADMUS: At daybreak.

[HARRY *comes up the stairs.*]

HARRY: Where are the girls, Forster?

RUPERT: Below.

HARRY: Well, what are they doing?

RUPERT: I've no idea.

CADMUS: You're drunk.

HARRY: No, sir. Not yet. But I'm on the way. And when I am I'll have me to talk to, see? That'll be fine because myself and me will have some very interesting things to say to each other. But until that happy time I want someone to hold my hand. You'd look silly doing that so it'd better be one of the girls. Where are they? [*He shouts*] Dido!

CADMUS: I'm told she's a friend of yours, Mr Lancaster.

HARRY: Dido? Well, I don't know about being a friend, but she'll hold my hand when the horror's on me, and I can only see the past and never the future. She's that sort of girl. A kind kind of girl, you know.

CADMUS: And you need her at this moment?

HARRY: Sure do. [*He shouts*] Dido!

CADMUS: Would she hold Forster's hand if he needed her?

HARRY: She's been doing that all day, so now I move up for a bit of comfort.

CADMUS: She must be a very extraordinary girl.

HARRY: She is. Dido!

CADMUS: Pay attention, Mr Lancaster. Why should Forster need the comfort this girl's given him today?

HARRY: Because he's a man, I guess. Beneath the splendour, you know – [*he is beside the bronze helmet: he taps it with his fist*] – empty. Hollow. Nothing. Nothing but a man signalling to be let out of the trappings of war. Asking to be taken back into the herd.

CADMUS: Is that so, Forster?

RUPERT: Lancaster has a liberal mind. To him no man is entirely evil. Not even me. And so he is compelled to mistake my gestures of defiance for signals of distress.

CADMUS: But Mr Lancaster says this girl has been with you all day.

HARRY: Holding his hand.

CADMUS: Where is she leading you, Forster?

RUPERT: Didn't we agree on that just before Lancaster came up?

HARRY: Excuse me. Were you two talking important when I broke in?

CADMUS: We were speaking of Forster's future.

HARRY: Oh, that. Well, I'm sorry for Kate, and in a little while I suppose I'll have to be sorry for Dido.

CADMUS: Couldn't you find a little sorrow for me, Mr Lancaster?

HARRY: Why? Is he breaking your heart, too?

CADMUS: He certainly is.

HARRY: Don't let him do it. That kind break more than hearts. They're not often caught as you've caught this one, and you don't often see the naked face out of its idiot covering. Don't let it go free.

CADMUS: But we're not, Mr Lancaster. Let me tell you: Forster is back here to be put on trial.

HARRY: Ah!

CADMUS: That makes you happy, I see.

HARRY: So they've finally caught up with you, Forster. What a chance for us all – all us little people – to take a smack at you.

CADMUS: Yes, Mr Lancaster, it'll give you all a splendid opportunity, won't it?

HARRY: Do I believe this? Are we moving into an age of enlightenment?

CADMUS: We can only hope so, Mr Lancaster.

HARRY: How y' going t' take it, Forster? You'll have to find the words to defend yourself now, not the actions. No more legend, Forster, hidden in the midst of an army or up in a camp in the mountains – just a man like any other. You're going to have to stand up and answer for what you did.

CADMUS: Yes, indeed, he'll have to be very truthful in the cross-examinations.

HARRY: I can't wait. I can't wait for the day when the whole world'll know what you are. How there was nothing back of those bloody murders but your lusting ambition. We only needed the opportunity, Forster – we just needed this to bring you down to our own level. That's all.

CADMUS: And when you've proved him your equal – what then?

HARRY: He may go off and live the best way he can. We'd be playing his game if we killed him. Mr Cadmus, I'd like to shake you by the hand. You're doing a fine job. Thank you, sir.

CADMUS: Thank you, Mr Lancaster. Well, Forster, he's given you a hint of the feelings of the ordinary people. I hope you'll respect those feelings.

[CATHERINE and DIDO come up the stairs.]

May I appeal to your good sense once more? Let go, give up and do what I ask.

CATHERINE: He says you have them with you, John.

CADMUS: Who says I have what with me?

CATHERINE: Your driver: the benzedrine tablets.

CADMUS: Have I? Probably. Well, Forster?

[RUPERT does not answer.]

Miss Morgen, will you help me down those stairs to the car?

DIDO: Of course. Aren't you afraid I might push you?

CADMUS: Why should you?

DIDO: I might be tired of the Government.

CADMUS: Who isn't?

[CADMUS and DIDO go below.]

HARRY: Kate, sweetheart, I seem to have run out of drink. I mean the immediate supply below.

CATHERINE: Haven't you had enough?

HARRY: No, Kate, I've not had enough.

CATHERINE: Then you'll have to to go to the kitchen. Ask for some. Take it to your room.

HARRY: I'll do that. Kate, how did you feel about the picture?

CATHERINE: Picture?

HARRY: The picture I showed tonight. My picture.

CATHERINE: It was very good, I think. Of course, it's old. Out of date now.

HARRY: That's right. Not much use now. It lacks the drama of these times. I should've put in a trial scene, eh, Forster? My, the newsreel boys'll have a hell of a time with you the next few weeks. Those cameras don't miss a thing – they pick it all up, you know, every bit of it. Wish I was going to be behind one. [*He goes down the stairs.*]

CATHERINE: What did all that mean?

RUPERT: That Lancaster thinks it a good thing I should be put on trial.

CATHERINE: How does he know about it?

RUPERT: Cadmus told him. And raised the rabble in him. It was done to frighten me, to make me understand what I must face when the time comes. As it seems it has.

CATHERINE: You've decided. It's terrible, you know, to watch a man going coldly along the edge of decision. You were beyond my reach. I was afraid to cry out and make you look back. Couldn't trust myself. I had to leave it to the girl. She could speak in a matter-of-fact way which you'd understand.

[DIDO *has come up the stairs into the room.*]

DIDO: That man – that old Cadmus man – he says there's going to be some sort of trial. Are you going to let them do that to you?

CATHERINE: There's only one other way out. Because of you he's not going to take that way.

DIDO: Because of me. What've I done?

CATHERINE: Enough. Thank you.

DIDO: I don't want thanks. Thank you, you say and smile. So, all right. I've made you happy. Rupert's come to a decision because of something I've said or done. Fine for you – yes! – but for me – ? Try to catch some of my bloody misery when that old man said –

RUPERT: What did he say?

DIDO: He said, 'You shouldn't have held him back. He had a chance to finish clean. Now, because of you, he's going to finish dirty and old and lonely and angry. Because of you.' That's what he said.

CATHERINE: John Cadmus thinks that. We know better.

DIDO: I don't know anything. I don't want to know anything!

CATHERINE: Then why did you stay?

DIDO: Oh, leave me alone!

CATHERINE: Alone? Is that what you want? Yet you're not happy. You're not even free.

DIDO: It'll do for me. As I am.

CATHERINE: For how long? It is the middle of the night. No time for envy or pain. Quite soon now the day will come when you'll have to admit that the anger and despair you feel is not because of other people. It is for them. [To Rupert] I suppose they'll send for you.

RUPERT: Yes.

CATHERINE: Call me. I'll be in my room below. [She has moved to the stairs.]

DIDO: Catherine!

[CATHERINE has gone from the room.]

RUPERT: First of all I must tell you – that old Cadmus man is an honest man. He believed what he said.

DIDO: You've been brought back for this trial.

RUPERT: Yes. John Cadmus doesn't want it to be. He wants me to take Catherine's 'other way out'. He wants me to die clean. That's what he meant when he spoke to you.

DIDO: And he thinks I'm stopping you.

RUPERT: Yes, but don't worry. The decision is entirely mine.

DIDO: It is, isn't it, Rupert?

RUPERT: Do you want me to live, Dido?

DIDO: I want you to do what is right for a man like you. Life's not everything, I know, for men of your sort. But you must decide.

RUPERT: I've told Cadmus I'll stand the trial. They're coming at daybreak to take me to the military prison in the city.

DIDO: You'll be in Arcady. It's just across the river from my place.

RUPERT: The questioning will begin there. The investigation of the past.

DIDO: Will you tell them the truth?

RUPERT: Yes, but they won't be interested.

DIDO: And when it's all over?

RUPERT: They'll let me go.

DIDO: To be old and angry and lonely. No!

RUPERT: You mustn't concern yourself. Keep free.

DIDO: All right. I love you, if that's what you want to hear me say. I love you. You seem to me a very good man.

RUPERT: I'd like you to stay with me through the rest of the night. Only a few hours.

DIDO: You will say exactly what you mean, won't you?

RUPERT: I mean only that. Stay with me until first light. Until they come for me.

DIDO: Long time since I saw the dawn come up. I was walking back alone from a party. I'd danced all night and I was a bit drunk because I thought I was in love again. I was going home the long way – making it last out. Restless, you know, because his arms had been around me as we danced. And I'd got a tune in my head and it wouldn't get out.

[*She sings.*]   Don't shut your eyes to,
                 You must get wise to
               The fact that we're in love.

I was singing it as I walked in the comfortable darkness when the dawn came up and smacked me in the face so hard I nearly fell on my back. Another day. They always take me by surprise.

RUPERT: I've always prepared for the day. I could never let myself be taken by surprise. The dawn's a time of great danger, you know. I remember how cold it was, summer and winter, and how still. The men about me whispered and a cough sounded like a shot. I would stand staring into the darkness towards the enemy and he would be looking into my eyes. Then, at the appointed time, the darkness would dissolve. Towards the end of the campaign I almost came to believe that it was the intensity of my vision which dispelled the night and the strength of my faith which lifted the sun into the sky.

DIDO: I'm not surprised they shut you up when you talk like that. You're dangerous.

RUPERT: I'm sane, you know.

DIDO: Yes, and they know it. That's the danger. You're safe with me. Here, with me. The Doctor and the Father are in bed, Harry's getting drunk in the kitchen, and Catherine's at prayer. You and me – here. That's fine. My singing in the streets and you staring into the East – that's the past. You going to Arcady and me going back to my room – well, that's in the future. But you and me, here. That's now.

RUPERT: Yes, we're safe.

DIDO: Of course we are. Safe.

RUPERT: How will you remember the time you've spent in this house? When you're free of it. Will you remember?

DIDO: I suppose so. Something'll bring it to mind. [She is crying.] Sorry. Doesn't mean a thing. For instance, always happens when somebody gives me a present. Stupid!

RUPERT: I've nothing to give.

DIDO: I don't want anything from you. Did your soldiers – those men who waited with you for those other daybreaks – did they expect you to reward them? That night seven years ago – after the fight with the children – were your men against you then?

RUPERT: They were with me.

DIDO: Well, then. So am I. What happened? [*A pause.*] I'm not just curious.

RUPERT: I didn't go on. I waited. On the wrong side of the river.

DIDO: Yes?

[RUPERT *does not speak.*]

Would you like to roll up and sleep for a while? I'll watch. Oh, come on. I'm not such a fool. You've trusted people before me. Rest. I'll watch. Sleep.

RUPERT: Yes, you have to trust someone. That's the comradeship of soldiering. The knowledge that you're a man. And need to be watched over in the last hours of the night. Protected. From hurt. And death.

DIDO: Rest.

RUPERT: Watch.

CURTAIN

ACT THREE

The scene is the same. The time is later the same night moving to dawn.

[RUPERT *and* DIDO *are within the room.*]

RUPERT: If you stand there I shan't be able to see the sun rise.

DIDO: Ah! that's cheating. I thought you were asleep. You haven't spoken for ages.

RUPERT: Do you like dancing?

DIDO: Oh, yes. Two things I like best of all are dancing and going to the Lido and lying in the sun. I'll do that all through this summer. I've been saving my pennies.

RUPERT: There was a lot of music for dancing in the old days, I remember.

DIDO: You remember. That's why you've been so quiet. Were those days good – so good?

RUPERT: No better than others.

DIDO: But you – did you have a good time, then?

RUPERT: I was a very serious young man deep in the study of war. But I loved Catherine very much and she liked the things you like and so, of course, I did them. I was stricken by the time they took from my studies, but yes, I enjoyed myself. I think I danced very well – especially waltzes. Do they waltz much now?

DIDO: Not very much. We dance to a lot of American music.

RUPERT: Catherine was beautiful when she danced. She's always been most beautiful when happy. You know, I wasn't in love with her when we first met. She was travelling in this country. She gave up everything she had at that time in her own country and settled down here. She seemed to find what she needed in me.

DIDO: It must've hurt you to tell her that it was over. Yesterday, I mean. Why did you do it?

RUPERT: I found her love for me remained, but it was the love of her young days.

DIDO: She thought you were going to be free.

RUPERT: Yes. She meant to take advantage of that and drag me back into the past. I was to live what should have been in the last few years if the war hadn't taken me away. But I want the present time as offered to me by John Cadmus. And I want it alone. I have to take it alone to make what I wish of it.

DIDO: What do you want to make of the present?

RUPERT: A triumph.

DIDO: Haven't you ever – in all your life – loved a small thing? Something I could share with you?

RUPERT: I've a great fondness for natural things. Flowers and things of young growth, of brief life. Through the war I collected wild plants. I kept little boxes for the purpose in my command wagon. The men knew this, and I think they laughed at me. But even though they laughed they'd bring me unknown flowers taken from the roadside and stand by whilst I identified them. My pride and happiness, Dido, has been that the soldiers loved me. Did someone call?

DIDO: Yes. Catherine.

[CATHERINE *comes up the stairway.*]

CATHERINE: Miss Morgen, will you come down? Harry's asking for you. There's been an accident.

DIDO: What's happened?

CATHERINE: Harry's burnt his hands very badly. So stupid. He put those rolls of film into the electric furnace in the kitchen. They flared up and caught his hands. I've got the doctor out of bed, and he's dressing the burns now, but Harry is asking for you. Will you go down? I'm afraid he's very drunk.

[DIDO *goes down the stairs.*]

RUPERT: Why did he do it? A quixotic gesture, surely. I mean, there must be more than one copy of a thing like a film.

CATHERINE: Apparently not. Everyone's forgotten it except Harry. That was the last copy. A personal possession.

RUPERT: It didn't remotely resemble life before the war. It was a fiction, a fairy tale with everyone in love and happy ever after.

CATHERINE: Perhaps it's unfortunate that life's longer than six reels of celluloid.

RUPERT: It's as well he hasn't the talent to make this new film. It's entertaining to misrepresent happiness, but there's nothing funny in lying about misery.

CATHERINE: He's not lying. That's the way he sees it. Why should you say it's wrong for him to take the world he knows and try to make something beautiful and tragic? Why should you say that?

RUPERT: I don't. I say it's unwise and dangerous to distort the world around you to satisfy your longing.

CATHERINE: There's more danger, you know, in trying to destroy it to satisfy your ambition. You made me say that. I don't want to drag up the past any more. The damnable part of it is that men of your kind shatter the ordinary, everyday human pride of people like me.

RUPERT: By that you're at last seeing me as I am.

CATHERINE: I believe so. Let me look at you.

RUPERT: It will be easier for you – in the future – if you understand me. At this time.

CATHERINE: If I understand you, see you for what you are – I'll not be in love with you. Is that what you hope? There's your true weakness. Believing love can be recognized, evaluated, made to fit into the situation of the moment. It's not so. Not so at all. Even at the height of your power you could never control that. Never.

[MATTHEW SANGOSSE *comes up the stairs.*]

MATTHEW: Catherine, I think you should know that the Chancellor's car has just driven up.

CATHERINE: Thank you, Matthew. [*To Rupert*] Did he say he was coming back?

RUPERT: No. I thought he'd just send the guard. I've nothing more to say to him.

CATHERINE: How's Harry, Matthew?

MATTHEW: Miss Morgen's with him. He's quieter now. His hands are badly burnt. I've done what I can in the way of dressing them, but until I can get out for more stuff he'll have to do. He's scorched one side of his face which makes him look rather comic, but that's not serious. He'll be better when he's sober.

CATHERINE: Thank you for all you've done.

MATTHEW: It's many years since I've been got from my bed to attend a case. Makes me feel quite a youngster.

[JOHN CADMUS and BRUNO HURST come up the stairway. BRUNO is a young man of twenty-two years.]

CADMUS: You look as if you might be attending someone in a professional capacity, Doctor.

MATTHEW: I have been. Harry Lancaster's burnt himself about the hands.

CADMUS: Combustion by righteous indignation, I suppose. Otherwise everyone is well. Forster?

RUPERT: Perfectly. Spare me your bedside manner.

CADMUS: I'm not trying to be kind.

RUPERT: Then shall we get this visit over?

CADMUS: Certainly. This is Captain Hurst who is now responsible for you. He is the guard commander and had better tell you of the arrangements himself. Shall we go down, Catherine? Forster is now a state secret and we mustn't listen. Come along.

CATHERINE: I shall see him before he goes?

CADMUS: Of course. This'll only take a moment.

[CATHERINE, CADMUS, and MATTHEW go down the stairs.]

RUPERT: Well, Captain Hurst?

BRUNO: Do you want to know the particulars of the escort, sir?

RUPERT: Is there anything out of the ordinary about them?

BRUNO: Nothing, sir.

RUPERT: Then I'll take them as read. Why aren't you in uniform?

BRUNO: My orders were to report in civilian clothes, sir.

RUPERT: You're very young to have reached your captaincy.

BRUNO: We are very young now, sir. Because of the re-formation of the army.

RUPERT: Is this a routine detail or have you special qualifications?

BRUNO: I've been on guard duty at the Chancellery.

RUPERT: And Cadmus took you from there today.

BRUNO: Yes, sir.

RUPERT: I'll try to give you my co-operation.

BRUNO: Thank you, sir. I'm to start thirty minutes after daybreak.

RUPERT: The details are not important.

BRUNO: Will you please take leave of your friends before that time?

RUPERT: Yes, Captain Hurst, I will. Is there anything else?

BRUNO: No, sir.

RUPERT: Very well.

BRUNO: I've orders not to leave you, sir.

RUPERT: I see. Then sit down, Captain Hurst. How long is it to sunrise?

BRUNO: Twelve minutes.

RUPERT: It will be light now over the mountain camp.

BRUNO: Yes. I found night duty out there worse than anywhere.

RUPERT: You know the place?

BRUNO: I was stationed in the Eastern Provinces last year.

RUPERT: Ah! Then you, too, have heard the goat-singers.

BRUNO: Yes, sir. [He laughs.] Those songs.

RUPERT: You know what they are?

BRUNO: The goat-songs? Of course.

RUPERT: Well?

BRUNO: They are obscene.

RUPERT: Obscene?

BRUNO: It's the goat-herd's expression of love – to his goats. The songs don't make sense.

RUPERT: Go on.

BRUNO: They're just filth. That's all. Did you hear them at the camp, sir?

RUPERT: What? Yes, I heard them there. [He is silent.]

BRUNO: Talk to me if it helps you.

RUPERT: What did you say?

BRUNO: I said, Please talk to me if you want to.

RUPERT: Thank you. Have you ever put your faith in love songs, Captain Hurst? Believing them to be something more. How did it go? 'Don't shut your eyes to, you must get wise to the fact – ' And do you like dancing and going to the Lido and lying in the sun? And being in love? Do you like being in love? [BRUNO *does not answer: he does not move.*] Forgive me, I'm in a privileged position. Yet I was a young soldier once, you know. Twenty years ago, I might very well have been you.

BRUNO: I have been you, sir.

RUPERT: What?

BRUNO: I have been you. I've been Rupert Forster.

RUPERT: Tell me what you mean.

BRUNO: I fought that last battle of yours several times. I fought it in the streets of this city. I was fifteen. I wanted to be a soldier. My command truck was an old bicycle, my troop of tanks were toys, my battleground was the waste around the railway yards. But my enemy, sir, was the same. All the howling children of the neighbourhood.

RUPERT: I hope you conducted the affair with more success than I did.

BRUNO: Every evening for weeks the shout would go up: Let's play Forster's game! They'd all run away and hide. Then, with six others, I'd pedal my way to the head of the street, dismount, and walk the length of the street. I'd hear them laughing in their hiding-places – they knew they wouldn't properly die. I'd go back to my machine, mount it, and be about to give the signal when they would be upon us. That was all very simple. You had set me an example. I'd only to follow it.

RUPERT: Not absolutely, I hope.

BRUNO: There were broken heads, nothing more. Perhaps a few pinched fingers. But after that I was lost. You had disposed of the children. The forward movement was poised. I wanted to go on but I couldn't because it was not your course. May I ask you something?

RUPERT: Yes.

BRUNO: Why did you wait for twelve hours before continuing the advance? The attack over the river which failed. Why did you wait?

RUPERT: Would you have gone on?

BRUNO: Yes. Every time I played the game and got to that point it was agony to hold back. The forward impetus was overwhelming.

RUPERT: I wasn't playing a game, Hurst.

BRUNO: Neither was I at the end. I was planning for the future. I don't want to be caught in the way you were caught. Think back. Why did you wait?

RUPERT: The armour moved on over the children and through the town.

BRUNO: Yes?

RUPERT: There was no more opposition. I had occupied the town by late afternoon.

BRUNO: You set up headquarters?

RUPERT: My staff had done so. In a deserted schoolroom. It was a convenient place.

BRUNO: You waited.

RUPERT: Until night. It had begun to rain. A little. Nothing much. They'd put my maps on a long trestle-table. The situation was there. Clearly marked.

BRUNO: You waited.

RUPERT: Reports began to come in. The room was very noisy. The footsteps of men were deafening as they came to me across the wooden floor. Someone put a meal in front of me.

BRUNO: You say reports were coming in. What did they show?

RUPERT: That everything was exactly as I'd planned.

BRUNO: Then why didn't you act?

RUPERT: I was trapped. Trapped by the memory of the child. I

237

couldn't free myself from that moment. The moment when I stood alone, sad, lost, childless, with the child in my arms. And looking down saw that it was a human being. Warm, as the bitter smell of its body struck up at me: dirty, fearful, brave, and – living. It was then the secret was forced on me. I'd shut it out until that morning by making my own prison, Hurst, years before they sent me to the camp in the mountains. A prison of pride and ambition. Then, when I caught the child to me, the secret was revealed. I suddenly understood what a man is. For I held it close.

BRUNO: If you felt this why did you shoot?

RUPERT: I had no choice. The way I'd chosen to live led to that encounter, which was in itself a challenge. Are you so great? Then fire! I fired, and the secret flew up leaving only blood on my sleeve. I became human. So I waited.

BRUNO: For twelve hours.

RUPERT: For twelve hours. It was my second-in-command who took the pencil from my hand and wrote the order for the attack across the river. It was too late.

BRUNO: You went over with them?

RUPERT: Yes. And lived.

BRUNO: Have you admitted this before?

RUPERT: Never.

BRUNO: You must consider yourself guilty.

RUPERT: I do.

BRUNO: Are you prepared to go on trial for this, to admit your error as you have to me, to be found guilty and to be sentenced? You'll serve the rest of time at the camp in the mountains. And your comfort will be the goat-songs.

RUPERT: You're exceeding your authority!

BRUNO: You did more. You misused yours. You had as your responsibility a part in a great conquest and you lost faith. I shall fight over that ground again in future years and next time the attack will go on.

RUPERT: I'm content to leave it in your hands. I'll fight no more.

[DIDO *comes up the stairs.*]

DIDO: I'm sorry I had to leave you. He's disgustingly drunk, and he's burnt his hands very badly.

RUPERT: What have you done with him?

DIDO: He's sitting down there talking to himself. He doesn't need me. He doesn't need anybody. They've come for you, have they?

RUPERT: Yes. This is Captain Hurst of the escort.

BRUNO: How do you do?

DIDO: Hullo. Is the old man here, too?

RUPERT: He's down with Catherine.

DIDO: Going to make sure they get you away, aren't they? How many soldiers?

BRUNO: Eight.

DIDO: Certainly making sure. Enough to carry you away if necessary with full military honours.

BRUNO: We're an escort, ma'am, not a bearer party.

DIDO [*she laughs*]: Did you hear what he called me? He called me 'ma'am'! [*To Bruno*] Are you doing the right thing?

BRUNO: That doesn't concern me.

DIDO: Not concern you. You just do what you're told.

BRUNO: Yes.

DIDO: Leave the room! Well, go on.

BRUNO: Don't be a fool.

RUPERT: You mustn't make fun of him. He's an unenviable job in front of him.

DIDO: Can't he wait downstairs? Oh, hell!

[HARRY *has come up the stairway. His hands are bandaged and the burns on his face have been treated with a vivid dye.*]

Go 'way, Harry.

HARRY: Peace, honey. Forster, I want to say something t'you. I want t'say something t'you. Listen – now listen. It's this. You're wrong, see. The whole way you've gone is'n insult to what y'could be. Don't ask me why it's wrong. I d'know why. But I feel it – here! Is that g'enough for you? I'm a man. All right, too, I'm a drunk. I've no pretty pictures left in me no more, I was born in a barn and my mammy knew my daddy just five minutes one hot afternoon – but I'm a man, Forster. And the way I've lived has been right, Forster, and the way you've lived has been wrong. You know something? You're wicked. That's it! You're just wicked. [*He sways at the head of the stairs.*]

DIDO: For Godsake, Harry!

HARRY: That's all, sweetheart. I've said it. That's all.

DIDO: Well, if you've said it just go off to bed.

HARRY: You want me to go to bed. That's funny. It's no remedy now, Dideeodo. No remedy at all. Can't draw the blanket of love over our heads now. Why can't? Because it's too late. Look, it's morning. Time to get up!

DIDO: Oh, you're –

HARRY: Drunk. I know. These damned stairs! They look to go so far down – they look they might go to hell.

DIDO: Try them.

HARRY: Hullo. [*He speaks to* CATHERINE, *who has come up the stairs.*]

CATHERINE: There you are.

HARRY: Here I am. You want me?

CATHERINE: No, I don't want you. What are you doing up here?

HARRY: Just looked up to tell Forster something.

CATHERINE: The doctor said you were to lie down. Try to sleep.

HARRY: Sleep it off? My hands hurt like hell, Kate. My hands.

CATHERINE: Well, what do you expect? It was a very silly thing to do.

HARRY: It was the only thing to do, surely. I just wanted you to feel something for me. Just anything – pity, or whatever you've got left over. [*He goes down the stairs.*]

CATHERINE: Captain Hurst, the Chancellor wants to speak to you.

BRUNO: I've orders not to leave General Forster.

CATHERINE: Who gave you those orders?

BRUNO: The Chancellor.

CATHERINE: Well, then –

BRUNO: Where is he?

CATHERINE: Immediately below.

[BRUNO *goes down the stairs.*]

Are you ready to go?

RUPERT: I'm ready when they are. They said daylight.

[*The first light has come to the eastern sky.* DIDO *has put on Harry's sheepskin coat and gone on to the balcony. She stands beside a man who can now be seen beyond the window.*]

CATHERINE: Will you need anything? Anything I can get for you.

RUPERT: I've everything I want. Did Cadmus really ask to see the boy, or did you invent that?

CATHERINE: No, he asked for him.

RUPERT: Why?

CATHERINE: I don't know. Now I'm trying to think of something to say that will keep you with me for a little longer. This seeing people off.

RUPERT: Walk away. Just let me go.

CATHERINE: I've always done that. First to war and then to prison. All in all, I've been a good soldier's woman, haven't I? And yet I wish I could have come a little nearer to you in the past few hours. I've failed. It's not a pleasant feeling. Have I been too concerned with myself? I wouldn't like to leave you with the thought that I've intruded my own unhappiness. Haven't you anything to say to me?

RUPERT: I don't think so.

CATHERINE: My God, couldn't you make up something for this moment? Dear, dear Rupert, there's nothing of the harlot player about you, is there? If you've nothing to say then you keep quiet. This is goodbye, Rupert – goodbye. When the trial's over you'll not come back here. I know that. We'll never see each other again. Never. I'm sorry. I'm behaving like this because I don't under-stand. I've tried. There are some things that are right to me and there are some things that are wrong. I can't tell you why they are right or wrong because I don't know. I suppose like most women

I feel – I don't reason. And it is the feeling for rightness which made me take you and will make me love you for ever. There. Now I just want to say goodbye.

RUPERT: Goodbye, Catherine.

CATHERINE: Goodbye.

[RUPERT *has moved to Catherine. He puts his arms about her for a moment. She whispers.*]

No, don't say you love me. [*She goes down the stairs.*]

[RUPERT *stands watching her. Then, he calls.*]

RUPERT: Time to go home, Dido.

[DIDO *comes into the room.*]

DIDO: I know. Funny – this morning didn't take me by surprise.

RUPERT: You were watching for it.

DIDO: I suppose so. Would you like this coat? We could steal it from Harry. He'd never know. It's warm. Keep you warm in Arcady, it would.

RUPERT: No.

DIDO: Can I send you things? Will they let me do that? Cigarettes and things.

RUPERT: I don't smoke.

DIDO: Of course you don't. Well, books and – oh, you know – cakes. I cook sometimes.

RUPERT: They won't allow anything to be sent.

DIDO: Letters?

RUPERT: No. Save your pennies.

DIDO: All right. You want to finish here and now.

RUPERT: Here and now. I want to give you this, that's all. [*He takes the jewelled box which was given to him by Cadmus from a pocket and holds it out to Dido.*] Take it.

DIDO: Thank you.

RUPERT: There's nothing in it, I'm afraid. Just a box. Do to keep your powder dry.

DIDO: Did it belong to Catherine?

RUPERT: No.

DIDO: Then I'll take it. Thank you very much.

RUPERT: I want you to go now. I want you to leave at once. Don't wait about. On your way give a message to Captain Hurst from me. You know, the young soldier.

DIDO: What is it?

RUPERT: Tell him he's mistaken if he thinks he has learnt or will learn anything from my behaviour. I faced the same problems over the same ground as that man – [*the wearer of the helmet*] – and young Hurst will face them in the future. They are unchanging but the time and place of decision is personal.

DIDO: I'll try to remember that. To tell him, I mean. Have you anything to tell me?

RUPERT: Only this. Don't stay caught in the memory of the past day. Escape. Get out.

DIDO: I will. [*She holds out her hand.* RUPERT *takes it with his left hand. Leaving Dido he goes to the upper room.*]

RUPERT: Goodbye, Dido.

DIDO: Goodbye.

> [RUPERT *enters the upper room. An Announcer on the public address system of the city speaks.*]

ANNOUNCER: The time is zero four one five hours. The time is zero four one five hours. It is now – officially – day. [*A bell is struck. The man on the balcony enters the room, crosses, and goes down the stairs. The* ANNOUNCER *speaks again.*] Attention! Here is a statement. General Rupert Forster is dead. General Rupert Forster is dead. Further reports follow later.

> [*A bell is struck.* DIDO *is staring towards the upper room.* CATHERINE *comes from below.*]

CATHERINE: Where?

> [DIDO *points to the upper room.*]

Is it true?

DIDO: I don't know.

CATHERINE: Go up. Go up there.

> [DIDO *moves slowly to the upper room.* CATHERINE *calls.*]

Rupert! Rupert!

[DIDO, *at the door of the room, looks back.*]

Go on. Please!

[DIDO *enters the room.* CADMUS, *alone, comes up the stairs.* CATHERINE *speaks to him.*]

You're lying! I don't trust you.

[DIDO *returns.*]

DIDO: It's true. There's a little stain at the corner of his mouth.

CADMUS: He'd only to break the glass before his face. He knew well enough.

CATHERINE: And you knew he'd do it.

CADMUS: Yes.

CATHERINE: Surely enough to tell them to say that over the speakers while he was still alive?

CADMUS: Yes. I gave instructions for the guard to be withdrawn and for that announcement to be made at daybreak. I gave those instructions some hours ago.

[DIDO *has come down into the room and now goes down the stairs.*]

The news of his return was beginning to get out. The morning papers might have got it. I couldn't allow it to happen that way. I could never have controlled the demand for him. They won't want a dead man. Also that was the only method by which I could tell the opposition of their failure. To tell them I was forced to tell everyone – even you – in that way.

CATHERINE: You were so sure? You can't have been! It was a gamble.

CADMUS: It was a certainty. I knew the man and I knew the situation. That was all I needed.

CATHERINE: Did you know him so well? You must have known him better than I did for I believed he would live.

CADMUS: I knew him as a man to be very much like myself. But he'd something I've had to put away whilst I'm in office. Honour. So I knew what the end would be.

CATHERINE: Honour. That means nothing. A word.

CADMUS: You're thinking of these last hours as a struggle between you and myself for his life. It was nothing of the kind. He was quite free to choose.

CATHERINE: Why do you say that? You wanted him to do it for a purpose.

CADMUS: I don't deny it. But I'm an old man, Catherine, and apart from the smallest things I don't do much to please myself. All I said of the situation in the country at the moment is true.

CATHERINE: You murdered him.

CADMUS: No. We're all victims of injustice, Catherine, every moment of our lives. We can shut ourselves up in the day and lie awake at night dreaming of revenge. But revenge against whom? Against each other? Why? Forster had great cause to dream in that way. It was an injustice that we had to imprison him, and he had reason to sit in that camp in the hills thinking up ways of reckoning. But he didn't do that. All he wanted was to be taken back into the service of the world. The world wouldn't have him and so he turned away. In acceptance. There was no hatred in him. He was a great soldier. Learn from him.

CATHERINE: Will you learn?

CADMUS: I can't allow myself to do so. At ten o'clock this morning I shall make a statement to the House and tell them the lies they want to hear. I shall belittle Forster's past achievements and say that he died under a burden of conscience. The sooner forgotten the better. That's the great thing. That he should be forgotten.

CATHERINE: Go, now. Go down and tell your lies.

CADMUS: Very well. Do I need to say how much your friendship has meant to me? In the past.

CATHERINE: Are you trying to tell me that you, too, have made a sacrifice?

CADMUS: I suppose I am.

[BRUNO *comes from below.*]

BRUNO: The guard is dismissed, sir.

CADMUS: Thank you, Captain Hurst.

BRUNO: You called me away from him, sir.

CADMUS: What's that?

BRUNO: You called me away. If you'd not done so this wouldn't have happened.

CADMUS: Wouldn't it?

BRUNO: I shall deny dereliction of duty.

CADMUS: It won't be necessary, Captain Hurst. What are you afraid of?

BRUNO: The incident was unavoidable, sir. I didn't want to leave him.

CADMUS: I called you away. The responsibility is mine.

BRUNO: Thank you, sir.

CADMUS: But some time – when you've nothing better to do – reflect on the consequences to yourself if I'd refused to admit it. Catherine, you'd better have someone here for a day or two. Hurst can make all arrangements for this and that.

CATHERINE: Very well.

CADMUS: May I call on you once again?

CATHERINE: I think not.

[JOHN CADMUS goes down the stairs.]

BRUNO: The house is no longer under guard, ma'am. You're free to go where you wish.

CATHERINE: Where do you suggest?

BRUNO: There's no need to concern yourself any longer with General Forster. All arrangements will be made.

CATHERINE: Then I'll forget him at once, Captain Hurst. At once.

[DIDO comes up the stairs. She has changed into her own clothes.]

DIDO: The old Cadmus man has gone, and now I must be going. I suppose that's all right.

BRUNO: Everyone in the house is quite free now.

DIDO: Well, I've come up to say goodbye.

CATHERINE: Did Rupert tell you what he was going to do?

DIDO: No. He just said goodbye and walked up there.

CATHERINE: You don't seem touched by what's happened.

DIDO: There was nothing else for him to do, was there?

   [BRUNO *turns to go from the room.*]

  I've got a message for you.

BRUNO: For me?

DIDO: From Rupert. Let me get it right. You're not to think that you learnt anything from him. You'll face the same problems – same place, perhaps – but you've got to find your own way out. All right?

BRUNO: Yes. [*He goes down the stairs.*]

CATHERINE: Did Rupert give you a message for me?

DIDO: No. He said he loved you.

CATHERINE: I'd like you to stay here.

DIDO: I can't do that. The life I live isn't much, I know, but it's the way I want it.

CATHERINE: And you think I'd take that from you.

DIDO: Well, I'd not have it in this place. Why do you want me to stay now? Good turn?

CATHERINE: Oh, no – it's for my sake, not yours. I'd like to try to live again. Help me.

DIDO: Please let me go now.

CATHERINE: Wait! I'm not offering the things I'd have offered before. Money, clothes, and amusement. I've learnt enough from you to know they won't keep you. I'm not offering you anything. Listen! You are the only person in nine years who has broken into my life against my wish. I've chosen others – people who wouldn't lead me away from Rupert. So, you see, they can't help me, but you can. Just for a little while, Dido.

DIDO: No! You'll eat me right up. Then you'll be fine, but where shall I be?

CATHERINE: You can have absolute freedom, I promise. Just live here.

DIDO: I like you, Catherine – always have. And you're good and strong, really. You can do it all without me.

CATHERINE: I'm not. Rupert's dead.

DIDO: Well, then, it's too bad. You'll just have to go downhill. Look, the sun's shining. It's going to be a fine day.

[HARRY *comes up the stairs.*]

Perhaps I'll walk out into the country and sleep through the day in the open. Who knows?

HARRY: You going? Hey! you can talk to me. I'm sober.

DIDO: I'd talk to you if there was anything to say, but there isn't. Goodbye. [*She goes down the stairs.*]

HARRY: I've been thinking, Kate. Let's sell up – sell out. You settled here because of him, that's all. Nothing to keep you now. Let's get away.

CATHERINE: No.

HARRY: All right. We stay. Kate, he wasn't any good. He wasn't worth waiting for. It wasn't what he was but what he did. You made a mistake anybody might've made and I'm sorry for you. Truly, I'm sorry for you. He walked out on you, Kate. I'm staying with you. Surely that's in my favour. And I'll get on with the picture. Honest.

[FATHER ANSELM *and* MATTHEW SANGOSSE *come up the stairs.* CATHERINE *has moved to stand looking through the windows over the city.*]

Hullo, boys. So here we are. Let's start the day. I'll do that with a bath. God! I'm filthy. Kate, can I go and freshen up?

CATHERINE: Do as you like. There's no need to ask me. Please go on as you've done in the past. There's all the time in the world now for us to be kind, for us to do good. Let me look at you. Come here. How shall we spend the time? All the time that's left. What shall we do with it? This fortune to be rid of. Shall we be charitable? Give me your part and I'll give you mine. But we have equal portions which makes it absurd. We shall end up where we began with no more and no less. There'll be no loss, no gain, but it will pass the time – the time we have to spend – it will pass the time, this give and take – it will pass the time. O dear Christ, I'm cold!

[HARRY *takes up the sheepskin coat and puts it over Catherine's shoulders. Then, with his arm about her, he leads her back into the room. The morning light catches Catherine's face: it shows her as an aged woman.*]

HARRY: Not to worry, Kate. We're here. We won't let anybody hurt you – not any more we won't. [DIDO *comes up the stairs.*] What do you want? Well, what d'you want? You back for something?

DIDO [*whispers*]: Go 'way, Harry.

HARRY: What're you back for?

DIDO: Changed my mind.

HARRY: So, all right, you've changed your mind. From what to what?

DIDO: Go 'way, Harry, go 'way. [*She moves towards Catherine.*] Catherine. What I know. Can it be taught? I'll try.

CURTAIN

MORE ABOUT PENGUINS

If you have enjoyed reading this book you may wish to know that *Penguin Book News* appears every month. It is an attractively illustrated magazine containing complete details of the month's new books. A specimen copy will be sent free on request.

Penguin Book News is obtainable from most bookshops; but you may prefer to become a regular subscriber at 3s. for twelve issues. Just write to Dept EP, Penguin Books Ltd, Harmondsworth, Middlesex, enclosing a cheque or postal order, and you will be put on the mailing list.

Some other books published by Penguins are described on the following pages.

Note: *Penguin Book News* is not
available in the U.S.A., Canada or Australia.

PENGUIN MODERN PLAYWRIGHTS

In this new series Penguins are publishing the very latest plays, wherever possible, at the time of their first production on the stage. The following plays have already appeared:

STAIRCASE
Charles Dyer

FANGHORN
David Pinner

LEE HARVEY OSWALD
Michael Hastings

MACBIRD!
Barbara Garson

TALKING TO A STRANGER*
John Hopkins

THE NIGEL BARTON PLAYS
Dennis Potter

AMERICA HURRAH and Other Plays†
Jean-Claude van Itallie

* NOT FOR SALE IN THE U.S.A.
† NOT FOR SALE IN THE U.S.A. OR CANADA

ALTONA, MEN WITHOUT SHADOWS,
THE FLIES

Jean-Paul Sartre

Born in Paris in 1905, Jean-Paul Sartre studied philosophy and took up teaching. After service in the Resistance he became a writer and edits *Les Temps Modernes*. His philosophical books – notably *L'Être et le néant* (1943) – have caused him to be regarded as the founder of existentialism, an attitude which is concerned with the absurdity of so many people's lives and the possibilities of human freedom. His novels, such as *The Age of Reason*, tend to stress the meaningless aspect of modern life.

His plays, on the other hand, deal more with human freedom. *The Flies* (1942) presents Sartre's interpretation of the Greek legend of Orestes, who killed his mother, Clytemnestra, and her lover, in order to avenge Agamemnon, his father, and set Argos free. *Men Without Shadows* (1946) is a brutal study of the effects of torture on captured members of the Maquis. *Altona* (1959) (previously published as *Loser Wins*) comments on the acquisitive aspects of capitalism as seen in a family of rich German industrialists.

Also available
Lucifer and the Lord *and*
The Respectable Prostitute

RHINOCEROS; THE CHAIRS; THE LESSON
Eugène Ionesco

Twelve years ago the plays of Ionesco, a Rumanian by origin, were being acted in Left Bank theatres in Paris and very poorly attended. Now regarded as one of the most important writers of the *avant-garde*, he has a world-wide reputation and his plays are translated into many languages.

Sir Laurence Olivier took the leading part in *Rhinoceros* when it was produced in London in 1960 at the Royal Court Theatre, where *The Chairs* had already been performed in 1957. *The Lesson* was produced at London's Arts Theatre Club in 1955.

Ionesco himself is hesitant to theorize about his work or assess its importance. His plays represent, he says, 'a mood and not an ideology, an impulse not a programme'. The substance of the world seems to vary, for him, between solidity and illusory unreality and he projects onto the stage, with a strangely universal effect of comedy, his own internal conflict.

His influence can be traced among the youngest generation of English playwrights.

NEW ENGLISH DRAMATISTS